MW01038325

CONVERSATIONS

Also by Steve Reich

Writings on Music, 1965–2000 (edited by Paul Hillier)

DAVID LANG

BRIAN ENO

RICHARD SERRA

MICHAEL GORDON

MICHAEL TILSON THOMAS

RUSSELL HARTENBERGER

ROBERT HURWITZ

STEPHEN SONDHEIM

JONNY GREENWOOD

DAVID HARRINGTON

CONVERSATIONS

ELIZABETH LIM-DUTTON

DAVID ROBERTSON

MICAELA HASLAM

ANNE TERESA DE KEERSMAEKER

JULIA WOLFE

NICO MUHLY

BERYL KOROT

COLIN CURRIE

BRAD LUBMAN

STEVE REICH

HANOVER
SQUARE
PRESS

**HANOVER
SQUARE
PRESS™**

ISBN-13: 978-1-335-42572-0

Conversations

This edition published by arrangement with Harlequin Enterprises ULC, a subsidiary of HarperCollins Publishe

Hanover Square Press
22 Adelaide St. West, 41st Floor
Toronto, Ontario M5H 4E3, Canada
HanoverSqPress.com
BookClubbish.com

Printed in U.S.A.

conversation

a talk between two or more people

- dialogue, discussion, observation, opinion, debate, give-and-take, small talk, reminiscence, exchange, questioning

...and man became a speaking spirit.

— *Genesis* 2:7, translation by Onkelos

CONTENTS

PREFACE

Whenever I thought about writing a book, one of my favorite music books always came to mind: *Stravinsky in Conversation with Robert Craft*. Stravinsky makes observations and recollections about his life and the great artists he was in touch with while Craft asks brief questions. While there was no one like Robert Craft in my life, that clearly opened up the inviting possibility of having many conversations. Composers, musicians, conductors, a sculptor, a choreographer, a video artist, and a record company president all came to mind, and it is my conversations with them that fill this book.

I spoke with David Lang, Brian Eno, Richard Serra, Michael Gordon, Michael Tilson Thomas, Russell Hartenberger, Robert Hurwitz, Stephen Sondheim, Jonny Greenwood, David Harrington, Elizabeth Lim-Dutton, David Robertson, Micaela Haslam, Anne Teresa De Keersmaeker, Julia Wolfe, Nico Muhly, Beryl Korot, Colin Currie, and Brad Lubman. I regret not being able to include conversations with artist Sol LeWitt, whose work and thinking somewhat paralleled my own, and impresario Harvey Lichtenstein, who presented so many of my works at the Brooklyn Academy of Music. Both passed away before this book was begun. All these people helped create the unique musical/

artistic environment in which I was fortunate to compose my works from the 1960s to the present.

Our conversations were almost all held via Zoom during the pandemic of 2020 and early '21. While we talked about my music in general, each conversation focused on one or more pieces that the other artist either performed or had a particular interest in. The order of the conversations is roughly chronological following the dates of the compositions discussed. Inevitably our discussions turned to the other person's work, as well, and given the variety of people involved, each with their own particular voice, every conversation inhabits a world of its own.

Steve Reich
May 2021

CHAPTER I

DAVID LANG

David Lang: In the mid-1960s you began composing all these great, radical pieces, but before that, you were a student in a music school, being educated to be a normal, well-disciplined, European-oriented composer. I wonder if before we get into all the things you've done since then, it might be interesting to find out what your life as a student was like. You went to Juilliard?

Steve Reich: Yes, but best to go back before that, to when I was fourteen and discovered the music that really changed my life. I had piano lessons when I was younger, and I had heard Beethoven's Fifth, Schubert's "Unfinished," Wagner's Overture to the *Meistersinger*, and lots of pop music, but at fourteen I heard a recording of *The Rite of Spring*, and it made an enormous impression. I had never heard anything like it. Then, a few weeks later, I heard a recording of the Fifth Brandenburg Concerto. Believe it or not, I had never heard any Bach before that. Finally, a bit later, a pianist friend played me records of Miles Davis, Charlie Parker, and Kenny Clarke, and we immediately said we'd form a band. I said I'd be the drummer and I began studying with Roland Kohloff, who later became the principal timpanist with the New York Philharmonic. All of those experiences starting when I was fourteen really laid the groundwork for the rest of my life. At sixteen I entered Cornell.

DL: You were young.

SR: I didn't know what I was going to major in. I was in a band playing drums on the weekends. I was listening to much more Stravinsky and Bach and discovering early music and Bartók, but I felt Bartók began at five and I was sixteen, so it was too late for me to become a composer. Fortunately, besides becoming very interested in philosophy and Wittgenstein in particular, I immediately took a history of Western music course with Professor William Austin, who was a musicologist, pianist, organist, and specialist in twentieth-century music. He taught the course as follows: first semester began with Gregorian Chant, went to the death of J. S. Bach in 1750, and then jumped directly to Debussy, Ravel, Stravinsky, and jazz. The second semester began with Haydn and ended with Wagner. Needless to say, I preferred the first semester, but more importantly, it clarified my instinctive attraction to Bach, Stravinsky, and jazz, showing how they all share a strong underlying rhythmic pulse and some form of tonal center. Nineteenth-century European Romantic music moves further and further away from both. Finally, the moment of truth came when I was a senior and had to make up my mind about where I was going. I applied to Harvard and was accepted as a graduate student.

DL: In the philosophy department?

SR: In the philosophy department. And I went to Austin and said, "I can't do this. I want to study composition." He said, "Why don't you study with Hall Overton, let me contact him." And he did, and I graduated from Cornell with honors in phi-

losophy and went down to New York City to study composition
with Hall Overton. You once mentioned you knew about him?

DL: Well, you know one of my hobbies, maybe my only hobby,
is that I'm a record collector. I collect LPs of musicians, American composers from the '50s and '60s. You run across his music
in a lot of really interesting places. You find him in the symphonic world, and you find him as Thelonious Monk's arranger.

SR: Exactly.

DL: So, by the time you would have been introduced to him,
he was already living a sort of dual life. Questioning the role
and the relationship of classical music to jazz.

SR: Right. Hall Overton taught in a loft in what was called the
Flower Market, which is lower Sixth Avenue. Later a book of
photographs was published, called *The Jazz Loft Project* because
on the floor below Hall Overton was W. Eugene Smith, the
photographer who constantly came up to Hall's loft to photo-
graph jam sessions with Thelonious Monk, Charlie Mingus,
Stan Getz, Phil Woods, Jim Hall, Zoot Sims, and all kinds of
jazz musicians of that period. Some of these famous musicians
also came to visit Hall as students to improve their musicianship, particularly their harmonic vocabulary.

DL: Wow.

SR: Hall was a capable and respected jazz pianist. But his greatest jazz accomplishment, as you pointed out, was with Thelonious Monk, who obviously thought very highly of him. Hall
had two upright pianos next to each other in his loft, and as my
friend and fellow student of Hall's, composer Carmen Moore,
described it, he and Monk would sit at the adjoining pianos

and play Monk's tunes. Hall would accent a detail and call out "Brass?" and Monk might respond by playing a slight variant of that detail as an affirmative with a slight difference. This remarkable musical dialogue, all recorded on Hall's funky 1950s tape recorder, eventually resulted in the arrangements for the concert of the Thelonious Monk Big Band at Town Hall.

Hall had studied at Juilliard, and later he taught composition there. He was a protégé of Vincent Persichetti, who was someone I studied with later at Juilliard, who was by far the most interesting teacher there. Hall started me off saying something like "You've been playing drums for all these years. I want you to go back to the keyboard and start with Béla Bartók's *Mikrokosmos* Volumes 1 and 2." And that was solid gold. Dorian mode, Phrygian mode, canons of all sorts. What are the modes? A lot of things which you may improvise, "Oh, that's interesting." And then you realize it's completely systemized…

DL: It's a thing.

SR: Yeah, it's a thing. It's a well-established thing for hundreds of years. Those little books of Bartók's were filled with imitative counterpoint, canons. Many years later canons became the backbone of much of my music. Phasing is just a variation of canonic technique where the rhythmic distance between the voices is variable. I remember the very first day Hall gave me a compositional exercise to do. He said, "I want you to write some melodies," and he went into my music notebook and drew it in pencil: "Write a melody that goes like this, down, another that goes up, and a third that goes straight." I looked at him, because this was the very, very beginning, and I said, "Hall, I don't think I have enough technique." And he looked me right in the eye and said, "You'll never have enough technique. Get to work."

DL: (*laughs*) Oh, that's such a great lesson.

SR: Isn't that wonderful? I mean, it's still true.

DL: It's still true.

SR: I'm gonna die and think, "Ugh, I was just getting started."

DL: That's like every composer's great fear, you know? "There are things I wish I could do, but I'll never be good enough to be able to do them."

SR: So, best to do what you can do and get on with it. Because you'll do that well, and who knows, you could get better.

DL: Yes.

SR: Working with Hall, besides the *Mikrokosmos*, we did study traditional harmony. He gave me the Hindemith harmony book, and the great thing about it was, there's hardly any text, it's almost all exercises. My compositions began to grow sometimes into imitations of Bartók. It was really an intensive two-year period. And I got a really positive attitude towards what I was doing. So then, with Hall's encouragement, I went to Juilliard and I was there from '59 to '61. During that period I spent a lot of time looking at the scores and listening to the Juilliard Quartet's recordings of Bartók's Fourth and Fifth Quartets. They're both in arch form, ABCBA, and that made a real impression on me, lasting all the way into the '80s, when I wrote *The Desert Music* and *Sextet*, and just two years ago in *Runner* and *Music for Ensemble and Orchestra*, all in that same arch form. In terms of teachers, I had lessons with Vincent Persichetti, by far the outstanding composition teacher there. I went in with a piece, might have been for violin and piano, and I said to him something like "I'm not sure how to analyze this. Maybe it's sort of free atonal?" And he said, "Hmm, I don't think it's atonal. It's really not free, either." (*laughs*)

DL: (*laughs*)

SR: And then he said, "I know it's difficult to put in the Roman numerals," meaning the harmonic analysis, but he said, "Here's a dominant, but you also use the lower two, and it's ambiguous about which is better. You've actually added lots of other notes, so it's an altered dominant." And I thanked him profusely. Also, I have to tell a very interesting story about Vincent Persichetti. Shortly after I graduated, I went to the concert of some young Juilliard graduate, I can't think of his name. This was some- where at NYU. I was sitting down in a small room and, before the concert begins, I see Mr. Persichetti walk in. And he sits behind me. I don't say a word, but I think, "Oh, that's inter- esting. He must have been a star student." And I listen to the concert, which was kind of neither here nor there, and when it was over, I turned around and I said, "Mr. Persichetti, how nice of you to be here." And he said, "Well, I try to keep up with my students." And then he says to me, "How's that dom- inant eleventh doing?" And I'm thinking, "This guy is amaz- ing, which piece is he talking about?" He goes, "You know, the one with the maracas and the organs?" Oh, *that* dominant eleventh! (*laughs*)

DL: (*laughs*) Even I knew which one he was talking about!

SR: Well, I froze up, you know? Because I'm facing this guy who knows everything.

DL: Well, that's also the power our teachers have over us.

SR: Yeah. So, I said, because it hadn't been recorded, "I didn't know you'd heard that." He said, "Well, I like to keep up." He had come to a concert of mine, quietly sat down and listened and left. Not to show me what a great guy he was, but because he was interested in the music!

DL: Yes.

SR: And then I turned around to him, we were finishing the conversation, it was time to leave, and Hall Overton had just passed away. So I said to him, "I guess you heard about Hall?" and he paused for a moment and said, "Well, you know, I don't really believe in death." And I shook his hand. If I'd been older and more familiar, I would have embraced him. That was the last time I ever saw Vincent Persichetti.

DL: Oh, my G-d. That's a beautiful story.

SR: Isn't that incredible?

DL: Beautiful.

SR: After that I went out to California to Mills College, to do my master's degree. Luciano Berio had just begun teaching there. Wait, I left something out. While I was still at Juilliard, Berio gave a concert at The New School in New York. So, I went to the Berio concert, and he started out with *Circles*, his setting of ee cummings.

DL: Which was written right then. It must have been in '60 or '61 that *Circles* was written.

SR: Yes, it was, it was fresh off the presses.

DL: It was fresh.

SR: And Cathy Berberian was there to sing it. It begins with "sssss," the beginning of the word *stinging*, and while she's pronouncing this, he's got sandpaper blocks imitating the sibilance. And I'm thinking, "Hmm, unpitched percussion imitates sibilance. Thanks! How much do I owe you for that?" *(laughs)*

DL: *(laughs)*

SR: And this is after hearing innumerable, sentimental settings of ee cummings by other American composers, completely missing the point, which is that it was about phonemes. Anyway, reconnecting with Berio at Mills College, the piece of his that impressed me was *Omaggio a Joyce*, which was again Cathy Berberian, this time reading *Finnegans Wake* and then him editing it into fragments. No one can read *Finnegans Wake* all the way through and understand what they're reading. If you cut it in pieces it's just phonemes, which is just exactly what Berio wanted. Still later he said, "I'm going to play you two pieces of [Karlheinz] Stockhausen, I want to get your reactions." First, he played *Electronic Studies* and then he played *Gesang der Jünglinge* and for me it was clearly *Gesang der Jünglinge*, because of the voice. And putting those three incidents together, when I started doing tape music, on my $100 Wollensak tape recorders, using tape loops like everybody else in the early '60s, I worked with speech loops. I began to realize that was a very rich acoustical source and it had meaning, so it's really interesting and worthwhile. So, I have to thank Berio for starting me on that path that led to *It's Gonna Rain*.

DL: It's so interesting that you say that. I always feel that one of the things that's so fundamental to those early tape pieces of yours is that they're not really about the technology, they're really about the people. There is something very human about them. If you look at them technically, we can see that there are tapes and they overlap in a particular way, and certain technological things happen. But what we hear is their documentary nature, that they're about the lives of people and about the speech of people. I think that means there's a bigger doorway into those pieces for listeners than there is for a piece like *Electronic Studies* by Stockhausen.

SR: Yes. At the time when I did *It's Gonna Rain*, and later *Come Out*, I thought, "This is my vocal music. But I'm not setting a text; I'm setting human beings."

DL: I think that's really great and really important. I also think those pieces show that you are learning as much from the civil rights struggles going on around you as you are from Berio. Maybe more. It's always a question of whether you get your best lessons from your teachers or your colleagues or just by paying attention to the world around you. Whenever I have to talk about who my greatest influence is, I always say it's Michael Gordon. Michael and I came up as students together at Yale and he was writing things that were so courageous. I couldn't even imagine that a composer could have that much courage. I learned a huge amount from his ability to focus on something, to commit to it. I loved my teachers and I got a lot out of them, but how you learn to commit to what you know is just as important as what you know.

SR: Right. Well, there are a lot of really important influences I had after Berio for sure. While at Mills I would obviously be in class most of the days, but during many of the nights I was listening to John Coltrane at the San Francisco Jazz Workshop.

His music and the intensity of his quartet made a very deep impression on me. It led me to compare most of my fellow student composers with their dense, serial scores, which they never demonstrated at the piano, to Coltrane, who simply picked up his instrument and the music came out. This led me to the conviction that, whatever my limits as a performer, I would do best to form a group and perform in my own compositions. This led to an early group in San Francisco and eventually to Steve Reich and Musicians back in New York. While still at Mills, around 1962 or '63, I heard Coltrane's album *Africa/Brass*. That particular piece was more than sixteen minutes just on the low E of the double bass. One harmony for over sixteen minutes. Certainly a forerunner and influence on what was soon to emerge as "minimal music." Also at Mills, I heard recordings of African drumming and shortly after that I discovered A. M. Jones's book, *Studies in African Music*. This eventually led to a trip to Ghana in 1970 after I had composed early pieces like *Piano Phase*, *Four Organs*, and *Phase Patterns*. The trip certainly encouraged me to continue my work with repeating patterns and phasing but also to return to my own background in percussion, which led to my piece *Drumming*.

After I left Mills I met Terry Riley, who was also a big fan of Coltrane. In 1964 I helped him put together the first performance of *In C*, which made a very strong impression on me. In turn, I suggested the pulse on the high Cs on the piano that became standard in performance. That was certainly a very important and formative relationship in my development.

Later, in '73 and '74, I studied Balinese gamelan Semar Pegulingan and gamelan Gambang on the West Coast with Balinese teachers. That undoubtedly had an influence on my *Music for Mallet Instruments, Voices, and Organ*.

A bit after that I wanted to know more about my own Jewish tradition, which led me to study cantillation of the Hebrew scriptures in New York and Jerusalem.

Now, whether all this adds up to my having been a "normal student at a normal music school," who's to say?

DL: So, you never wanted to be a teacher yourself?

SR: No, not really. While I was at Mills I was a graduate assistant to Professor Robert Erikson and then later I taught briefly at The New School in New York. I really wasn't interested in teaching, so eventually I just got jobs out in the world. This allowed me to concentrate all my musical energy on my own music. In San Francisco I was a cabdriver for a year and then spent another as a postal clerk. Back in New York I worked briefly as a soundman for films, and then Phil Glass and I had a moving company at one point—I think you've written a piece about it?

DL: *Chelsea Light Moving.*

SR: Right. Well, while all this was going on, I completed the tape pieces *It's Gonna Rain* and *Come Out*, and things began to happen. Through my friend, the composer David Behrman, *Come Out* was recorded by Columbia Records and released around Christmas 1967, along with over twenty records of new music by Boulez, Stockhausen, Cage, and many others. *Come Out* received a lot of very positive attention. At the same time I was working on *Piano Phase* and forming a small group with Jon Gibson, Arthur Murphy, and sometimes pianist and conductor James Tenney. We began giving concerts, including a significant one in 1967 at the Park Place Gallery, run by Paula Cooper. Later, Steve Chambers and Philip Glass joined the group so we could perform *Four Organs* and *Phase Patterns*, which was also for electric organs. It was shortly after that, in early 1971, that I made my first trip to Europe with this group, and we played in Paris and then in London at the ICA. That began the possibility of making a living as a composer who played his music with his own group. I put all my energy into writing, rehearsing, and the group grew. The complete *Drumming* needed twelve musicians, and by 1976, *Music for 18 Musicians* was completed. With these pieces we began to tour the world. Performing my music with my own ensemble proved to be the answer of how to survive as a composer.

But as to teaching, David, you have had enormous success as a composer. Your Pulitzer Prize–winning *the little match girl passion* opened up so many choral music performances for you, and then your music for the film *Youth* with Michael Caine and Harvey Keitel was nominated for an Oscar, and I'm sure it's still playing all over the world. Then you wrote the music and very uniquely staged and directed *the loser*, your setting of some of the novel by Thomas Bernhard. It seems you don't really have to teach, so I guess you really like teaching. Did you know early on that you also wanted to teach? Did you know that you had that gift, as well?

DL: When I began as a composer, I became interested in everybody in the world who was writing music, and I thought that one of my responsibilities was to be a booster for composition in general. I was supposed to love all composers and love all music and spread the good news about how great it is to write music, to everyone who would listen. When I was an undergraduate, I was a chemistry student. I was supposed to go to medical school and, like you, I had to decide whether or not I was going to dedicate myself to composition. I would have been a terrible doctor, so I'm happy I made the decision that I did. But I remember thinking that I wanted to continue my studies with a teacher whose music I really loved, so I made a list of the composers I was listening to, in order to see where they taught. And none of them taught, anywhere. None of the composers I was listening to were teachers. They were all practicing composers, they were out in the world doing what they were supposed to do. That was great for them but really disappointing for me. I remember thinking then that there is a value to being someone who can be enthusiastic about music in all directions—to the people around you and the people who are older than you and the people who are younger than you. You know, it's important to figure out how to pass the knowledge down. I really love talking about music, and I love talking about it with you and I also love talking about it with my students. I probably love talking about it way too much.

SR: Judging from the Sleeping Giants group of composers and lots of other composers who have passed through Yale with you and Martin Bresnick, it's not just a place where composers learn, it's a place where composers go and then come out and do wonderful things in the world. When you were a student, do you remember when you first heard my music?

DL: When did I hear your music? I was working at a music store, my high school job, 1974. I worked at a record store in Westwood, California, which is a store that is no longer there. Not that there are record stores anywhere, but...

SR: (*laughs*)

DL: This was not a particularly good store. I was their classical music stock boy. I was a really nerdy classical music–loving person, and my job was to keep track of the department. I would reorder records when the stock got low and file them when they came in. If something interesting came through the remainder bin, I would just take it. And basically, that meant any composer whose name I didn't know, I would take their record, or I would buy their record. So, your record showed up, the one that has *It's Gonna Rain* and *Violin Phase*. I'd never heard of you, I'd never heard of this music, I didn't know who you were. I was just a high school student. I took the record and listened to it. *Violin Phase* didn't shock me because it's a violin—I thought, "I know what a violin is." Then I heard the flip side, *It's Gonna Rain*, and I thought, "I've never heard anything like this in my life." I had been writing music since I was nine and I never imagined that music could be made out of speech, or could be made with machines, or could be made without changing harmony. The piece really challenged so many things I thought I knew. I became immediately very curious about you and your world. I started researching, reading the *Village Voice*, buying more records. I found out about Philip Glass and Meredith Monk and La Monte Young. Someone who knew a little more about new music told me, "You know, the really funny thing about all the composers that you are listening to is they all live within a few blocks of each other in lower Manhattan." Well, I'm in southern California, I'm seventeen years old, and I make a vow at that moment that I'm going to live in that neighborhood, someday. And I have lived in that neighborhood for thirty-eight years now. You are responsible for a lot in my life! I became a big groupie of yours. In 1974, *Drumming* came out, the recording on Deutsche Grammophon. My sister asked me what I wanted for my eighteenth birthday. I said, "Look, I don't have any money. You can get me this recording." Deutsche Grammophon records were $5.00 a disc then, which was a million dollars to me. And that is what my sister gave me. I still have the record.

SR: I do, too.

DL: The things I heard in your music were really important to me. They represented a different way of understanding how pieces get made. I started writing music because I had heard and loved Shostakovich, and that made me love melody and harmony and those traditional dramatic shapes that are based on nineteenth-century music and on the very nineteenth-century idea of how life works. Hearing your early pieces opened a window for me into a different definition of what a composer could be and what a piece of music could be. I basically have lived with that definition ever since.

SR: Mea culpa.

DL: (*laughs*)

SR: Okay, now jumping to your piece *The So-Called Laws of Nature*, which overlaps our mutual interests in several ways. The title is a quote from Wittgenstein and I've heard the piece, first recorded, or part of it recorded. And then I saw it when we were together recently at Lincoln Center. What struck me was that the setup, the lines of instruments were clearly reminiscent of the lines of marimbas, drums, and glockenspiels in *Drumming*. The music, however, is very, very different. I've got the score right here. I was looking at it and thinking, Sō Percussion said to me that this is hard, but this is not hard. This is *really hard*.

DL: (*laughs*)

SR: So, tell me, what's the story?

DL: First of all, my piece is a very conscious attempt to follow up on your piece, *Drumming*. Of all your pieces, *Drumming* was a major milestone in my life. It's a piece I've thought about more than a lot of your other pieces. At least to me, in my imagination, it's a really important and transitional piece for you, as well.

SR: You're right.

DL: Sō Percussion, when they were still students, wanted to commission a piece from me. One of them had gotten a grant from Yale, where they were all studying, and that grant would have allowed them to commission something very small from someone. They came to meet with me in New York and they said that they didn't have very much money, and they were hoping it might be enough to commission a tiny piece from me. What I told them was, okay, since you don't have a lot of money, you have to let me write whatever piece I want to write. And what I wanted to write was a piece that was gigantic, and would be so hard that they would have to work on it for an entire year.

SR: (*laughs*)

DL: Well, I thought, they're students. All they're doing in school is practicing anyway, they might as well spend their time practicing my piece. For this amount of money, they would have to let me make them work.

Their original conversation with me was about how important *Drumming* was for them. They told me that *Drumming* was the most significant piece in the repertoire for them and that their goal was eventually to do a program where they would tour *Drumming* and add my piece. I have to say, this was terrifying to me, to write a new piece that could be on a program with *Drumming*. But it put me in the mind from the very beginning that I had to figure out a way to make a piece that was strong enough to hold its own, next to your piece. And it also made me think that my piece could be a comment in some way on what I learned from *Drumming* in particular and from your music in general. The Wittgenstein quote that gives my piece its title is of course a nice pun that has the ensemble's name in it. And it is true that I first heard about the Wittgenstein quote when I was a chemistry student at Stanford, from some friends who were taking a philosophy class, who were totally obsessed with Wittgenstein's notion that the laws of nature might be mere descriptions of the things that are important in the world but not the things themselves. But it is also true that the title is a reference to the Wittgenstein quote in *Proverb*, which is another of my favorite pieces of yours. So there are many connections to your music in my piece. Certainly, having everyone playing the same instruments in each movement, paying attention to how people set up and where they stand and how they move, paying attention to the visual and theatrical attributes of the performance. I don't think I would have paid attention to these things if I hadn't already paid attention to them in *Drumming*.

SR: Well, you sure took off on the theatrical part. I mean, in your later works. You designed the unique set for *the loser* which puts the solo performer on a tiny platform enormously elevated by a crane from the stage up to the front of the balcony, and people can only sit in the balcony with most of the theater empty. Everyone is sort of in this intimate "cabaret in the balcony."

DL: I love the theater, and I have a theater background. It's really important for me that live performance acknowledges that musicians make music while you watch them make it. The nineteeth-century classical music idea is that performers are the vessels through which the gods communicate to us. And the gods are a few men who lived in Vienna in the early nineteenth century.

SR: *(laughs)*

DL: And that the job of a performer onstage is to be the mediator, the conduit through which the genius of the past can flow. In reality, if musicians are on a stage and we are watching them, there is no fundamental difference between their performance and a Beckett play or a ballet. A composer might want to take advantage of the fact that we experience music in a theatrical environment. My piece tries to do that. It asks the players to use the same hand motions, to turn at different times, to move in particular ways. The performance instructions govern how the theater of it is supposed to look.

CHAPTER 2

BRIAN ENO

Brian Eno: I first heard *It's Gonna Rain* quite some time after you released it. I think it must have been about 1971 or '72, something like that, that I first heard it. I don't know when you first released it. Was it 1968 or '69, something like that?

Steve Reich: Yeah, it was first on Columbia, in '68, I believe.

BE: So, it was the Columbia release that I heard, and I heard it in the house of my friend Peter Schmidt, who was a painter. He's no longer alive. Peter and I spent a lot of time together listening to new music. One night he put on that piece, and it was, I have to say, one of the three or four really life-changing musical events of my life. Everything I thought I understood about music needed to be revised (*laughs*). It had a very, very big impact on me. It really set me thinking again about what music could be, and what the act of listening consisted of, because it made me realize that listening was a very creative activity. It wasn't a passive activity. The assumption of classical music had been that you sit back in the seat and the music washes over you and it's all carefully made and perfectly done, and you sit there quietly and don't do anything. Basically, you're a receiver. But one of the things that really struck me about *It's Gonna Rain* was that the most active thing in the room besides the music was my perception, which was constantly changing. I was always hearing new things. But, of course, I knew how the piece was made and I knew the amount of sonic material in it was actually very, very small.

Now, at this time, in the midseventies, we had just moved into the era of multitrack recording. And so, everybody was putting as much stuff into the music as they could. You know—"There's a track free, what could we put there? Let's have some strings or a synthesizer or something," and music was getting fatter and fatter (*laughs*). It had this kind of obese quality to it. And then this piece came along with just about the very minimum of sonic material in it—and so much was going on! I thought, "This is amazing: so much is happening here and so little is being used!" Now, I've always been very fond of economical composition both in painting and in music, and this set a new standard for me of what economy meant. I mean, I was never a big multitracker or anything like that—never went for big, inflated compositions—but this really shocked me. I haven't listened to that piece many times in my life, actually—it's not a fun piece (*laughs*)—not something that you put on when you're cooking dinner or something like that, you know? It's a piece you put on when you really want to have an experience of some kind, a sort of significant experience. So, I save it for those occasions. If I'm going to listen to it, I sit down, I make sure nothing else is going to happen for a while, and I listen to it again. I've played it to a lot of other people, and I've found that is not a good idea unless they are also in the state of being ready to welcome something quite big to happen to them. So, I don't play it lightly, no. (*laughs*)

Compositionally, the other thing that really interested me about
It's Gonna Rain was this: almost the whole history of music is
about creating sonic events that happen in a fixed relationship
to each other. If you look at the notation of music, you get the
bar line that keeps everything tied together, and in fact, probably 99% of music is constructed in that way. The project is to
make a set of sonic events that are kind of bolted together, and
that act in concert with each other, and the job of composing is
to bolt them together in good ways. And suddenly there's this
piece, where the elements are not bolted together but are allowed to run free. That was absolutely a breakthrough to me.

Now, funnily enough, I had been doing something a little bit
similar myself with playing with tape recorders. But I wasn't
really conscious of what I was doing. In fact, it was probably a
default position because I didn't have available to me any more
conventional ways of making music. At art school I'd gained
access to a tape recorder which had three recording speeds and
I made my very first piece of music by striking a large metal
lampshade and recording it at all three speeds.

All I did was I'd hit the thing, wait until it finished ringing,
and then hit it again. And I did that on three separate tracks. I
didn't make any attempt to synchronize the different takes to
each other—and I liked the random cascade that resulted. So, I
got a result which was a very crude version of "asynchronistic"
music, you might say. And I didn't think much about the fact
of the asynchrony. It wasn't until I heard *It's Gonna Rain* that I
thought, "This is a thing. This is something important." Breaking that fundamental, ancient musical rule, of having all the elements stuck together with each other and moving together,
breaking that rule suddenly liberated a whole lot of music. And
actually, of course, it liberates the listener into a new way of
listening—because every new form of music is really a new form

of listening, as well. So, then I started copying that piece: in fact, a lot of the work that I did after hearing *It's Gonna Rain* is really based on that experience of allowing things to exist asynchronously and become what I went on to call *generative*.

Generative means that, instead of starting out with a precise sonic plan, "I want the music to sound like this at this point, this at that point"—specifying the whole thing in advance, which is how composition normally works—instead of that, saying, "I'm going to invent a system of some kind, a musical system, and I'm going to let that system play out. And I'm going to listen to the result." So the composer becomes sort of the audience, the first audience for the piece. You let the piece run. You listen to it. And if you don't like it you change the rules and try again (*laughs*). It's basically a different assumption about what "composing" means. Is composing something like architecture, the careful putting together of all the elements of a plan to make a finished building, or could it also be making a set of rules and materials and procedures and seeing how they react together—which is more like gardening. The point is that you, the composer, don't know exactly what the end result is going to be—and it might be different each time the piece is performed.

So, I think what I'm trying to say is that the difference between this kind of composition and let's say normal or classical composition is, first of all, that you start out in this type of composition by inventing. The composition is really inventing this system. You don't specify precisely what it's going to do. The piece generates itself. And in fact, it's arguable that you couldn't have scored *It's Gonna Rain* in any conventional way. The score would be a description of how you make this piece come into existence. In the case of *It's Gonna Rain*, you may say, "Take a small loop of tape, play it on two tape recorders which don't play at exactly the same speed." That would be a sort of description of how to begin to get that piece. But that's a description of a process, you know, it's not a description of the sonic experience or exactly how the piece plays out.

SR: Exactly. Two questions. One, did you realize how important—for me, at least—the slowness was, the glacial slowness with which this was happening, and that that was essential? That if it happened quickly it would be, "Who cares?"

BE: Yes, absolutely. If it happened quickly it would be like a nice trick, a novelty of some kind. But because of the gradualness, you were sucked into that process and you started hearing these tiny shifts, these tiny differences. Now, I had been reading a cybernetician called Warren McCulloch, who cowrote a brilliant essay called "What the Frog's Eye Tells the Frog's Brain." A frog's eyes don't scan like ours. Our eyes scan all the time, they're always in motion. And they do that so that they don't habituate to whatever they are looking at. But you can practice habituation. If you stare at something for a very long time and don't move your eyes, you'll find you cease to be able to see it. The reason the frog stares fixedly at the landscape for a very long time is because everything that isn't moving becomes invisible—and anything that moves becomes intensely visible—and if something moves the frog eats it. The frog uses the fact of habituation to distinguish the parts of the environment that are live, that are moving. When I was listening to that piece, I was thinking of that Warren McCulloch essay because what was happening with my ears was that anything that was common was starting to recede in the background of my attention and the little tiny, tiny fractional differences from moment to moment were starting to become more and more important. I remember very, very clearly hearing birds, lots and lots of birds at one point. Now, I knew nothing had changed in the mix of the music. I knew you weren't sitting behind a mixing desk saying, "Let's bring up the birds now." (*laughs*) What had happened was in my attention. What had happened was a change in how my perception was working. I can really remember having the shivers when this happened. I thought, "This is a piece of music that is playing my brain. It's playing my perceptions. It's making things happen in my mind that are, in some sense, optical illusions or aural illusions, if you like." I was focusing in on the really minute changes that were happening and which were a result of that very long process. Of course, the other thing I have to say is that I wasn't having just a technical experience like that. I wasn't just sort of sitting there thinking, "Now what's going on? Is this perceptual…?" No. I was thoroughly, totally immersed in the piece of music. And completely lost in this huge world of sound that had opened up to me from this tiny fragment. That was really what was fascinating to me, that there was so much to be found in a tiny moment of sound. It was the biggest gift. I can never stop saying thank you for it. (*laughs*)

SR: You're very, very welcome. (*laughs*)

BE: Thank you.

SR: A lifetime of welcomes. Question two, did you ever go on to hear the very depressing second half of the piece?

BE: Do you mean *Come Out*?

SR: No, no. *It's Gonna Rain*. There's a first movement and then there's a little pause, and then he says, "They didn't believe it was gonna rain, but sure enough…" and then this huge loop begins to come apart and it's really like the world's coming apart as you listen.

BE: Yes, yes. I didn't listen to that at the time, because the first time I heard *It's Gonna Rain* I just didn't want to hear anything else for quite a long time (*laughs*). I was so in that world and it was probably some months before I heard the second piece. The second part. Yes, that was quite a different prospect, but I also loved that, as well. Yes, and it was sort of apocalyptic, actually. In fact, that would be very interesting to listen to again now (*laughs*). Very good music for this point in time, I think.

SR: It was shortly after the Cuban Missile Crisis and that was hanging in the air and here he is talking about the end of the world. *It's Gonna Rain* begins so that you know it's from the biblical Noah story. Did that play any role at all, maybe even subconsciously, while you were listening?

BE: Well, what I was very aware of was that this voice, that preacher's voice, was absolutely freighted with all sorts of history. I knew that it was biblical, the reference, or I assumed it was. But what I most thought was the choice of that particular voice, and the fact that it was recorded with a lot of other ambient sound around it, was actually very important to this piece. It took me a while to realize that, because one of the first things I did, after I heard that piece, was made my own version of *It's Gonna Rain* using a recording that I got off the radio of the actress Judi Dench.

SR: Oh! Wonderful! Love to hear that.

BE: And there was a line that she used—it was in a radio play—and she said at one point in the play, "You don't ask why." And I thought, okay, I'm gonna do a Steve Reich with that phrase (*laughs*). And I replicated exactly what you did on *It's Gonna Rain*, and it was nowhere near as good. One of the reasons it wasn't as good was because his voice, the preacher's voice, carried within it so much baggage. There was so much history in that voice. For me, as an English person, it was also kind of an unfamiliar, exotic voice in a certain way. But there was a lot of pain and angst and emotion in the voice. Whereas Judi's voice, which was lovely, was like a nice, British voice, very sweet. And, of course, it was recorded in a radio studio, so there was nothing else going on. So, I then became aware of how important the choice of that particular type of fragment was. The fact that it was a found piece, it was something that hadn't been done for recording, something where you hadn't excluded all the other stuff that was going around it. And in fact, it's the stuff that's going on around it that you start to hear more and more as the piece goes on. You stop focusing so much on his voice and you start hearing traffic, and there's one point, I remember at one point I hallucinated a huge brass section in there (*laughs*). I don't know what that was, but it sounded like horns. It was as clear as anything.

SR: It's overlapping vowels which are all fairly clearly pitched in D major—I chose that because of the speech melody and the intensity of that speech melody.

BE: Okay, yes. Well, it was a very brilliant choice, I think. So, as I became familiar with the piece, I realized the most important compositional decision probably was the choice of that particular loop. That was the piece that distinguished it from me fiddling around with Judi Dench or whatever I tried. (*laughs*)

SR: Did you listen later to *Come Out* or did you feel "It's nothing new"?

BE: Oh, yes, yes. I did hear *Come Out*. Of course, it wasn't quite such a revelation to me in the sense that, as I said, the real revelation for me about *It's Gonna Rain* was this astonishing fact that within a tiny fragment of sound was a world. A very rich, busy, fertile world. So, having heard that, I sort of expected it (*laughs*). How quickly we become *blase*! But the shock was *It's Gonna Rain* for me.

SR: You use the word *ambient*, which of course has become closely associated with you. Did *It's Gonna Rain* play any role in moving you toward what became ambient music?

BE: Yes, a huge role. So, ambient had some roots in what I had been doing anyway, as I told you, about these kinds of ways of making pieces of music asynchronously. But the thing about *It's Gonna Rain* that really crystallized that thought was, okay, what about having a number of cycles that run independently of each other? And why don't we choose cycles that don't easily come back into sync, in mathematical language, are incommensurable? So, instead of choosing a cycle of four-somethings and six-somethings and ten-somethings—which is all going to come back into sync in 240—whatever the somethings are— why not choose cycles that will never get back into sync again, that will constantly be reconfiguring over each other and generating new clusters? And that idea was what all of the ambient music I did was really based on, the idea of saying, "I shall choose a number of musical elements, quite carefully, and then I shall set them into motion to play against each other and to constantly be throwing up new clusters and new combinations." And if I don't like it, I'll change something and do it again. So, the composition was a sort of empirical process, starting with the idea of setting a number of asynchronous processes in motion but then allowing myself the possibility of correcting them, of saying, "That bit doesn't work, leave that out. Now let's try this instead." I was familiar with the process music world of the 1960s and the '70s, I guess, and I was fascinated by it. But I wasn't so happy with the results always. I thought, why not get it right? (*laughs*)

SR: You composer, you! (*laughs*)

BE: Yeah, I did let the side down a little bit there, I think.

SR: I want you to know that there were at least three or four different versions of the first part of *It's Gonna Rain* based on exactly how slow they should be paced. Too slow? Boring. Too fast? Trivial. And then, "Ah, got it just right." That's aesthetics amidst the process. In other words, there's an irreducible aesthetic judgment that enters into the strict process.

BE: Yes, and I think what I objected to with some process music there was this kind of feeling of "Okay, we've got the process running, mustn't touch anything." And I would think, "Well, for fuck sake, you're composers! Your life is involved with touching things, with making sounds work!" Why not step back and say, yeah, it could be a little bit better or it could be different, it could be other ways. I'm not at all surprised to hear that you experimented with this and with getting it right because you're a composer, you know (*laughs*). But it seemed to me that a lot of the people who went into the process music world sort of were very nervous about actually engaging their compositional senses at all. As if the process should be sort of pure and intact on its own.

SR: Right.

BE: I mean, this is sort of a legacy of Cage, I think.

SR: I was just about to say that, yes.

BE: Cage was very doctrinaire about that and it was very much to do with, "This is the piece of music that the universe wants to produce at this moment, who am I to interfere with it?" sort of thing. (*laughs*)

SR: Cage could be very inhibiting in that respect.

BE: Yes.

SR: After this period, much of your life that followed was as a producer for several famous groups. I'm thinking particularly of when I was in Vermont about forty years ago and my son must have loaded into the car CD player or tape player U2's "Where the Streets Have No Name." You know that long, droney opening?

BE: Oh, yeah.

SR: And I heard that and I thought, "What's going on here? I'm not on drugs, so what's going on?" (*laughs*) And then I was impressed by the tune, the performance, and obviously I suspected... Did you have a hand in that opening? I had a feeling that must be Eno.

BE: Well, that is all centered around that guitar part (*imitates guitar melody*). Which was entirely invented by Edge, the guitar player.

SR: Wonderful musician.

BE: So he had already written that before I ever heard the song, so that was actually the beginning of the song. And that had started before I got there. So I think that the only contribution I made to that was to encourage them to keep it long, to make it long. And that certainly could have been an influence from you, in that I got used to listening to these long, repetitive, unfolding processes. But the actual musical content was pretty much established before I had anything to do with that particular piece. And I have to say, I don't know whether The Edge had ever listened to *It's Gonna Rain* or any of those pieces.

He may well have done, he's a keen listener. But we never discussed you at that time, not in that regard.

SR: Yeah, The Edge always struck me as a great minimal guitar-drummer (*laughs*). I mean, I'm paying him a real compliment. Usually you think of the drummer propelling the group, but in this case, it's The Edge propelling the group.

BE: Yes.

SR: What are you working on now?

BE: Well, I'm still making music. In fact, the reason I was late for you today is because I've just been working on a new piece, which I'm very, very pleased with. And I just completely lost track of time.

SR: Good.

BE: And suddenly thought, "Fuck!" and ran over here. (*laughs*)

SR: No, no. Fucking good! You got lost in a piece!

BE: We'll be good, I promise. But I've also been doing a lot of visual work for the last forty years or so—I trained as a painter, actually, not as a musician.

SR: I know, I remember that. I remember giving a concert at Queen Elizabeth Hall in the '70s. It might have been *Four Organs*, it might have been *Six Pianos*, something in there. And after it was over, you came up with RoseLee Goldberg, you had long hair, and you said, "Hello, I'm Brian Eno." And I thought, "Great! When I was his age, I was listening to Miles Davis and

John Coltrane, and here he's listening to me." Must have been Roxy Music time?

BE: Yes, that's right. That would have certainly been around that time.

SR: So here we are, still in touch.

CHAPTER 3

RICHARD SERRA

Richard Serra: I met you on the street one day, must have been around 1966 or '67, and you said, "Do you want to come up and listen to a recording?" And I said, "Sure." And you invited me up and you played *Come Out*.

Steve Reich: Right, right. What was your reaction to *Come Out*?

RS: I had never heard anyone deal with music or language in that way, turning language into music that had political content. I was completely floored by it. I remember you telling me about this Black kid who had been accused of murder, arrested, and taken up to a precinct in Harlem where he was beaten up. That's when the kid uttered that phrase, something like "I had to open the bruise to let some of the blood come out, to show them so I'd be taken out of the cell and cleaned up." And then what happened is you looped the phrase, and the phrase successively turned into music. I was amazed by it. That was the first phase piece I heard.

SR: It was the second one I ever did.

RS: I didn't hear the first one.

SR: *It's Gonna Rain*. I think you must have heard it later on, maybe not.

RS: I thought *It's Gonna Rain* came after *Come Out*?

SR: No, *It's Gonna Rain* was made in San Francisco before I left, and then when I came back to New York and got that place right around the corner from you, that's where I did *Come Out*.

RS: *It's Gonna Rain* doesn't have political content, though.

SR: No, *It's Gonna Rain* is just the end of the world using the Noah story. I did it in '65 just a little bit after the Cuban Missile Crisis. So the whole feeling of the end of the world was not so abstract for me, and I think maybe for others at that time, especially in the second part of the piece, which really got pretty dark. It certainly caught the tension of the time.

RS: Very contemporary.

SR: I haven't touched a tape recorder in...well, there are no tape recorders! (*laughs*)

I remember I gave you the score of an early version of *Piano Phase* about that same time, which showed basically what was going on in the tape pieces. Did you ever look at that? Because it makes the process graphically clearer.

RS: I think I still have it, but I think it's in Cape Breton.

SR: Right, but at the time, did you have any thoughts about the structure of what was going on in *Piano Phase*?

RS: If I remember correctly, the structure is based on adding a sixteenth, is that the one?

SR: Well, one performer gets slightly faster than the other and slowly moves ahead a sixteenth, not by adding anything but just by accelerating a little bit. In other words, you and I are in unison, you stay put and I get ever so slightly faster than you until I'm 1/16th ahead of you. And that's the phasing process. I thought it was impossible for people to do, but I found, hey, I can do it, it *is* possible.

RS: But doesn't it make a full return and then it's back in sync?

SR: Yes, if you keep on going. If you start in unison and go one ahead, two ahead, and so on, you finally get back in unison.

I guess the next thing that you were involved in was *Pendulum Music*. What is your memory or take on *Pendulum Music*?

RS: That would have been '69?

SR: '69 at the Whitney, it was you and Bruce Nauman and Michael Snow, and Jim Tenney releasing the mikes, and I was running the amplifier.

RS: I see *Pendulum Music* as a paradigm for the process movement because of the way you used process in relationship to material and time. My recollection was that performers—I don't know how far apart they were, maybe twenty-five feet apart—you probably know…

SR: It was about that. It fit the Whitney.

RS: And the speaker was placed, I think, right at the center of the room, the center of the circle.

SR: No, everybody had their own speaker.

RS: You are right. And each performer had their own mike tied to a cord attached to the ceiling. Then we pulled the mikes back and released them in unison. After we did that, we turned up the amplifiers. As the microphones passed over the speakers, it allowed the feedback to occur. None of them passed over at the same moment exactly so the feedbacks were out of sync, the performers stepped back and just let the piece come to a standstill as the mikes stopped swinging, that is my recollection.

SR: Yes, exactly. What was your take on that in terms of sculpture?

RS: I thought it was similar to Nauman falling in and out of the corner. The work caused a certain kind of dislocation of our sensibility, not in terms of space but in terms of sound. I thought it really slipped right into the middle of that whole process movement and brought it together—and it was so simple, too.

SR: (laughs) Yes, it was. Absolutely. Well, good ideas are often simple ones, as you seem to have noticed. Bringing us up to date, you mentioned in your email about your piece *Combined and Separated*, which Beryl and I really got attracted to in that recent show you had. And you said somehow it might have had something to do with my music, and I was wondering what you had in mind.

RS: Well, in that piece you have two juxtaposed sets of three forged rounds that are fifty tons each. In one set, they are right up against each other, and at the other end of the space the rounds are each standing alone, separated from each other by, say, two feet. I think the interval between them is what gives them their substance. The interval somehow relates to the structure of the sound in your music. And I think it has a lot to do with tempo, and timing. You can tell me if I'm wrong. I see timing as a value in itself. It's either quick or slow or concentrated or contracted or extended. In your music there are layered temporalities and in this sculpture there are layered ways of dealing with space. Time is subjective time. It's different than literal time in that it's more of a durational time. I think durational time is subjective, it's more psychological. And that compares to the viewing of the sculpture.

SR: Well, for me, actually, you had a small version in the side room? I think there were three or four pieces that were close to each other and three or four pieces that were spread out. But I mean, on a table, it wasn't like the main piece in the big room.

RS: *Nine*, the main piece in the big room consisted of nine forged rounds of different heights but identical weight, fifty tons. The rounds placed in the center were higher and more narrow, the lower and wider rounds were placed on the periphery. The higher central rounds prevented you from looking across the entire piece and made you meander through it. The piece was laid out in a circle which was impossible to discern, because you never got an overview of the entire sculpture. Most people preferred this piece to any of the other pieces in the show. You were one of the few people that liked *Combined and Separated* better. I thought that was an interesting observation because I tend to think of that piece as more abstract.

SR: Well, first of all, my gut reaction to the *Combined and Separated* was that the separated was relatively relaxed and the combined was very tense, even threatening.

RS: Yes.

SR: The separated were more spread out. They were like out in the country (*laughs*). And the combined were like lower Manhattan. They're in a sardine can. And I felt psychologically trapped, a very dark feeling of being unable to move because of the tightness in the combined part.

RS: I think that sardine analogy gives pieces that are juxtaposed a greater weight and a greater density.

SR: Yes, they definitely are dense as opposed to having a lot of space in between.

RS: Well, in that sense, it doesn't differ from a lot of your music which does that. It can contract and be very dense and then open and be very light.

SR: In musical terms, it's called *augmentation*, which is "da–da" becomes "daaa–daaa." You can literally expand quarter notes to half notes to whole notes etc., etc., etc., or go the other way. And in a number of my pieces, not *Come Out* or *Piano Phase* but particularly in *Four Organs*—you must have heard that one. It's for four rock organs and maracas?

RS: Yeah, I've heard that one.

SR: It was literally one musician shaking these maracas. He was the timekeeper, he was the clock, he was the energy moving the piece ahead. And then there were these attacks of all four of us together (*imitates electric organs*). And then individual notes begin to stick out like a bar graph in time, and then finally, fifteen minutes or so later, you have these long, held chords that are coming apart with this (*imitates maraca rhythm*), still going, the clock is still running. But you go from a very short series of chords that are jammed together to long, spread-out chords, like we're in Montana as opposed to Manhattan. And that to me was the analogy between the *Combined and Separated*.

RS: I never went as far as Montana. (*laughs*)

> *Serra gave the following speech when Reich was presented*
> *with the Edward MacDowell Medal in 2005.*

There emerge at various times and places manifestations of art which transform the realm of possibilities. New York in the late sixties was such a place. To invent, to originate something new was the pressing need of the moment. The group of young artists that would bring about the change came from different practices. They were musicians, dancers, sculptors, painters, filmmakers. I'll mention a few amongst others who were insistent on bringing about a break, a rupture: Michael Snow, La Monte Young, Philip Glass, Yvonne Rainer and the Grand Union, Trisha Brown, Bruce Nauman, Robert Smithson, Bob Ryman, and I have to add Steve and myself to this list. We were each other's audience and critics. The interchange of ideas nourished the new approach to materials, to time, to context, to process. We were all involved with process. Trisha did her *Accumulations* piece, Bruce fell in and out of a corner, I wrote the *Verb List* and splashed molten lead against the wall, Steve wrote his *Pendulum Music* for microphones, amplifiers, speakers, and performers. I was one of the performers when *Pendulum Music* was played at the Whitney in 1969 as part of the *Anti-Illusion* show, a show that summed up the activities of the moment and confirmed them as a movement. One could call *Pendulum Music* a paradigm for process art. Let me read a paragraph of Steve's notations:

"The performance begins with performers taking each mike, pulling it back like a swing and then in unison releasing all of them together. Performers then carefully turn up each amplifier just to the point where feedback occurs when a mike swings directly over or next to its speaker. Thus a series of feedback pulses are heard which will either be all in unison or not depending on the gradually changing phase relations of the different mike pendulums. Performers then sit down to watch and listen to the process along with the audience."

Steve's early work has had a lasting effect on me. *Come Out, It's Gonna Rain, Clapping, Drumming, Piano Phase* refuse to be eradicated from my mind, although I have no precise recollection of how the pieces develop. Listening to Steve is being in complicity with his process. Comprehension is a matter of complicity. My experience lags behind my anticipation, which has to do in part with the speed of sound. It keeps me alert, sometimes annoyingly so. Even after having heard a piece many times, I can never predict with any assurance how it will develop as I am listening. The density and saturation of sound, the specific gravity, prevents recollection.

Sometimes, as the music evolves, patterns change so swiftly that its logic evades me. I am unaware of its consistency, particularly in the later work where I only experience the emotional effect and I completely give myself over to the rush of sound. Yet I am aware that there is an exact weight to the lightness of the sound. Although there are varying durations, the power of Steve's music has a lot to do with its speed. I find my ear and mind being flooded with ideas and emotions which follow in quick succession. Tempo counts. Tempo, timing may be a value in and of itself, and it's of particular importance to me whether the pace is quick or slow, contracted or extended. It's the same subjective time that conveys meaning to perception as you walk through an installation which I recently completed in Bilbao titled *The Matter of Time*. It is based on the idea of multiple or layered temporalities. Duration, not time on the clock, not literal time, is the main organizing principle that drives the work. The time of experience can be fast or slow, which depends entirely on bodily movement. The listening time of Steve's music is subjective time, psychological time, durational time, and comparable to the viewing time in my work.

Some of the music places me in a constant state of unease with its continuous, relentless, incessant modulations. It forces me to follow its trajectory. It gains power through the building of similarities connecting them one after the other so that the process of adding produces a kind of layered rhythm: forward, forward, backward, forward. As the pieces develop, the sound includes and connects all that you have previously heard in its elastic stretch. It is as if the sounds begin to roll forward, pitch backward and then forward again, shift and repeat. I understand that the form is a round but that is not what I hear. This is not the "Alouette" I learned as a child.

When I recall *Come Out* or *It's Gonna Rain*, I don't recall the structure or concise logic of the pieces. What I retain is a feeling of alienation and discomfort. It might seem strange but the discomfort that arises from a rethinking of form is what I cherish in art, whether it's Schoenberg, Feldman, Newman, or Pollock. Let me try to explain what I mean by rethinking of form in relation to Steve's early pieces where he uses prerecorded language. He starts out with a seemingly simple premise: a found voice, a sentence uttered. But as he subjugates this found language to his structure of overlays, as it is repeated again and again, the detail of the detail begins to resonate. I find that I am drawn into the infinitesimal, the infinitely subtle quick moving variations. It is then that I realize that I am lost in the infinite vastness of the whole. As the voices spin out, they become something other than language. The words are transformed by rhythm into emotion. Words sing as pure sound as they reach the end of the path that they trace through their phased diversions and combinations. The result is music, not language. Language is being pushed to the breaking point where the meaning of the word has been obliterated so as to allow its potential for music to emerge. It's as if the original word or phrase has been stretched along an abstract infinitely variable line dissolving its original meaning in a process which allows for new meaning to emerge. [Robert] Smithson loved Steve's work. I can still hear him say: Oh, yeah, I get it, the disintegration of language into a vortex of entropy.

It takes an effort to sustain listening to Steve's music. That's its virtue. You might say great composers need great listeners. Steve was never tempted by commissions for operas or symphonies. He says at the end of his interview with Jonathan Cott that life is too short to just write the next orchestral commission. "Best to do what you have been assigned to do. I have been given my assignment just as everyone has his or her assignment." I don't think I am wrong when I assume that Steve looks at his assignment as given by a higher power. Whether we believe in assignments, whether we are secular or religious does not matter. In Steve's case, his belief translates into conviction. It is his conviction that makes the work compelling.

Having taken this tack, I want to compare two major composers of the second half of the twentieth century in terms
of their philosophical underpinnings. Steve Reich's belief
of having been given an assignment to fulfill differs radically from John Cage, who stated: "I have nothing to say
but I'm saying it." I always thought Cage's statement was
somewhat disingenuous in that he used an attitude of indifference and a denial of meaning to bolster his musical the-
ory based on chance. The ability to believe and to confess
to a belief is a quality. Art, music, poetry would not exist
without belief systems. Belief systems are not synonymous
with ideologies. I do not mean to suggest that art ought to
communicate a specific ideology. Art is purposefully use-
less. It must refuse to serve. However, non-service does not
negate the ability or necessity for an artist to have a belief.
It may be a mere belief in self or a longing for belief. It may
be a belief in making a contribution. Assumptions, specu-
lations, all kinds of superstitions qualify as belief systems.
I simply don't believe that art can come out of an attitude
of indifference. That's where I take issue with Cage. We
all have fantasies, we all imagine, we all project. Making
art is an act of faith, a manifestation of hope.

I always felt that Steve had an ethical grounding which in
his early work translated into social and political respon-
sibility, whereas in the later work the emphasis is on the
historical and the spiritual. Steve didn't choose the words
for *It's Gonna Rain* or *Come Out* by chance. *Come Out* was
a political choice of content, echoing the concerns of the
Civil Rights Movement. I never got over the desperation
of a young Black man who was wrongfully arrested for
murder and after having been beaten in a Harlem police
precinct squeezed his bruised leg till blood came out so that
he would be taken out of his cell to be cleaned up. I came

upon his cry for the first time when Steve played the tape loop for me in his studio. Conceptually I begin with process, form, and structure. Here I found myself listening to a work where the form was content driven, where the account of the boy—"I had to like open the bruise up and let some of the blood come out to show them"—was turned into the sound of sheer anxiety. It floored me. *Come Out* violated any notion of music that I had held. It was with these early works that Steve became the key figure in creating a new music for my generation and the generations that followed.

CHAPTER 4

MICHAEL GORDON

Michael Gordon: I wanted to start by telling you how I discovered *Piano Phase*. I was fifteen and I got this book called *Notations* by John Cage. It's got a completely white cover, very minimal, and it just says "Notations" and "John Cage" at the bottom. The book is basically one page of a score from about 300 different composers. Now, as opposed to most of the pages that were overloaded with notes or incomprehensible graphics, there was one page with a complete section of a clearly notated piece.

Steve Reich: (*laughs*)

MG: And I could play one of the parts.

SR: Right.

MG: It wasn't some impossible thing that took months of virtuosic practice.

SR: It's one pattern and it's relatively simple.

MG: It's one pattern, but it's a completely different way of playing the piano. And I had been studying the piano since I was five and I was playing Beethoven piano sonatas. And I came across this and this is not the way you play the piano.

SR: *(laughs)*

MG: Can you imagine how attractive that was to a fifteen-year-old? Because it feels great, you know? One hand is going back and forth between two notes and one hand is doing a three-note pattern, and as they circle around, they're making a tune.

SR: And that's only one of the two parts.

MG: It requires a completely different skill set. You're playing the piano like a percussionist. One person has to lock into a steady tempo, which is a hard skill set, and in the late '60s that was a much harder skill set because people didn't focus as much on rhythm. And then the other person has to slowly speed ahead and then lock into the next pattern. You were asking the performers to do something that up until that point people had not been asking performers to do.

SR: That's right.

MG: I would imagine keeping steady is the harder part.

SR: Exactly. I always did the moving part, but Art Murphy, who I played it with, he did what I considered the hard part, which is trying to stay still when your impulse is to follow the person who's getting faster.

MG: There's a fascinating fight between consonance and otherness. I don't want to call it *dissonance*, but I want to call it *other-*

ness. The tune is very simple and identifiable, but as the one keyboard player moves forward, it goes into a completely different type of harmonic world.

SR: Right.

MG: It seems almost impossible to do. As the pianist is moving forward, it seems like there's a magnet pulling you to lock in.

SR: That's a very good description. It feels like a magnet.

MG: And that's a really interesting, amazing moment in a certain sense. We've got this shift from "I can do it with tape recorders" to "Can I do what the tape recorder does with people?"

SR: Right.

MG: The big thing about *Piano Phase* was the idea that here's this piece of music going through these shifts from sixteenth note to sixteenth note until it gets back to the beginning, on one hand very conceptual and process oriented, yet it brings forth something very mysterious, something bigger—out of simple elements comes a wondrous journey.

SR: Well, that depends on the notes, the subject, the pitches. You can't make good counterpoint out of a bad subject. There were a lot of rejected parts of the piece, and finally there are three parts. You were playing the first part, which is what Cage published because that's what I sent him, but in the whole piece there's a twelve-note pattern, an eight-note pattern, and a four-note pattern. They're all sort of contractions of the original. In other words, it's a mixture of a brand-new conceptual way of thinking. And at the same time, it brings in very old-school musical values, i.e., the notes and the rhythmic structure of the piece. Without those musical values, it would be an interesting experiment, but what else have you got?

MG: Let's talk about the rejects. Where is that file?

SR: Whatever still exists would be in my archive in Basel, in the notebooks from that period of time, and I have no idea. They're all similar. I think the hand-over-hand thing appealed to me right away and the idea that you'd go back and forth with the right hand, but because I'm left-handed, the more active role is in the left hand.

MG: Okay, so I do the opposite.

SR: Right. I had been fooling around with hand-over-hand patterns for a while. Just improvising patterns like that, but the real problem for me was: I did the tape pieces *It's Gonna Rain* and *Come Out* and I thought, "This is a great thing—but I want to do live music—but people can't do that—but it's such a great musical result." And back and forth and back and forth, until I said, "Okay, I'm the second tape recorder." And then I made a tape loop and played against the loop, and then finally I asked Arthur Murphy, who was a very good pianist and a composer at Juilliard, and I said, "We've got to try this." It was thrilling to go out to New Jersey, to Fairleigh Dickinson College at night to rehearse for a concert we were supposed to do, and to try it for the first time ever on two pianos. It was like "Look, ma! No tape!" (*laughs*)

MG: And that was '67?

SR: That was in 1967.

MG: So you played the part that went forward.

SR: I did.

MG: And later, when you started touring the piece—I've never seen you play this piece, so...

SR: I played the piece with Arthur all the time from when we started to tour. Later, Nurit Tilles, the pianist, came on board, and shortly thereafter Ed Niemann did, too, and they became the two-piano team Double Edge. They could play it much better than I could. As I got older, I found that it made me increasingly nervous.

MG: Talking about being nervous playing a piece: *Four Organs*.

SR: Not so bad. Just a huge amount of counting.

MG: I had the pleasure of playing *Four Organs* many times. I also should mention that we presented it on the first Bang on a Can Marathon in 1987. I didn't play on that. Petr Kotik played that with his group, the S.E.M. Ensemble. Later, Bang on a Can recorded it and I played on that.

SR: Yes, I know that recording. It's very good.

MG: Speaking with you about *Four Organs* on and off over many years, I think there were times when you felt like "Okay, it's a kind of a severe piece." Maybe the most severe piece in your catalog?

SR: I would agree, yeah.

MG: I was just wondering, when you look back, how do you think of it today?

SR: I think probably I was cooler on it at the time you and I were first talking about it, years ago. I look back, and it's a very good job of doing something that no one else, to my knowledge, has done. It came out of working on this electronic device that I had been spending a year on. There was this organization called EAT, Experiments in Art and Technology, back in the '60s, which Rauschenberg started with people at Bell Labs in New Jersey. I got involved and I made this plastic box I called the Phase Shifting Pulse Gate, which is not worth going into at great length,[1] but one thing about it, electronically, was a capacitor on each channel that would determine if the pulse was a short beep or a long beep or very long beep. And that interested me. The other part of the equation was a rediscovery of Pérotin, the twelfth-century French composer who I had learned about when I was at Cornell back in the '50s.

MG: That has a big effect on you later, but how did that affect *Four Organs*?

SR: Well, the biggest effect Pérotin ever had on me was *Four Organs*. I mean, *Proverb* is a conscious homage to Pérotin, but *Four Organs* is totally about augmentation. A short chord becomes long, very long. In a nutshell, what Pérotin is doing, especially in the big four-part organa, is taking a melodic line from the chant, and then stretching it out, so that instead of a melody note, it becomes a kind of drone. Not an endless drone, but a drone for a long time. And then the next note of the melody becomes a new drone or really a harmonic center, because in the twelfth century, harmonic centers were in the tenor voice. There were no lower voices. That's a very radical idea. Melody becomes drone becomes harmonic center. In *Four Organs*, a chord played for one eighth note gradually becomes 256 beats

---

1   For more on the Phase Shifting Pulse Gate, please see Reich's *Writings on Music 1965–2000*, pp. 38–44.

of held tones with slowly staggered released notes. That would never have happened if I hadn't had the Pérotin in my head as a kind of a basic model. Also, it's the longest V–I cadence in Western music. (*laughs*)

MG: Well, I think there are several ways of listening to the piece. There's a way where you hear the starkness and the severity and also the slowness of the narrative unraveling. I also think that if you have the right hall, the right kind of reverberation, it's a very beautiful sound. I've heard people say, "It reminds me of Debussy."

SR: (*laughs*) Good!

MG: I'm sure that's probably something that would come as a surprise to you.

SR: Yes, a pleasant surprise.

MG: But now I'd like to talk about *Music for Mallet Instruments, Voices, and Organ.*

SR: Can't wait.

MG: And especially about the voices, Steve. The voices in *Music for Mallet Instruments* led to *Music for 18 Musicians* and then to *Tehillim*, and that had a big effect on my writing and, I think, much of the vocal writing of many composers today.

SR: Perhaps it did. It offered an early music or jazz voice as an alternative to the operatic voice.

MG: Exactly. And until then, people weren't singing contemporary music with a clear straight tone. Just recently I wrote an hour-long piece for chorus, *Anonymous Man*. I had a great experience with The Crossing, a Philadelphia-based choir led by Donald Nally. I couldn't have imagined ever writing a choral work when I was younger. But the way people sing has changed. The way choruses sing has changed. A lot of that is due to how you use voices. Also, what constitutes text has changed. Your string quartet *Different Trains*, which was so radical in the way you wrote for strings and samples, it's about you!

SR: Yes, it is.

MG: And *Anonymous Man* is basically a memoir that I wrote about my life on Desbrosses Street, where I've lived almost the entire time I've been in New York. The piece is about my experience there as the neighborhood changed, and meeting Julie there. The text revolves around the lives of two homeless men who have lived on my block. Unfortunately, in many parts of New York, people are homeless. One man who has lived on my block for more than a decade is an erudite person. I stop and speak with him. He's always reading history, philosophy, in French, in Spanish, in English, and many times books I wish I had read but hadn't gotten around to. *Anonymous Man* is about my life on that block. Musically, and especially in terms of the singing, I think the clear sound makes it possible to have a direct connection with the singers and the text. I use very tight, canonic writing in the piece. In the fourth movement, "It's Julie Passing Through Town," there are twelve voices in a 1/16th note canon. It becomes very reverberant, cloudy, and mysterious. I can't help but think of the canonic writing in *Tehillim*. I hope I've done something good with it. (*laughs*)

SR: Well, I certainly enjoyed listening to *Anonymous Man*.

MG: Now, going back to *Music for Mallet Instruments, Voices, and Organ*, there are two things that strike me about that piece. One is the sound. In a certain sense, you found the sound. There's some real magic right at the beginning of *Music for Mallet Instruments* that says: this is something different, a monumental shift. You're always going back to that sound and building on it.

SR: Well, *Music for 18 Musicians* is certainly, as you say, the direct descendant of *Music for Mallet Instruments, Voices, and Organ.* When I finished *Music for Mallet Instruments*, I thought, "I want to continue this," and I started having rehearsals and expanding the ensemble, but I wanted to get rid of the electric organ and make it all acoustic. So, the strings, the violin, and cello in *Music for 18* became the sustaining instruments and replaced the organ. The voices grew from three to four. The mallet percussion and pianos increased. But you're right, everything I had done since 1965 except for the last part of *Drumming* was multiples of the same instrument against themselves. That was necessary to achieve an interlocking web of counterpoint where you couldn't separate out different voices by timbre, by which instrument was playing. There was just one giant contrapuntal instrument made of the combined identical instruments: two pianos in *Piano Phase*, four violins in *Violin Phase*, four organs in *Four Organs*.

MG: Six pianos.

SR: Six pianos in *Six Pianos*, which was written at the same time as *Mallet Instruments*, by the way. But at the end of *Drumming*, drums, marimbas, glockenspiels, voices, and piccolo all play at the same time. *Mallets* was just saying, "Just dive in!" and like you mentioned, why wait? Dive in right at the beginning. I loved the sound, the overall sound, the richness that comes from the normal idea of instruments of different timbre played simultaneously. Hey, what's new about that? Well, at the time, it was new for me and therefore very exciting.

MG: About three and a half minutes into the piece, you do something I think for the first time, which is that you change chords.

SR: That's right, at least the first time since 1965.

MG: We've talked a lot about staying on the same chord.

SR: Yes, absolutely.

MG: And I've heard you talk about songs like Junior Walker's "Shotgun"—it doesn't change chords, right? But then at that moment, how did changing harmonies feel?

SR: It felt great, it felt like liberation. It felt like "Oh, I can do this, too." In other words, it's kind of one step forward for me, one step back into Western tradition. And that process basically goes on for a good, long time. But you put your finger on it. There are four sections set off by changes in harmony.

MG: Well, I think after modernism and after the kind of minimalism that you were doing and that other people were into, I think that chord change, it seems like the whole history of Western music breathed a collective sigh of relief.

SR: (*laughs*)

MG: They were cheering or something. "Yeah, finally! It's been like twenty-five years, someone actually changed harmony!"

SR: Well, let's see, for me it was 1965 to '73, a little under ten years.

MG: It's a beautiful moment. And you don't go back. From then on your music shifts back and forth between sections where it hovers in one place harmonically, moving the patterns around and finding interest on a micro-scale, and then the harmonic shifts. I think of harmony like rocket fuel. It's such a big event. Your harmony changes in time. I think it's more than ten years to '84 and *Sextet*.

SR: Right, it was 1984.

MG: Now, *Sextet* is a completely different piece. I have to say I love *Sextet*—it's beautiful, it's fresh, it's radical, but it's also real chamber music.

SR: Yes.

MG: And it's structured, not necessarily like music of the classical period is structured, but it's structured like Bartók might structure one of his string quartets.

SR: Exactly.

MG: All the rhythmic relationships are organically related to each other as you slow down and speed back up. Five sections, ABCBA. And right away at the beginning, the chords start to shift. In that first movement, I think of that first movement as two outer sections and the inner section. The outer sections where the harmony is shifting, and those beautiful...

SR: Bowed vibraphones?

MG: Yeah, incredible. And then the middle, which is the stasis, in a sense. Here are the patterns and the patterns are shifting and changing and the musicians are doing all of these detailed things. You have to listen closely, and then back to the shifting chords. And then on to movement two.

SR: I think one thing that really needs to be said is that right before I wrote *Sextet* I wrote *The Desert Music*, which was a huge undertaking, taking well over a year, where, because of the subject matter, the harmonies get a lot darker, a lot more chromatic than in any other piece of mine, unless you go back to when I was a student, and I was imitating Bartók. But from *It's Gonna Rain* to just before *The Desert Music* it's what you could call *modal harmony* with very little chromatic dissonance—well, there's a few things in *Tehillim* here and there, but *Desert Music* is the big shift. Now, *Desert Music* is for a big orchestra, chorus, and it's not going to be done that often. I spent most of my life as a touring musician with Steve Reich and Musicians from about 1966–2006, and I thought, "Wouldn't it be great to have a piece that had those kinds of darker, interesting, chromatic harmonies, that we could tour with?" That was one of the major motivations for doing *Sextet*. Taking the harmonic world of *Desert Music* and putting it into chamber music with two pianists and four percussionists. Now, for me the best thing in the piece is the last movement.

MG: Oh, you like the last movement. Yeah, that's interesting. The second and fourth movement seem darker. Does *The Desert Music* have darker sections than that? I mean, that second movement is pretty dark.

SR: Well, *The Desert Music* varies with Williams's poems, but the answer is that they are similar.

MG: And how did you find the bowed vibraphones?

SR: There were no strings, so how can I get a sustaining sound without using the synths? So I just tried it myself. I had a bass bow, and I got some rosin. I had vibes at home, and I said, "Wow, it's like a very, very pure, non-vibrato string sound," which is exactly what I like in strings anyway. So, the vibraphone was a very good stand-in. It's challenging because the players have to play it with a bow in each hand, and they have to do it up-bow on the edge of the bar. You have to do it just right or you'll pull the bars off the instrument. I think it really works. It's a surprise. You don't think of the sound as part of a percussion piece.

MG: You also have the bass drums, which are so beautiful. You use a lot of bass notes on the keyboards. There's that one section at the end of the fourth movement, where it's just the synths playing the bass notes. It's one of the more unusual spots where you're featuring bass, and I know there are a lot of, I would say, frustrated bass players who wish you would have included basses more in your early music. It's not until much later that you do.

SR: Well, when you're writing for a touring ensemble, the last instrument you want is a double bass (*laughs*). And when I finally got into basses, I often got into electric bass just because of sound, and at that point, I was writing for other ensembles primarily and not as concerned about the touring part. That end of the fourth movement, which is just the very low synths doubled by bass drum and these interlocking chords between the two vibes, is, I think, very dramatic in a sparse way.

MG: It's gorgeous. And all these pieces, we've performed many times at Bang on a Can, but I have a score of *Sextet* and I must have gotten it before the piece was copied, because it's actually a photocopy of your handwritten score.

SR: Right.

MG: It's a great period of music, very exciting period. I feel fortunate that that was the period of music that I grew up in, and that I stumbled across it.

SR: I think we all meet who we're supposed to meet and encounter what we're supposed to encounter, and how that works, we don't exactly know. By the way, you have a very different percussion piece called *Timber*, which is not even for musical instruments. What about that?

MG: Yes, it's really for six 2x4s or any kind of wooden planks you can get. The fancy name for the instrument is simantra, and when I was workshopping the piece with Slagwerk Den Haag, they said, "Oh, we've got these incredible instruments, these incredible simantras." And they brought out these 2x4s and I said, "Those are 2x4s!" And they said, "Yeah, you can get them at a lumberyard." Actually, I wrote that piece back in 2009 after a long period of people calling me up and asking, "Would you write for orchestra?" I thought, "I'm tired of this. I want to get back to the music I love, get back to basics." I decided that the six percussionists were each going to play one instrument only. The instrument was going to have one pitch or sound only. And the instruments, the simantras or 2x4s, were going to go from high to low. I thought of the piece as a kind of ritual journey out into the desert, where everything was stark. The planks of wood have beautiful ringing overtones. When you amplify them and drum on them, they create clouds of harmonics. *Timber* starts with a sweep going from high to low very slowly. I use tiered dynamics to bring out each instrument in succession. Then this downward sweep contracts. It speeds up and expands. As it goes from high to low, from percussion 1 to 6, each successive percussionist plays a syncopated rhythm at a slower speed. With a minimum of material, so many variations of color are revealed. I was so happy to have found that sound and that piece.

SR: I listened to a couple of different recordings, the American group Mantra Percussion and the European group Slagwerk Den Haag, and I noticed that the pitches are very, very different. When you specify in the score, which I didn't see, do you say how long the 2x4s are, do you give instructions for that? Are you thinking about pitch or areas of pitch when you do that?

MG: I only ask them not to tune them, not to do anything consciously in relationship to diatonic scales. Basically, they're just randomly cut. And from ensemble to ensemble the planks are pitched very differently. The European sound really is a lot more elegant, I think, and the American sound is a lot heavier and darker. Different groups have played it and gotten very different sounds.

SR: But you want high to low. Isn't that dependent on the length of the 2x4?

MG: Yes, you cut them short to long. Every successive player has a longer slab of wood or a longer 2x4.

SR: And that's in the score.

MG: That's in the score.

SR: Well, the result is really great, and I enjoyed both versions of it, and thank you for all the homework you did preparing for this conversation.

MG: Well, I live with your music all the time. I don't think it was homework. I did sit down and think about it. I was glad when you said you wanted to talk about *Piano Phase* because I had forgotten.

SR: I've sort of forgotten about the *Notations* book and that someone might be introduced to the piece not by hearing it but by seeing that one-page score.

MG: I was in Miami and there weren't a lot of record stores that carried this stuff. There was a record store in downtown Miami, Specs in Coral Gables, which was about an hour from my house. Once in a while my sister Jeannie would drive me there. I would buy two or three records. I remember in '73, the recording of *Four Organs*, the one that was paired with Cage, *Three Dances*.

SR: Oh, the one with Michael Tilson Thomas and myself on Angel? All of us looking up at the ceiling.

MG: Yeah, yeah. That recording I listened to many, many times.

CHAPTER 5

MICHAEL TILSON THOMAS

Michael Tilson Thomas: Steve, I first heard your music in a loft in downtown LA, I think. And it was in a party situation and there was music on, and there were some people listening to it, some more closely than others. And I think it was probably *Come Out*, so it's way back. And shortly thereafter I heard *Violin Phase*, and then *It's Gonna Rain*. And those became big records, especially *It's Gonna Rain*, that I played a lot.

Steve Reich: Did you play both halves of it?

MTT: Both?

SR: Halves. There were two movements and one of them is *It's Gonna Rain* coming back into unison. The other one is the disintegration of the world before your ears.

MTT: Right, it gets more and more stretched out... Yeah, of course, I listened to both movements.

SR: Because some people just listen to the first and they think, "Oh, that's *It's Gonna Rain*."

MTT: Well, I thought that was the commitment that one was having to make. Maybe sort of symbolic of many things in your music, that there was this initially kind of entertaining, bouncy game-like thing, and then it went in a direction that was much more profound, even disturbing.

SR: As a matter of fact, it was so disturbing that for a while I thought, "Why should I inflict this on people?" And then I came back from San Francisco to New York, and I thought, "No, it's really good—all of it."

MTT: But in the early days when that was a central piece of your repertoire, did you go around to lofts and play that tape piece, give an introductory talk and then play it, or how did it work?

SR: No, no. In '65 I was busy moving back to New York and in early 1966 I got approached by the activist Truman Nelson to do a Civil Rights piece which became *Come Out*. That swallowed me up through most of 1966. After *Come Out* was over, I remember thinking, "What is this? Am I gonna be a mad scientist trapped in a loft with a tape recorder?" So, I immediately thought, "I've got to return to live music."

"But you can't do the gradual phase shifting that was in the tape pieces with live musicians, because it's only possible with tape recorders."

"But I want to make live music." Back and forth like that, and finally I said, "I'm the second tape recorder." And I recorded the first *Piano Phase* pattern, made a loop of it, sat down at the piano, closed my eyes, and found, "Wow! I'm not as perfect as the tape recorder—no news there—but I can do it!" And doing it is really incredible because the only way I can do it is to close my eyes and listen as closely as possible so that I don't move two sixteenths ahead, or just get stuck in unison. And so, there were concerts where a taped piece would sometimes be played in addition to the live music.

MTT: Well, let me just say that this process you just described of the sort of, what one would call, the discovery of the delights of phase shifting (*laughs*), of being a human phase-shifter. There is that wonderful feeling that just feels that you're just slightly leaning forward maybe.

SR: Exactly.

MTT: But that's such a wonderful place and you get to enjoy it. The more incremental, the slower it is, the more fun it is because there are the moments when your brain is still organizing it one way and then (*imitates phase shifting*) now it's organizing itself the other way. It's a very gradual process and that's the whole delight of what it is.

SR: The virtuosity of that technique is, "How slow can you make it happen?" Because it's very easy to just suddenly jump ahead. You hit the nail on the head, as usual.

MTT: But you're right, so I wonder if that has any relationship, probably not, but when I listen to Balinese musicians, they have this ability of playing so that you're hearing a passage that has quick sixteenth notes but it really is two people playing eighth notes who are able to instantly interlock them.

SR: Well, interlocking or hocketing is one thing, and gradually increasing your tempo to move slightly ahead of another musician is another. I certainly listened to Balinese gamelan. It was played for me, at Cornell, way back around 1954 by Professor William Austin in a Western music history course, along with Pérotin and a whole lot of other formative stuff. But I was trained as a drummer. I studied with Roland Kohloff starting at fourteen, and the exactitude of rhythms and the feeling of a rhythm was essential to me, from the get-go.

MTT: I don't know this very well. But I know that African drumming was a big influence on you, as well.

SR: Oh, yes. Later, in the midsixties, I heard recordings and I discovered a book with accurate transcriptions of African drumming—*Studies in African Music* by A. M. Jones. He invited a Ghanaian master drummer by the name of Desmond Tay to the London School of African and Oriental Studies, where he had built a machine that had moving graph paper and two metal plates on either side. Every time you tapped a metal pencil on a metal plate it made a mark on the moving graph paper. Tay would teach Jones to play, let's say the bell pattern (*demonstrates bell pattern*), and then Tay would begin to play drum one against the bell pattern. And everything was marked on graph paper. Rewind, play the bell pattern and drum two and so on. What evolved were really accurate scores of Ghanaian drumming. Jones was a good enough and honest enough musician to know that if he did it by ear, he would distort it as a Westerner, and move all those individual downbeats so they're all together, but they weren't. They were all in different places. So, that made an impression on me, even though I only looked at the opening sections of the book and I thought, "I should study this music live myself." And in 1970 I got to spend over a month in Ghana before I got malaria and had to come home earlier than I had anticipated. But I took daily lessons which I recorded and then transcribed. Later, the experience of playing

Balinese gamelan with Balinese teachers in '73, '74 out on the West Coast, was also very important.

MTT: Yes, that's wonderful that you had the flavor of that, because I was saying, the little experience I've had with that, as well, it's a very liberating, different kind of space of music-making compared to the one in which we were reared.

SR: Exactly, exactly so.

And then, getting back to New York many years ago, there I was living at the corner of Broadway and Canal Street in Manhattan and the phone rings, and it's this already famous young conductor, Michael Tilson Thomas, in I guess late 1970, or early '71, saying something like "Hi, I heard your music and what have you got for the Boston Symphony Orchestra?" And I pause and then say, "Well, I've got this piece called *Four Organs*." And I briefly explained that it was for four rock organs and maracas, and you said, "Please send me the score," and in those days a tape which was actually a tape. And now I'm asking you, when you looked at that score and heard that tape, why did you call me back?

MTT: Well, it was part of a series called Spectrum Concerts that I was introducing with the Boston Symphony, which was designed to take music into far-flung realms. And the different concerts had different themes, and one of them was called Multiples.

SR: Right.

MTT: And it was like, Bartók's [*Music for*] *String, Percussion, Celesta*, J. C. Bach's *Double String Orchestra*, and it was Gabrieli's *Double Brass Choir*, and it was Liszt's *Hexameron for Five Pianos* *and Orchestra*, and it was various other things. And so, I thought, "Well, here's this piece for four Farfisa organs," and I thought, "This is perfect!" It fits right into the idea, and besides which I loved the notes and I also was fascinated that it achieved its goals essentially by subtracting rather than adding. Mostly you think of a piece of music that you play some notes and then you play more notes, then you play more and more notes. But in this case you played all of the notes from the very beginning, but then it was a question of which notes you sustained, and then gradually when they were all sustained, as you released a note, the releases were so exact that a melody emerged from the subtracting of the notes.

SR: Exactly.

MTT: I found that all fascinating.

SR: By the way, did you ever make any connections between *Four Organs* and Pérotin?

MTT: Does that relate to one of the organa in *Sederunt Principes*, or whatever?

SR: Well, basically *Four Organs* is about augmentation. I mean, I woke up in the middle of the night at one point before I wrote the piece and wrote down a sentence in my music notebook: "short chord gets long," went back to sleep, and that was basically it. Much earlier, William Austin, my music professor at Cornell in the early '50s—who played the Balinese gamelan recordings—also played Pérotin, I was immediately taken. I didn't know Pérotin or the whole Notre Dame school, but I thought, "This is gorgeous. What's going on?" So, I went to the library, the music library, which in those days was actually books on a reserve shelf. And there was *Masterpieces of Music* *before 1750*. And inside was a Pérotin *Alleluia* score. The tenor notes were so long, they extended for two pages. Jumping to 1970 just at the time I was beginning to write *Four Organs*, there was a new edition, by Ethel Thurston: *The Works of Pérotin*, in one volume, a very slim volume. And there you could see these enormous lengths, which no one tenor could sing alone, they had to be handed off to a co-tenor to keep the sustain up. The idea that augmentation could be more than going from two-to-four and four-to-eight. That it could be irregular, and to enormous proportions, to completely change something which had started melodic, and then became so augmented that it became a series of shifting drones, creating an enormously slowed-down harmonic rhythm. All of this was in my head. Pérotin deserves a lot of credit not only for *Four Organs*, but he influences *Music for Mallet Instruments, Voices, and Organ, Music for 18 Musicians*, and *Proverb* in 1995 is an homage to Pérotin. *Viderunt Omnes* was on my piano as I wrote it.

MTT: In this music, it's the tenor part, which really means the held part, in the tenor part of polyphony, that something you heard perhaps as a chant melody is now slowed down syllable by syllable. And then there's a whole world that is explored and opened up around each new tone. I think it was the clausula, the troped clausula, something like that, which was usually the pitch outline of the Hallelujah, which was taken and then around those individual (*sings vocalise*), each one of those became a world…a universe.

SR: Yes, and there's also a part with the clausula, where all the voices move together.

MTT: But part of what happens in that piece, a little bit related to *Four Organs*, as well, is that we have three or four parts singing, but there are only maybe six available notes that are in the scheme of things. So inevitably there is a great deal of overlap, people singing the same pitches but it being part of different lines, different lines moving in different directions. The same pitch is overlapping, and that produces a feeling of a kind of overhanging harmony or chord that's present, even though the moving lines are happening.

SR: Right, right. And six tones are the number of pitches in *Four Organs*.

Now, completely shifting gears to sociological considerations: In 1973, when we went to Carnegie, did you have any conscious idea that *Four Organs* might cause a riot given the fact that it was a BSO subscription concert with the Liszt *Hexameron*, et cetera?

MTT: I didn't really because, as you remember, when we did the concert in Boston—it was controversial, but quite successful. Maybe it was because we had gotten a certain audience there. I actually had these little flyers for the Spectrum series that had a kind of *S* with a rainbow on it, prophetically. And Betty Walsh, my wonderful assistant, and I took about several hundred of those flyers and staple guns and we went all over Cambridge, Mass., and stapled those on every bulletin board and on every telephone pole and on everything we could possibly find. And I think as a result of that, there were a higher proportion, perhaps, of Harvard, MIT, and so on students who may have been at that concert. So, the general temper of the audience, somehow or another, was a little bit more receptive, adventurous. But in New York the audience was a very, very tried-and-true conservative audience. I think a lot of people went to Boston Symphony concerts in New York because they thought, "Well, this is all the real music and all these vulgar New York people, back in Boston we know better." And so here was this piece which couldn't have been more in-their-faces, so to speak.

SR: Right. But were you plotting this to occur?

MTT: I didn't plot it deliberately at all. Interestingly, in my archives here is my *Four Organs* folder, in which there is my original part from that performance!

SR: Right, which is not the Universal Edition, the published version, but it's probably in my manuscript.

MTT: It is in your manuscript. And it has, at various points, all these little notes to myself. You know, arrows going from line to line. It's very easy to lose your place because you're seeing all four parts and, "Oh, wait a minute. I'm playing part number three, so that means I'm here." (*laughs*) And then various eyeglasses at particular changes which must have been more difficult than other ones, you know? Nod, two nods. My instructions. But what people need to realize about this piece is that the gradual sustaining and then precise releasing of the notes by the different players is what produces the effect. And that the numbers of counts are like (*demonstrates steady, rhythmic beats*), right?

SR: You're counting the maracas, yes, the eighth note.

MTT: Yes, you're counting maraca strokes. So, I'm just looking here toward the end, and the numerical scheme is 24–20–16–14–12 and so on. So that means that initially you're trying to keep yourself hitting the new bar, and you think, "1–2–3–4–5–6–7–8–9–10–11–12–13–14–15–16–17–18–19–20–21–22–23–24, 1–2–3–4–5–6–7–8–9…" and so when we were doing this, rehearsing it, we could quietly count to ourselves. You always counted moving your lips, I remember. Some of the rest of us counted interiorly or by tapping our feet or whatever method we used. But, of course, in the Carnegie Hall performance, the audience, even while we were playing the piece, became so unruly that in spite of the fact that it was heavily amplified, we couldn't really hear one another anymore! So that's when I began really shouting out these numbers (*shouting*), 17–18–19–20–21–22–23–24, 1–2–3–4, you know, really shouting the numbers! And only in retrospect I realized that that's exactly the description that Stravinsky had of the performance of *The Rite of Spring*, when Nijinsky was standing on a chair in the wings yelling out the numbers to the dancers of what count they were on. And Stravinsky describes how he was holding Nijinsky's tailcoat and Nijinsky was out there (*laughs*) yelling out the numbers. Which was more difficult, because in Russian, numbers are very polysyllabic, so 18 is "восемнадцать" (*laughs*). So that's much more difficult to say those numbers! But nonetheless, that evoked the whole thing so that when we came off stage and you were white as a sheet, I said to you, "This is *The Rite of Spring*! Nothing like this has happened since *The Rite of Spring*." All those thoughts were in my mind. But it was a really startling cultural event in the history of Carnegie Hall, in the history of New York. And I think only one of many for which you have been responsible. (*laughs*)

SR: None of that magnitude in terms of scandal.

MTT: We did it at Ojai, too, didn't we?

SR: That was very soon after Carnegie. Ojai became well-known with Stravinsky and Lawrence Morton, so they were expecting something new. And afterwards we recorded it for Angel at the Capitol Tower.

MTT: Yep, yep.

SR: But then there was a hiatus and we played it in San Francisco years later, at which point it had already been recorded and the audience applauded and it was just a piece that people really liked. It was a quasi-chestnut. (*laughs*)

MTT: But meanwhile, I was doing quite a lot of your music, in Boston and other places, pieces like *Music for Mallet Instruments, Voices, and Organ*. That was like Smokey Robinson & the Miracles compared to *Four Organs*! (*laughs*) People just totally loved that! That was very user-friendly. And that's the one—when we were rehearsing that and the rehearsal was late at night, it was not on the regular Boston Symphony rehearsal schedule. We just had a separate schedule. So, it was late at night, and there was a terrible snowstorm, and you were onstage and you heard this buzzing noise. And I think it's important that your admirers and fans really have an understanding of just how precise, how particular, you are about the way you want something to be. In this case, there was this noise, and we determined that it was the patch cords that were causing this buzz. And so this was now about eleven o'clock at night, and you said, "We've gotta replace these patch cords." I said, "Okay, fine. It's a snowstorm and it's Saturday night, and we don't do the show until the matinee tomorrow. Whatever, we'll get up and get the patch cords." You were not having it! "We have to find a place that's open, we have to go get the patch cords, and we have to bring them back and check them out to make sure they'll work!" And that's what we did.

I think that when people hear your music sometimes, because of its expansiveness and because of its generosity, people imagine that you, the person who created it, must be this very floaty, very "hey, anything goes," kind of person. Nothing could be further from the truth.

SR: By the way, we were talking about *Music for Mallet Instruments, Voices, and Organ*, and I was at rehearsal. And there was this fantastic Black singer, Pamela Wood, who is no longer with us, I'm sad to say. And she was amazing. So, at the end of the rehearsal I went up to her and said that I was working on a new piece, which was *Music for 18 Musicians*, and would she consider coming to rehearsals, and I'd cover the expenses, for sure. She was interested, she came down for a rehearsal, and she was in our ensemble for many, many years. And just recently Pamela passed away. She was an instructor in Kodály method, actually, at MIT.

MTT: Lovely person, lovely artist. I'm so happy that that happened.

SR: Yes!

So, here we jump from the seventies to the mideighties, to *The Desert Music*. When you were conducting these many, many rehearsals, do you remember any particular problems and did the instrumental setup, the arrangement of the orchestra, make the crucial difference that I thought it would make?

MTT: Yes. I want to say a word or two, about the intervening years, speaking of different pieces you were doing and there were these little events. One event that I remember was very touching. We had a friend who was named Jack Roman, who was the head of Baldwin Pianos.

SR: Oh, yes! He let me and my ensemble into the Baldwin store at night, across the street from Carnegie Hall, to rehearse *Six Pianos*. No one on earth would do it but him.

MTT: Exactly, and then there was sort of an open rehearsal of that at Baldwin. You guys played the piece and then there was champagne afterwards, and it was a very charming kind of New York social event.

SR: Right. And you were down there for that, weren't you?

MTT: Yes, and I'm just thinking of the way in which, in different levels of society, different levels of the concert world, the academic world, in which your music became known and kind of woven into an evolving culture in a really nice way. Because people must remember that at the time you were writing this, in the '70s and the '80s, which was still the time of the really doctrinaire, avant-garde conception of what music should be, which was total serialization of note values and rhythmic values and all these very forbidding—highly complex rhythmically— although you probably couldn't really discern that there was any rhythm going on. But highly fragmented note values and patterns, and moreover, there was a certain kind of mafia in England, you know, Sir William Glock, and in various other cities people could name, there was a sort of threshold of intellectual density and respectability, which you had to go past or else your music wasn't really considered serious. It takes me back to those years, I barely experienced them, but in New York when there was the League of American Composers and...what was the other group?

SR: The Group for Contemporary Music?

MTT: There was the sort of Varèse crowd on one hand, and the sort of Sam Barber whatever on the other. And so, there was this between the avant-gardists on one end, more hard-edged people, and the more neoclassical, romantic people. And then some people like Aaron [Copland] were straddling a little bit those two groups, and Roger Sessions even at times went back and forth between one group or another. But people have to remember that when these major pieces of yours were coming out that there were people who were very, very devoted to them, and for whom they almost were a spiritual antidote for other things. Because some of us who were also playing this very, very complicated, hyperintellectual stuff, we were doing that, but then we all could sit down and play one of your pieces which was a kind of like (*takes deep breath*) "Ah, we get to love and experience harmony again, we get to love and experience playing together again." It was a lovely experience, and it meant a lot to people, even though there were some people in these ensembles, the second viola, saying, "Oh, I can't believe I have to play (*imitates repetitive viola part*), you know, 149 times at least!" But then they discovered this thing, which I know I said to you, I said that the way that I knew that I had finally learned one of your pieces was when it had stopped hurting (*laughs*). That initially in playing it I was trying to grasp it and grab it and trying to achieve it by tension, and then I gradually realized that you could get into this place where it was more like loping along the savanna. That it all happened, it was all under control. And you must remember that when *The Desert Music* was scheduled at Brooklyn Academy of Music it was already presented by Harvey Lichtenstein, I guess, and it was understood that it was going to be a major cultural event even before it happened. It was very much on everybody's radar screens of something that was going to happen. Even though the actual premiere took place in Germany, Peter Eötvös did it…

SR: In Cologne, it was a disaster. Total disaster. I mean, the orchestra was left over from World War II and the chorus was straight out of *Tannhäuser*, so, I mean (*laughs*)… It was people who you couldn't go up to them and say, "Excuse me, dear, it's small voice, no vibrato" because they were born to sing Wagner and you could go straight to you-know-where. So, I just sat back and Peter Eötvös looked at me and just shrugged his shoulders like "Hey, I'm trying."

MTT: Because he is a very, very serious and able musician.

SR: Oh, superb, and a wonderful guy, yes.

MTT: Wonderful composer. But of course, I think the very first instruction on the very first page of *The Desert Music* it says, "The vocal parts should throughout be sung with no vibrato." That's one of the very first instructions. So, I can imagine some of those life-contract chorus members in… What was it? One of the radio stations? Where did it take place?

SR: It was the West German Radio in Cologne, their orchestra and the local chorus. If the shoe fits, wear it. If the shoe doesn't fit, you're stuck.

MTT: Because they were singing. (*imitates singer with heavy vibrato*)

SR: Yes, it was something along those lines. And I realized, there's nothing I can do about this.

MTT: But anyway, the reverse was true when we did it in New York because it was really a kind of handpicked group. It was the Brooklyn Philharmonic, but it was also a lot of people that you and I knew from various parts of the contemporary music scene.

SR: The deck was stacked, absolutely.

MTT: And we rehearsed it, it was kind of like Camp *Desert Music* (*laughs*). I don't know how long, but a couple of months before the performance, we started having these workshop rehearsals out there in Brooklyn, even I think sometimes with just the mallet instruments, sometimes with just the strings.

SR: A lot of sectional rehearsals, right.

MTT: And very much getting each half of the stage to be comfortable playing with itself and then learning to play with one another across the whole length of the stage—it's in such small, little increments sometimes—and being able to again find that sort of lope-like inner rhythm in which it all lines up comfortably and makes sense. And it was extraordinary for me to watch the musicians because some of them initially were, "Okay, this is a gig and we play a lot of different gigs in New York. And it's a slightly vexing one because we have to do this stuff a lot of times, or whatever." But then it was remarkable that over a period of time, they really got into it. Their bodies, their spirits opened up a lot. And they began to really very joyously, enthusiastically, energetically be a part of it. And I think everyone felt that because we are all out here in Brooklyn at Camp *Desert Music*, that we all are part of something that is special, and certainly the piece has a very powerful, spiritual message. So, it was really deeply meaningful for everyone involved.

SR: Very good of you to say all that and to bring back those memories. That was all back in the '80s, over thirty-five years ago. *The Desert Music* was done recently by the Sydney Symphony in Australia with David Robertson, and *The Rite of Spring* was on the same program—and it was a great success. The BBC Symphony did it at the Proms a few years ago, and just recently the Swedish radio did the chamber version with distanced seating. So by now lots of musicians know what's involved and can enjoy performing it.

But going back to my original question, about the special orchestral/choral seating arrangement specified in the score. It obviously makes demands on the stage crew and means the piece has to be the entire first half or second half of an entire concert. So it's not going to be done every other week, for sure. But it seems to me that the seating diagram, although it does make for a lot of stage preparation, was absolutely necessary for good ensemble playing. Did you feel that to be a reality when you were conducting? Where the different string groups were and where the mallets were—where everybody was?

MTT: Oh, yeah. It does make a difference; you definitely feel certain parts of the stage are taking the lead, more or less at different moments of the piece because of the register in which they're playing, perhaps, and just the nature of the movement. The conductor in that situation needs to be a kind of inspiring, hopefully, least common denominator, in that you have to kind of lay this pulse down which is precise enough but which has enough space inside of the ictus, so that the ictus is not so narrow that it will cause ensemble problems because people don't have enough room. In other words, as I'm fond of saying, "There's all kinds of now." There's some now that's going (*imitates short, staccato bursts*), you could barely hear it, it's just a little barked-out instant, and the same tempo could be (*imitates longer, sustained notes*), which gives a lot more room for things to happen. Interestingly, I learned a lot about this from the couple of times I was on the road with James Brown. He was a monster about that, about in each song how wide he wanted the pulse to be in terms of the trap drummer being on the front edge, the hand drummers being on the back edge, and the bass player being in between. And that sort of sandwich, he would adjust just how narrow or wide that sandwich would be. And that relates to what it's like in conducting a piece like *The Desert Music*, and also, it's a different thing for a conductor because conductors very often are used to hearing something that's happening and making a very quick, immediate correction of that problem. You cannot make quick or immediate corrections in something like *The Desert Music* because it will just have consequences of knocking everything into a greater confusion. All you can do is you can look at the people who perhaps are causing the problem and give them, perhaps, an eyebrow or a shoulder or a little slightly encouraging and/or cautionary sign that says, "Maybe move along a bit, maybe just stay where you are, maybe more like that…" and then it'll come back into focus again. That's a very interesting ensemble situation and it's also a piece where so much of it is about people looking at one another, people looking into one another's eyes. I found particularly with me and the percussionists that we'd hit a particular change at the moment that we made a metric modulation to the next section, which of course is really crucial, and we were on. They knew their parts by heart and they'd just see where their mallets initially had to be and then our eyes were absolutely locked waiting for the change. And there was this nice feeling in one another's eyes either of "Yes! That's right!" or "Oh, my G-d! What's happening?" (*laughs*)

SR: Well, in that piece and in others of that period, is the conductor conducting or is the conductor following the percussion? I mean, how would you describe that?

MTT: I think a lot of the time what a conductor does is to confirm things that are happening. That's a very important role. Something's been rehearsed a certain way and decided a certain way and now in the performance a certain thing is happening, and you're looking at people and you're saying, "Yes, that's right. We're on track. Okay, now the next thing that has to happen is you're gonna do this, right? Right." Right? Right. That's a lot of what can go on particularly in a piece like that. Because the thing about *Desert Music*, the thing about your music, is that, yes, it has a certain tempo and usually you give a certain range of, you know, between 162 and 164 or whatever it is.

SR: Maybe wider than that.

MTT: A little range of possible tempos. But then it's really a question of the feel of it, which is vitally important.

SR: You bet! I was going to ask you about tempos. I think there are some conductors who tend to, at least in my experience, play my music, who generally feel that the key is play it fast. It always seems to me that what you're doing is assessing the situation and saying, "Well, let's see where we are here and what we really want." What you really want, I think, is that bodily feeling of solidity that holds an ensemble together. And there will be a range of tempos in there, but there will be a point where if you go too fast, hanging on by the fingernails sets in, which is never a good feeling when you're playing or listening. Or on the other hand feeling, "Can't we get this thing going?"

MTT: It's a really interesting thing that I'm working on with young conductors, like if they're conducting a piece like *The Firebird*. There's a piece in the complete *Firebird* called "Dance with the Golden Apples" [sic]. It's an up-tempo piece (*demonstrates staccato rhythm*), something like that. And then it has these wonderful little interlocking things where muted trumpets play a three- or four-note little repeated note figure, and then a solo violin, harmonics, and a celeste play an answering figure. And then the trumpets do it again, and this time a clarinet and flute do that, and the harp does something, and there are these miraculous little calls and responses and challenges that are taking place. If it is done too fast, it is impossible to hear all those things.

SR: Right.

MTT: So, then you just have the excitement of the tempo (*imitates steady, rhythmic tempo*) but you don't hear that (*imitates more complex, intricate music*), you know, this whole miraculous world. That's a little bit like in one of your pieces where, let's say, there are mallet instruments, what they're playing is sometimes "dead strokes."

SR: Right.

MTT: So, there has to be enough time allowed after the dead stroke to appreciate that moment of silence before the next thing is going to happen. That's the kind of feel, flavor of it.

SR: Exactly. There's a piece of mine now called *Runner* and there was a recording made by a European group and it's very fast. It's exciting when you first hear it because of the tempo. But it's as if everything inside the piece, you can't open it up and look inside or hear anything because it's moving too fast. So, you get an initial excitement, which after a while gets a little boring because all the detail that was written in is no longer there.

MTT: Well, I have a question to ask you about *The Desert Music*, which has this opening series of chords (*playing piano*), which actually you very kindly, after those performances, wrote out.

SR: The first movement, yes.

MTT: Because I had said, "Oh, this would be such a nice chorale," and you very nicely said, "Well, I'm sorry it didn't make it into a chorale in this piece, but just for your own pleasure, I wrote this out for you." A very sweet thing to do. What I want to ask you is, what state of mind are you in when you write those chord progressions? Because on the one hand they're hanging in space, on the other hand they're highly pulsed and made of all these little increments of time. But how do these chord progressions develop? In what sort of tempo do they happen?

SR: There's no tempo at all. When I'm working on the chords, it's as if there is no such thing as rhythm. Literally, if you look in my notebooks, they're written with just a dot, there's no stem. And it's just to ascertain the movement of the pitches, the voice leading, the spacing, which octave notes are in... It all seems so trivial, it's absolutely crucial. *The Desert Music* was a conscious thickening of the plot harmonically. I had been, as you know, writing basically in a modal nonchromatic harmony from the '60s through the early '80s. In contrast, much earlier in the late '50s, as a student I was more chromatically inclined because I had a real interest in the Bartók Quartets, particularly Four and Five. *The Desert Music* forced me, because of the nature of the text, to go back to that, to get more chromatic harmonically. Setting a text, as you well know when you compose, forces you to consider things that you would not otherwise consider. So, it pushed me to think about darker subject matter, which called forth more non-scale tones as part of the harmony. It was also necessary to make chord cycles where the last chord led back to the first. I composed four cycles. One for the first and last movements, another for the second and sixth, still another for the third and fifth, and a separate cycle for the central fourth movement, "It is a principle of music, to repeat the theme." *The Desert Music* begins with the possibility of a D-dorian-minor center and gets more and more harmonically ambiguous as the piece progresses. Finally, at the end you have the women's voices, violins and mallets all pulsing the notes (*reading up*) G—C–F—A with nothing in the bass leaving the possibility of an A altered dominant, D dorian minor, or F major. I really enjoy that particular ambiguity!

MTT: What period of time, how long did it take you to come up with the cycle of chords for the first movement?

SR: Who knows? I'd have to go to my archive at the Sacher Foundation in Basel and look at my notebooks where they're sitting and try to reconstruct it—probably, Michael, it could have taken anywhere from four or five days to two or three weeks, and I really don't remember. I think in those days, *The Desert*

Music was written pretty concentratedly because I knew I had a lot to do and I better stick with it. So, I would tend to think it went fairly quickly, though I had to do a cycle for the various movement pairs, as I mentioned. The truth is, I can't answer your question. It could have been days; it could have been weeks.

MTT: So, would there have been a point, let's say, in your process where you would have these little dots on the page of what the notes are, no stems, no nothing, and say, "Okay, I like that one, I like that one." And then there's two, and then there's three, and then there's a group of them. And then the next day you come back and you say, "Well, I'm still sure about one and two, I'm not sure about three." And then you just continue to fiddle around with three?

SR: Absolutely, absolutely. I was talking with Sondheim, and I asked him, "How do you get this marvelous continuity, it seems to just pour out of you." He said, "I could ask you the same question. It takes an infinite amount of hard work to make something sound like it's effortless." And I totally agree. There is more in my garbage can, whether it's on the Mac desktop or the one filled with paper, than there is on a printed page. And it's always been that way. I am my own worst critic. There is no critic who can compare to the criticism that I have inflicted on myself.

MTT: So, as you're writing the cycle, are you carrying on other kinds of work or kinds of rhythmic patterns or melody patterns or anything else?

SR: No, I'm a real plodder. I've got to do this first. When I get done with this, then it's time for that. In my whole life, I only wrote two pieces simultaneously once, which were *Six Pianos* and *Music for Mallet Instruments, Voices, and Organ*. That might have been because rehearsals for *Six Pianos* were so constrained being in the Baldwin piano store at night, when Jack Roman could let us in. But outside of that in 1973 when I wrote those two pieces at the same time, I've always just done one thing after the other.

MTT: See, that's really interesting because I think for all of us to imagine that something as intricate and as long as *The Desert Music* was at a point in its development just these series of static harmonies, which you were somehow interiorizing and deciding how authentic they seemed to what your vision was. And then only when those were right, you then embarked on this highly rhythmized conception of time in which they're ultimately presented.

SR: You're right. Originally there were these, if you like, chorales. In *The Desert Music*, the opening pages are basically a chorale, but presented as pulses. The chords are all there, all the notes are just as they were as dots in my notebook, but they're presented rhythmically instead of held tones, as you get in a Bach chorale. The idea of pulses I was stealing from myself from the opening of *Music for 18 Musicians*. Only here the notes were more chromatic.

However, if you want to go back to the real beginning, the very first thing, it had nothing to do with music. It had to do with getting the text right. And I literally remember having excerpts from William Carlos Williams typed out, printed on paper, and laid out on a four-octave marimba. And I was moving these pieces of paper around. And spending probably a week or two, or more, figuring out which excerpts really make sense here, and what is their order, and when do they repeat, and which repeats where. The basic idea of arch form goes way back to Juilliard and Bartók's Fourth and Fifth Quartet, as I said, but this particular application was the very first thing in *The Desert Music*. Then, okay, first movement, "Begin my friend…" and then "Inseparable from the fire…" at the end. Now, where is the harmonic world that these words will live in? Now, I may have done a lot of the first movement as soon as I had that first progression or I may have gone on—the only way to find out would be to go back and look at the notebooks and see what I did.

MTT: Sure, because there were very different tempi, very different feels in these different sections. Then let me ask you about the section which actually is quite different from the rest of the piece, which is the "It is a principle of music" and "Difficult." So those two sections are very much in contrast to the rest of the process and piece.

SR: Right. They're very syllabic settings of the text, which of course the piece is in general, but in the Williams poem originally here it feels like prose. "It is a principle of music to repeat the theme, repeat and repeat again, as the pace mounts. The theme is difficult but no more difficult than the facts to be resolved." And it's almost like, "And now the nightly news!" (*laughs*) That's what I actually felt. And "Difficult" was just my personal scream—"Oh, no, there's so much to do!"

MTT: I think those sections are both in the best possible way a kind of composer showing off, too.

SR: (*laughs*)

MTT: I can do this; I can do this. This is really hot, intricate stuff, and I can do this.

SR: Well, I told Beryl, I said, "One of the candidates for my tombstone is the 'Difficult' canons." (*laughs*)

MTT: And so then very much in contrast to that, think of other moments. The moment with the viola glissandi.

SR: Right, the alarm.

MTT: Because that came in during the rehearsal process, you may remember.

SR: Well, actually, I was composing the piece in Vermont in a town just outside of Dartmouth on the Vermont side of New Hampshire. And while I was finishing "Man has survived hitherto" the second time, a fire alarm went off in the town. And I was right at that point and I thought to myself, "That's it! That's it!" I'm thinking about the bomb and here's this alarm. And then I thought, "You know, I don't want to get involved with recordings, enough of that." And then I thought, "Well, hey, glissandos. Violas are free. Put a contact mike on!"

MTT: I don't know if you remember that in the very first rehearsals of the piece, it wasn't there yet. It could have been that you had thought of putting it in, weren't quite ready to make the leap to do that, and then you did do it.

SR: That sounds like a real possibility.

MTT: Because I certainly think that I remember that maybe at the end of that first rehearsal period—anyway, at some point you told me, you told the two solo violas, there's going to be a solo viola part here. So, of course, they were imagining Brandenburg Six or something was awaiting them. And instead these long, long wailing glissandos. It took some work for them actually to do it as together and as expressively, it's not easy.

SR: It really matters how they pace it. There's a beginning and ending pitch which you really have to move steadily towards to achieve tonal consistency with what's going on. So, yeah, you're right. But finally, it really worked.

MTT: Now, another moment which is again a very telling moment is, of course, the whole setting of the "Man has survived hitherto."

SR: Right.

MTT: Which is very kind of Bach/Berg chorale. The words are so serious and profound and sadly prophetic. That's such a stirring moment. That could perhaps be the darkest, most pessimistic moment in the piece. Now, when I think of that chord progression, "Now that he can realize them, he must either change them or perish." And that harmony change that takes you into the word *perish* is very, very dark and hopeless feeling.

SR: When I first encountered that text, Williams had recorded the poem, and I thought, "I can't set this. This has to be Williams himself." But then I thought, "No, the recording's a cop-out. I've gotta set this thing." And, as I remember, that setting came fairly rapidly. I just really got into it. I think I was in Vermont. Where I was, I don't really remember, but I realized, "This is it. I've got it. This is the right setting. This is the way it should be." And it will be repeated, and it has a very different feeling when it's repeated. I'm glad that you expressed that emotional reaction because that is one of the high/low points of the piece, for sure.

MTT: And then, in contrast to that, of course, is the evocation of the light.

SR: Right.

MTT: The end of the work.

SR: "Inseparable from the fire, its light takes precedence over it. Who most shall advance the light, call it what you may."

MTT: They're totally wonderful words and beautifully set by you. Now one little memory I want to share of rehearsals of that moment. When we come to the light, the rhythmic part stops.

SR: Right.

MTT: And the chorus just sings a cappella "The light, the light, the light." And I think it's marked *mezzo piano* or something like that, I can't remember. And when we were doing that, I was so intoxicated by that moment and I thought, "Oh, good, we should *molto diminuendo* here and then we should come to 'the light' and it should just fade out completely and then there should be a moment of silence and then (*loudly*) 'Call it what you may.'" You just said, "Nope, nope, it's *mezzo forte* and it's exactly this many beats, and then it comes in! 'Call it what you may.'" You were having none of my sentimentality.

SR: Well, that may be, but I will remind you of a contrast, which is that in "Well, shall we think or listen" there are these rhythmic sections of threes and twos in the brass, the trumpets in particular, which are just written without accents. And you looked at me, you said, "Look, you have all these obvious accents, why not *sforzandi*." And I said to you, "Michael, pretend I'm dead." Because I knew you were on to something!

MTT: You said that to me more than once. (*laughs*)

SR: And sure enough, it's dynamite. And it's just what the doctor ordered. It's implicit, but you made it explicit, so one of my many belated thank-yous. I'm usually not a yes man, but when I am, I'm very enthusiastic!

MTT: That same idea I've seen operative in your thoughts in other pieces, as well. There is such feeling in the notes that you write, which is one of the reasons we all love the music and why we as Americans recognize a connection to something which is really part of our heritage. And that's just there. You wanted to say, "Just let the notes say what they have to say and don't try and oversentimentalize them." It was only my Thomashefsky instincts at that moment that were saying, "Oh, we could have this rapturous moment here." So, my caveat was good, it's just that it wasn't what you wanted (*laughs*). Because you're always thinking, and this says so much about you, that even though people are getting lost in the big, floating vision of the piece, that you, in your mind, have a very, very clear purpose in mind at all times.

SR: By the way, I heard there was this performance of *Clapping Music* in San Francisco with two old guys on a park bench. Now, that was definitely the Thomashefsky at work but in a very understated way. How did you come up with that?

MTT: I had that vision of the design of *Clapping Music* being able to be something which is, the people who are clapping have been around the track many, many times. In the way people sing an old familiar song, they sing it just like "Oh, yeah, here's the song." And that's what we were going for.

You know, I think at this moment in time we're in the middle of this pandemic and we're also in the middle of probably the most challenging moment socially-politically in the history of our country. And people are very happy now if they can do a piece for 3 1/2 musicians put together somehow online. So, the idea of this big assemblage of people, *The Desert Music*, this kind of community of people that was put together to make this piece happen and this kind of expansiveness of human thought

and generosity, and thinking of the positive attitude of the society in which it came into being makes me kind of tear up.
The feeling we still had about ourselves and society when this
piece was written, in spite of some of its cautionary messages,
"Together we can do this."

CHAPTER 6

RUSSELL HARTENBERGER

Steve Reich: Were all the rehearsals of *Drumming*, in that dilapidated loft on Broadway on the corner of Canal—looked like the *Cabinet of Doctor Caligari* (*laughs*) leaning to one side, with the elevator that clanked two floors below. And you started coming to rehearsals there?

Russell Hartenberger: Yeah, I came to the first rehearsal, I think in the early spring of 1971, and the first thing I saw was you, Steve Chambers, Jon Gibson, and Arthur Murphy practicing the bongo section. I think by that point you had written the bongos and were just beginning to work on the marimba section.

SR: Right, because you mentioned, when you were looking at my diaries in the Sacher Foundation in Basel, that you saw that the first rehearsal for *Drumming* was on December 3rd, 1970?

RH: According to your diary, that was the first.

SR: So, when you came in the spring, some of the marimbas had been done, and I was rehearsing with Joan La Barbara and Jay Clayton to do the vocal patterns?

RH: That's right. The marimbas were set up and we were starting to rehearse that. I don't think the whole thing had been done. I know you were working on the resulting patterns with the singers.

SR: Right, because that was always a separate rehearsal with tape loops and everybody singing or jotting down what they heard.

RH: My recollection is that I would come in each week and you would have composed something new. We never saw music notation, at least the percussionists didn't, and you would demonstrate the part, whoever's part it was. And we would play it until we got it and then attach it to what we had learned the week before.

SR: How did that strike you? That way of working, of rehearsing?

RH: The thing that struck me about it was that I was also starting African Drumming and Gamelan at Wesleyan. And it was exactly how I was being taught those musics. Just imitation and repetition, the teacher would show me something and I would just play it until I got it, and then we would move along. It was curious that here was a piece of Western music by a traditional Western composer, being taught in the same way that I was learning non-Western music. And all at the same time, for me.

SR: Right, I had the same experience in Ghana taking lessons and I would record them, to review and transcribe. I'd play the part, "No." Play it again, "Okay, now you've got it." And the same thing with Balinese gamelan, first in Seattle and then later on in Berkeley.

So, let's see, later on in our rehearsals… Jim Preiss came into our ensemble pretty quick.

RH: He came in shortly after me and then he brought some of his students in as you needed more people.

SR: Right. When did Bob Becker come in? He came in through you.

RH: That was not until the fall of 1972.

SR: Oh, so that was already going into *Music for Mallet Instruments* and *Six Pianos*.

RH: Yes, you realized you needed actual percussionists because you were starting to think about *Music for Mallets*, and *Music for Pieces of Wood*.

SR: Right.

RH: That's when Bob Becker came in and that's probably when Glen Velez came in, too. I think Glen Velez came in for *Six Pianos* and *Music for Mallets*. And then a little bit after that Gary Schall came in.

SR: So, you've noted while you were in Basel, there were sixty-seven weekly rehearsals of *Drumming*?

RH: Well, I counted from your diary! (*laughs*) That's counting all the separate ones you had for vocal rehearsals and for the piccolo patterns. But yes, there were a lot of rehearsals, at least one a week throughout the year.

SR: Right. And after the first few you asked me about my background.

RH: Yeah, as a percussionist.

SR: Well, as I mentioned to you, I studied with Roland Kohloff, who was of a different school than Hinger, who you studied with along with Alan Abel. But I remember you were interested that I got into the *Stick Control* book. When you were studying, was *Stick Control* an important part of your training?

RH: I think it's a basic for almost every drummer, every percussionist, and still everybody that I'm familiar with has worked through it at one point in their lives. And a lot of people still use it as sort of a warm-up book, warm-up exercises. It's a basic book, probably the most basic book for a drummer. And it was really curious to me that you had worked through that, and according to what you said, it made an impact on you.

SR: Well, hand alternations create accents and suggest patterns.

RH: Yes.

SR: Besides hand alternation, you have hand repetition, and when those are mixed together, you get patterns. I mean, my favorite rudiment is still paradiddle, left-hand lead![2] Of course, you do right-hand lead. (*laughs*)

RH: That's the one thing people don't understand about *Drumming*: everything's a left-hand lead because you're left-handed. (*laughs*)

---

2 LRLLRLRR

SR: That worked its way into all the percussion parts and I inflicted that on everybody (*laughs*). But everybody seemed to adapt pretty well!

RH: Yeah, yeah. But *Stick Control*, that was a basic thing. You've talked a lot about the basics of hand alternation. Obviously even in *Piano Phase* it's there, and in a lot of the other pieces, too. It implied other sorts of patterns.

SR: Exactly, and later on when I got into the threes and twos in *Tehillim*, that also became a big part of it, too.

RH: One of the things that I learned from looking at your manuscripts in the Sacher archive in Basel is that when you were working out the *Drumming* pattern in your notebooks, there were sections where you just put *R*s and *L*s for right-hand, left-hand, creating little rhythmic patterns. And then from that you would go into actual music notation, so it seemed like it had a pretty important impact.

SR: Yes, I was thinking that way, and it definitely came out of *Stick Control*.

RH: That's interesting.

SR: Do you remember anything about the premieres of *Drumming* at the Museum of Modern Art or at BAM or at Town Hall?

RH: Well, I think we had full houses, as I recall, at every place.

SR: Not at BAM. In those days BAM was in the boondocks.

RH: (*laughs*) Well, that's the truth.

SR: But at the Museum of Modern Art it was absolutely chock-ablock.

RH: Yeah, yeah. And enthusiastic audiences. I don't have a whole lot of memory (*laughs*), but I also remember we performed some of *Drumming* in your loft.

SR: Right.

RH: For invited audiences, I guess, for people that you knew downtown came to it. Mostly artists, probably some musicians, but mostly artists.

SR: Donald Judd, the sculptor, was at one of them. I'm not sure if Betty Freeman came in that early, I guess actually she came later when we were doing *Music for 18*.

RH: I was just learning about those people. I knew nothing about any of the so-called minimalist artists, but I know you had that sculpture by, who was that, Richard Serra?

SR: Yeah, the *Candle Rack*.

RH: *Candle Rack*, and you had a Sol LeWitt drawing, as well. Those were actually the first artworks from those people that I ever saw.

SR: Sol came down at one point when I was working on *Drumming* and he was interested in buying a score and he ended up buying *Four Organs*. Onion skins in the old days, when I did scores with ink on vellum. And the money that he gave me for that, I used to buy the glockenspiels for *Drumming*. The Sol LeWitt Memorial glockenspiels.

RH: I'm kind of interested in how you got to know people like Sol LeWitt and Richard Serra and of course Michael Snow.

SR: Well, before I lived at Broadway and Canal, I lived on Duane Street right off of Greenwich. Before Tribeca was called Tribeca, it was called the Washington Market because it was a vegetable market that was there all night long. And I was right across the street from the vegetable market, on the top floor of the loft building that some engineering company had. And they thought I'd be a good night watchman. (*laughs*)

RH: Boy, did they have you pegged wrong! (*laughs*)

SR: I paid $65 a month and I was always late, but they were very forgiving. Today you couldn't get a doorknob there for $65. In any event, when I was down there, Richard Serra was on Greenwich Street, just around the corner. We ran into each other in the street and just started talking. He came up and I played him *Come Out*. And he was completely taken with it. Then he had me come over and showed me a piece where he rolled up a sheet of lead and used it as a prop to hold up another sheet of lead on the wall. That was one of his first prop-pieces, which is the first thing that he became known for. So, we were kind of in on the ground floor of each other's work. Michael Snow lived on Chambers Street just a block and a half away. I saw his film *Wavelength* and thought, "I've got to meet this guy." And I don't remember how, maybe somebody said, "He's on Chambers Street" or gave me his number, but we met and he said, "You did *Come Out*!" So, he knew *Come Out* and I'd seen *Wavelength* and that began our relationship. Sol LeWitt, I saw his work in 1966 when there was a show at the Jewish Museum called *Primary Structures* and it was the first show of minimal artists here. I think Sol had a number of pieces there, these white or gray sculptures of open cubes, very elaborate. I liked them immediately. He lived over on the Lower East Side on Hester Street, and I don't remember how, but I got over to his studio loft and he came to rehearsals, too, later on. I guess certain people were on the same wavelength. I've often thought, it's as if some artists of the same generation have receivers built into their brains, so to speak, and if they tune in to the same stations, they bond together. There is something literally in the air. Artists will pick up on that, and for all kinds of reasons, whether they're listening to non-Western music or early Bob Dylan or Junior Walker with a repeating bass line or the first prelude of the *Well-Tempered Clavier* with the same rhythmic pattern repeated or Pérotin with those long held tones. All kinds of things seem to lock in.

So, anyway, that's how I got to know those people at that time.

RH: That's very interesting.

SR: Well, let's see, the next thing was we started to go to Europe.

RH: Yeah, that was very soon after the premieres, I think it was late January of '72.

SR: We premiered *Drumming* in New York in December of 1971 and—we were off! First concerts were, I think, in Paris and London?

RH: Yeah.

SR: And we used to go over, as I remember, by Icelandic Airlines.

RH: That's right! I'd forgotten about that. Stop in Reykjavík.

SR: In the middle of the night!

RH: Go in the duty-free shop for a few minutes.

SR: And then collapse and wake up in Luxembourg, remember that?

RH: Luxembourg! Then we would rent trucks. Panel trucks. You had shipped the instruments and the electronics over before by air freight.

SR: I was the roadie, well, we were all roadies.

RH: Right, that's when we did everything. I think you and Arthur Murphy set up the electronics while we were setting up the marimbas and the bongos.

SR: This was when we screwed wires in the back of a tube amplifier and had spare tubes.

RH: And you always brought a spare because something always went wrong.

SR: Mostly with the electric organs. We'd travel with five, we needed four, and two would break.

RH: I remember in England, of course you only took a core ensemble, the singers, a piccolo player, Jim Preiss, me, Steve Chambers, and Arthur, I guess.

SR: Right.

RH: So we needed other people to do all of *Drumming.*

SR: Right.

RH: In England you brought on some of the composers you knew.

SR: We brought on Gavin Bryars, Michael Nyman, and Cornelius Cardew. And they became a part of Steve Reich and Musicians.

RH: For a short time, yes.

SR: Nyman actually arranged some of the concerts for us.

RH: I think he did.

SR: We played *Drumming* at the Hayward Gallery, inside the first major installation of Mark Rothko's paintings in the UK, and Nyman actually set that up.

RH: And I think that's the tour when we were in Oxford and we were supposed to drive to Bristol the next day. I think you saw on your map that we were not that far from Amesbury, where Stonehenge was. And, as I recall, you suggested we all get up early in the morning, so we could drive to Stonehenge and see the sunrise.

SR: I remember that, yes.

RH: We got there early. In those days, you could just walk among the stones. You could touch them.

SR: Exactly.

RH: There was nobody else there, just us. That was great.

SR: It certainly was. And it was built to be an observatory.

RH: Yeah, that was a really memorable moment from that tour. Almost as memorable as going out to the Spanish restaurant in Brussels. (*laughs*)

SR: You mean that flamenco spot in cloudy, foggy Brussels? Right. We all got pretty drunk, and then two women came out and, as I remember it, they sang and played the guitar, but when they started to clap we all looked at each other like, here it comes!

RH: Yeah, that was great, and I remember, it was after a concert when we had been schlepping all the instruments. You leaned over to me once they started clapping and said, "That's fantastic! There's a piece with no instruments to carry! Just bring your hands!" I remember, after we finished eating, we all went outside, and started fooling around with clapping patterns.

SR: Exactly.

RH: I don't know if *Clapping Music* was a direct result of that, but maybe it had some influence on that?

SR: It did! We had 2,000 pounds of equipment and it certainly had occurred to me all the things that could go wrong. Also, we were working in the early '70s with bongo drums with skin, and marimbas with wood, and glockenspiels with metal, while Stockhausen and Cage were twisting dials on electronic equipment. Clapping seemed to continue the direction we were going in. Just bring your hands. But I also remember later on when you and I started to rehearse it, that we both assumed this is going to be another phase piece, because that's what we did, right? I remember we started out (*demonstrates clapping rhythm*) and then

I began to slightly speed up, while you held the tempo, and it was extremely difficult and kind of ridiculous because there we were doing the simplest thing you could possibly do, and then trying to superimpose this difficult phasing technique. And then I said, "Look, I'll continue, and you just move up an eighth."

RH: Just skip to the next measure and forget the phasing.

SR: And it worked! And that was the end of phasing—right there in 1972.

RH: It took me a while to figure out why that was so difficult, and I think the reason is when we phase in *Drumming*, if you're the person phasing, you keep your sense of one. The beginning of your pattern is always one, even after you phase and you're on the other person's six, you're still feeling like your first note of the pattern is one. When you do *Clapping Music*, when you skip to the next measure, to me, you think of it as a new pattern instead of thinking of one. So, if you try to keep your sense of one you get very disoriented, and that's when we collapsed on the floor laughing because we couldn't do it!

SR: Where is one! That was the prime question in many rehearsals, right? We had all kinds of strategies, I remember, when we did *Drumming*, when the piccolo player would come in. One musician on the glockenspiels would nod to the piccolo player, and I would sit next to them and subtly nod my head and give them the one. And all of us at one time or another would get lost.

RH: Yeah.

SR: I think phasing is easier if you're playing continuously, and there are so many rests in *Clapping Music*.

RH: That's exactly right.

SR: (*demonstrates consistent rhythm*) That's easier, *Piano Phase* is the easiest of all. I mean, none of it is easy, but you're just playing, and nothing gets in your way. Once you have rests, you introduce a real problem with the phasing process.

RH: The other thing I remember about our concerts in Europe is, I think that was the first time I had an inkling of how momentous this music was or was going to become. The audiences went nuts over there. In fact, as I recall, we played the fourth section of *Drumming* as an encore.

SR: Right, I remember we went backstage to discuss exactly where we were going to start the fourth section.

RH: Yeah. The audiences in the United States were good, but in Europe they just went nuts.

SR: Yeah, that's true.

RH: You don't really appreciate the significance of it, but so many people with *Drumming* and *Music for 18* basically said it changed their life, or changed their outlook on music or the way they compose or the way they think about things. So, it's pretty amazing that we were in there on the ground floor for all of that.

SR: Here we are, as we're talking now here in 2020, getting ready to do *Drumming at 50*. You sent me this great tape of you and Bob Becker and Garry Kvistad and Bill Cahn.

RH: And the Sō Percussion guys.

SR: It's our generation and the next generation, and very important percussionists of both generations, playing this piece beautifully and very much with the aural tradition, because you and Bob and Garry were there, knowing how we used to do it. When I went over to London about ten years ago and heard Colin Currie, who had put together a group, do it, my jaw just dropped. I thought to myself, "We couldn't have ever done that!" (*laughs*) They grew up with it. It was just something that was out there, and they brought a whole new energy. That's so encouraging. The music meant something to people we didn't know anything about.

RH: Yeah, it's great that there's the Boosey and Hawkes score and people can learn it from that. For the first two generations, we learned it from you that way and I taught it to my students and other percussionists the same way, by rote. It's one of the few pieces that still works better learning it that way.

SR: I think people forget, there's always an aural tradition. When I went to Juilliard, Eduard Steuermann was on the piano faculty. He was pretty old, he was very nervous, and he wouldn't play in public, his hands would shake. But he made a recording of the complete Schoenberg piano music which he learned with Schoenberg, for their private performances. I've heard Glenn Gould do it, but somehow when Steuermann plays it, that's the real deal. He's coming from where it started.

I was listening to our Deutsche Grammophon recording the other day, *Music for Mallet Instruments, Voices, and Organ*, and I just remember the feeling of playing it. It's wonderful that it's recorded. There are people who can do it, quote, "better than we did," but we were the original instruments. (*laughs*)

RH: Well, we had magic time, as you put it.

SR: We've left out Kenny Clarke!

RH: Kenny Clarke, that's right. You and I did this interview a few years ago and that's when I first heard that term you were describing. I said, "Who did you listen to?" And of course, Kenny Clarke was one of the first people you talked about. Not that he had so much technique. I mean, Max Roach and some of these other people had more chops.

SR: Exactly.

RH: But Kenny Clarke had a time feel that was magic.

SR: You also explained to me, and maybe you could explain again, how he completely revised basic timekeeping in jazz.

RH: Well, I didn't realize this until you brought him up and I started investigating what it was or how he came to play that way. It turns out that pre-bebop, actually, the drummers would play their right foot-pedal bass drum and they would play almost every beat like 1–2–3–4. Then they would cross their right hand to play a high-hat cymbal on their left, maybe playing after beats or something. But Kenny Clarke moved his right hand to the ride cymbal on the right and started playing (*imitates jazz rhythm*) on the ride cymbal and didn't play all those beats on his bass drum, so it gave a floating sense of time. A sort of over-the-bar-line kind of feel, rather than a marchlike, 1–2–3–4 kind of feel. That's, I think, how Kenny Clarke came to be able to play with that sense of time.

SR: We call it the "ride" cymbal.

RH: The ride cymbal, yes, he's riding it.

SR: It was a new way to ride. The whole band was literally just riding on that cymbal.

RH: Well, I think as you were teaching us *Drumming*, for example, you demonstrated every part and you had a certain lilt to your playing, a certain feel. We all either consciously or unconsciously tried to imitate that same kind of phrasing, or the way you played the patterns. In retrospect, I think it was sort of a jazz kind of feel. Your experience as a drummer was more as a drum set player, a jazz player, and your influences were like that. Up until that point, I'd played orchestral style, which is a little bit more strict.

SR: Right.

RH: It didn't have that kind of lilt. And I remember you saying that when other people started learning *Drumming* or other pieces of yours, they didn't quite have that feeling yet that we had because of the sensibility or the sense of time feel that you were giving it when you demonstrated the parts.

SR: That was increasingly clear when European musicians would do it.

RH: Exactly.

SR: And there were a lot of specific things, a tendency to play rhythmic music too staccato (*imitates staccato rhythm*). I've always said, I want to get a T-shirt that says *tenuto sempre* (*laughs*). In other words, give each note its full value. An eighth is not a sixteenth note, a quarter note is not an eighth note, and that really matters. Don't get misled by the fact that it's fast and rhythmic. Because if you do, the notes will be too short, the harmonic interest will shrink, and the emotional power will diminish. You'll be like a waiter whose shoes are too tight. (*laughs*)

RH: I think that's important. The drummers that you brought into your group all came from the same school or studied with a lot of the same teachers. Jim Preiss and Bob Becker and eventually Garry Kvistad. We all learned to play with a certain kind of sound, a lot of depth of sound, a lot of center to the sound, which is what you're talking about, in a way. So, I think we were able to understand what you were talking about and bring that sensibility to your music.

SR: You got that from studying with Hinger, right?

RH: With Hinger, right. Before that, Alan Abel. And Jim Preiss studied with Hinger, Bob Becker studied with Hinger's teacher, Bill Street.

SR: Right, up at Eastman.

RH: Up at Eastman, right. So it's all the same school of playing.

SR: It's also a very American thing. It took another generation or two for people in Europe... The Ensemble Modern got it. They're one or two generations younger than we are and they got it. But the people before them really just didn't have it and you really couldn't ask them to do it, because it wasn't in their bones.

RH: Right, right. I remember with Ensemble Modern; they were the first group other than Steve Reich and Musicians who played *Music for 18 Musicians*. They're the first ones who played it with the Boosey and Hawkes scores.

SR: Right.

RH: You brought Bob Becker and me over just to kind of supervise. (*laughs*)

SR: To bring the aural tradition in to supplement the written notation.

RH: And, of course, they played great.

SR: They did.

RH: It was probably helpful to have people who had done it so much.

SR: Absolutely. I know they expressed to me how important it was that you and Bob were there and what a contribution that made.

I used to go over and play with them. I'd play *Drumming* Part 1, and *Music for 18*, and whatever I contributed, it was helpful.

Another thing we forgot to cover was *Six Pianos* and *Music for Mallet Instruments*. I remember *Six Pianos* was an unusual rehearsal process, I mean, where do you find six pianos? In a piano store! (*laughs*) And there was Jack Roman, who was the head of Baldwin Pianos back in the early '70s. In those days, Baldwin had a piano store just opposite Carnegie Hall. And somehow, I don't remember how I got to him, probably through Michael Tilson Thomas because they knew each other. I gave him what I thought was this unlikely request, "Could we come in when you close up and rehearse?" And he said, "Yeah, great!" I remember, we started off with twelve concert grands and it was a supernova of confusion!

RH: Well, *Six Pianos* also started off as a phase piece, too. We were trying to phase fifteen yards apart or something. It just wasn't working.

SR: It wasn't, but we whittled it down to six spinets close together. And then later we did it on six interlocking grands, once we got it together. I remember we had an open rehearsal there, too. Because I was talking to Michael Tilson Thomas and he said, "I enjoyed coming to that open rehearsal of *Six Pianos*," and I had completely forgotten about that.

RH: Yeah, that was great and, of course, *Six Pianos* along with *Clapping Music* were the last two pieces that started out as phase pieces. No more phasing after those two.

SR: Phasing was over. It wasn't a decision, it just evolved. Composing went on and it didn't work with the new musical material, so we didn't continue it. *Drumming* is the last phase piece.

RH: It's kind of interesting. You're known for phasing but it was only from, what, '67 was *Piano Phase*?

SR: Yeah, from '67 to '71. Except I discovered it with the tape pieces in '65 and '66.

RH: It was a really short period of time.

SR: Right, I haven't done phasing in over fifty years. But I think musicians who play *Drumming* or *Piano Phase* nowadays enjoy the challenge of that.

RH: Exactly, it's a technique that at least percussionists, and probably a lot of other musicians, have to learn. It's one of those things you have to learn to be able to do. Because all percussionists play *Drumming*. Of course, *Piano Phase* now is probably more often played in the marimba version. We call it *Marimba Phase*.

SR: Where were you and Jim fooling around with that?

RH: This was on the first tour. We were recording something for BBC in London, I forget.

SR: *Four Organs*, I think.

RH: Yeah, maybe *Four Organs*, and there was a break, and Jim and I were just fooling around. Because you'd been doing *Piano Phase*, I guess it was you and Arthur Murphy on that tour.

SR: Exactly.

RH: So, Jim and I realized, "Well, we can do that, too." (*laughs*) You're not playing chords, you're just playing a single line, so we started fooling around, with *Piano Phase*. You were there listening to it and you said, "That sounds pretty good. Why don't you guys work it up?"

SR: Right.

RH: So, we did that and then we played it, I think it was at The Kitchen. Jim Preiss and I played *Marimba Phase* on two of the concerts and Bob Becker and I did the other two.

SR: I don't have my ear to the ground now as much as I used to. Does it get done on marimbas with any frequency, so far as you know?

RH: Oh, all the time, in university percussion studios. It's a standard thing. I think everybody at least practices it at some point.

SR: All right, *Music for 18 Musicians*. Two years, two years of rehearsal… It was twenty-one musicians in 1975 when we played the first half.

RH: After that performance at The Kitchen, I think you were starting to think about the tour to Europe and the expense with all those people. I mean, that's a lot of people to fly over, and you can't just bring over English composers to play some of these parts. There's clarinets and violin and cello and all that. So, you realized at some point you didn't need all those people if people would double on other instruments. At one point Jay Clayton started to play piano and some of the percussionists played piano. You played piano and marimba. People moved around.

SR: Yes.

RH: During the rehearsals, this was a little different because we actually had little scraps of manuscript paper that you would bring in, with our next pattern, and it would say something like "Play this, then cue Bob here," or "Look at bass clarinet for cue." Everybody had little notes on their scraps of paper about who to look at.

SR: Right, exactly.

RH: And I don't know if you actually had a score. I don't know how that worked.

SR: No, there were only parts. I wrote *Music for 18 Musicians* in my notebook, each individual part, and only on tape had I combined them, so that I knew they worked. And then I would write them out individually for rehearsals. And the score didn't happen until years after. I went through the whole recording process without a score, we all did, and then when it was being edited and mixed with the producer and engineer, I just had it all in my head. I wasn't looking at a score during the editing and mixing of the piece.

RH: Wow.

SR: So, that may be part of why it worked so well. (*laughs*)

RH: You know, it was interesting for us because I think all the players felt they were more a part of it. Somebody might say, "Maybe this other person should play that part and I can go do something else... If I cue Jay, then Steve Chambers will know what to do." Just from being inside it and working through it as a performer, we would make suggestions to you and then you would incorporate that. Those were great rehearsals and really different from the *Drumming* rehearsals.

SR: There were more people involved.

RH: A lot of people.

SR: A lot of people, who really got to know each other. You and Bob were seniors, I don't mean in age, I mean you had been there from the beginning and everyone recognized what great players you were. What I loved about the whole situation was that there was such honesty. Everybody recognized the realities in the room. And went along with that. I may have been the composer, but I deferred to you and Bob and Jim as better players. Everyone acknowledged what was best for the music. We recorded the beginnings of the rehearsals, maybe an hour's worth or more because it was a long piece. We'd relax for, what was it, apple juice and cookies? (*laughs*)

RH: That's right!

SR: And listen to the tape.

RH: That's right, we did listen.

SR: And everybody would go, "Oh, no. Did I do that?" And that's another interesting lesson. You don't have to criticize musicians. Just let them listen to themselves. And everybody will generally be self-critical, and will try to improve things. That carried over to our many real recording sessions. We always went into the control room to listen. Everyone would zero in on themselves, trying to hear what they had done that they could improve. That may account for the fact that the recordings were by and large very good, and done in a very reasonable amount of time.

I remember our rehearsals as enjoyable, too, because sometimes it would be so screwed up you could really get a laugh out of it. (*laughs*)

RH: Well, I think that's one of the genius ways you handled the group. You let the players make decisions when necessary and you accepted their opinions. You weren't autocratic in your handling of the group. You respected that some people were great players and had good ideas about things. And you would accept that and allow the piece to evolve from the suggestions of the players. And it made us invested. I felt some kind of ownership. In fact, with *Drumming* in particular, it was hard to let go (*laughs*) when other people started playing the piece, you know? In fact, when I teach the piece, I don't teach it as Player 1, Player 2. It's Jim's part or Bob's part.

SR: Who do you want to be?

RH: Yeah, exactly (*laughs*). And the students like that.

SR: Everybody likes that.

RH: *Music for 18*, that was a special kind of a community experience.

SR: I think that carries through in performance, too. I think that's in the piece. Technically it's in the piece, because one of the key decisions was "No conductor."

RH: Right. Exactly. Did you ever think there would be a conductor, or did you know from the beginning?

SR: It was one of the very first things that I was absolutely clear about: no conductor. We'll figure it out with a lot of inside-the-ensemble cuing. *Music for 18 Musicians* is basically a large piece of chamber music with all that typical performer interaction. Even when we did *Four Organs*, somebody would be doing the nods to change bars, and it wasn't always me. Same thing with the organ player in *Music for Mallet Instruments*, and in *Drumming* you would nod when we all had to switch to the C-sharp drum. That background made me feel that whatever happened, we'll work it out, and we did.

RH: Then, of course, you wrote some of that into the piece, like the vibraphone part.

SR: The vibraphone is closest to being the conductor. The part is written to signal changes. But it has to be a good musical line, too. Also, the first bass clarinet gives cues during the less exactly measured changes during the pulsing sections.

It's interesting, the duration of *Drumming* went from an hour and twenty minutes for Deutsche Grammophon in the mid-seventies, and by the time we did it for Nonesuch in the mid-nineties, it was fifty-six minutes, and nobody said anything to anybody! It was the *zeitgeist*, the spirit of the age, or whatever had changed. Our mentalities had changed and we all naturally paced it faster. *Music for 18* was not that way. It was always around fifty-five to sixty minutes.

RH: Exactly.

SR: And nobody said anything about that, either. That communitarian reality, in the piece, seems to continue. And I think that's one of the things people really enjoy when they see it in live performance.

RH: I've heard many people comment on the fact—same with *Drumming*—seeing it is different than listening to it in your living room on speakers. When you see the choreography, see the involvement of the players, it's a different experience entirely.

SR: I think that's true of all music, but it's particularly true of those pieces.

RH: I think the thing about *Music for 18* in particular is the impact it has on the players as they're playing. It's basically, every time, an emotional experience. For me, anyway. And I think for everyone.

SR: For me, too.

RH: And somehow that comes through. I know certain spots like—I forget the section number—when Liz [Lim] and I are playing, I'm playing marimba and she's playing the repeated pattern on violin. Anyway, we just look at each other every time. It's like there's some kind of...

SR: "Here we go!"

RH: Here we go, let's go on with this, let's ride with this.

SR: Right.

RH: The feeling at the end, it's nothing like… I mean, I've had great feelings from other pieces, but nothing quite like that. The audience always senses that.

SR: Oh, absolutely, the audience really is keyed in. The attitude of the players is directly communicated to the audience. In any concert. And it determines how you receive the music.

RH: Now, when you were writing *Music for 18*, did you have any sense of that? I mean, obviously you're listening to playbacks and tapes and you're hearing how it's going, but I just wondered if you really had an awareness of what that was going to be like for a player and for the audience?

SR: Well, there were all our rehearsals, and that gave me and you and everyone else in the piece a good idea of exactly what was going on. Also, going back to *Music for Mallet Instruments, Voices, and Organ*, we rehearsed that in 1972–73. I remember the third section; I was aware while we were rehearsing of how other people were responding to what I had written. And if I felt involvement and energy in it, great. But the third section, everyone was like, "When do we move to the next section?"

RH: *(laughs)*

SR: And so I rewrote that whole section. And I often say that the only music criticism that matters is the reaction of musicians playing your music. Just watch them carefully and take it seriously.

RH: That's really true. I don't know if we were gonna get into this, but after *Music for 18*, did you ever think about trying to write another kind of *Music for 18 Musicians* piece?

SR: I think, yes. But there was a roadblock.

RH: (*laughs*)

SR: We did a tour of *Music for 18.*

RH: Oh, yeah, we toured it all over the place.

SR: Very successful tours in Europe. I remember the one that took us to Venice. Beryl came with us and Bob Becker's mother came. And I came back and I guess that was 1977–78, and I hadn't written a thing for a year. I'd been on the road. And I sat down, and in those days there was a very unhealthy attitude. You can't repeat yourself in any way, not even influence yourself. Everything has to be something new, new, new! And I couldn't think of anything new! (*laughs*) I had this huge experience I'd been through. But I can't repeat myself in any way, I can't repeat myself. So I went back and forth with that, just getting more frustrated, and finally, between thinking of *Music for Mallet Instruments*, and thinking I've just got to do something, I wrote *Music for a Large Ensemble*. Now, some people like it. Fine, I'm glad they do. But for me, at least it was a new piece. Maybe the most interesting thing in it was the sustained trumpets. In any event, once I got through that, I was improvising at the piano, moving in fifths up and down, and I came up with this piano pattern that grew to be the underpinning of what was first called *Octet* and later became *Eight Lines*. And that piece really felt, "Ah, I'm somewhere else." Then the next piece was *Variations for Winds, Strings, and Keyboards*, which had a lot of harmonic movement and a lot of sequences. Anyway, I remember we did all three pieces at Carnegie Hall in 1980, we filled Carnegie Hall. You looked at me and said, "Well, Steve, I think *Octet* is the best of this batch." (*laughs*) And you were right. It was the smallest, the shortest, and the best.

Going back, do you remember the open rehearsals for *Music for 18* that we used to have?

RH: That's right, a lot of famous people came to those rehearsals. John Cage came to one of them. And I saw him go up to talk to you, so I kind of edged over there to hear what he was going to say, and the only thing I heard him say was "It changed." (*laughs*) And I of course had no idea, I still don't know exactly what he meant.

SR: Well, neither do I, but my hunch is that either he had heard *Drumming* and it stayed in six sharps for an hour. Here there was harmonic movement. That might have been one thing. Or the fact that, instead of being multiples of the same instruments, it was this sort of unusual chamber orchestra, many different timbres. And that might have been it, too. But it remains a mystery.

RH: Which is probably just fine with him.

SR: I don't think he would have wanted anything else.

RH: Those open rehearsals were really interesting, mainly because of the people who came, artists, musicians. I think Morty Feldman may have come?

SR: Yeah, Morty Feldman. And Betty Freeman photographing. She took a couple of the best photographs of us playing in those rehearsals.

RH: Right, right. Those were exciting times. I forgot what we played at The Bottom Line.

SR: It was *Music for 18*. When the recording first came out on ECM, which was in '78. We recorded it in Paris in '76 on a European tour. The same tour I think that we played in Berlin, where David Bowie was. The recording sat in the can because Deutsche Grammophon recorded it, but they ended up selling it to ECM. Deutsche Grammophon felt it would do better on a jazz label than it would on their label. It wasn't until '78 that it was released, and Bob Hurwitz, who has been president of Nonesuch for many years, was then at ECM, and he arranged for us to give the performance promoting the record at The Bottom Line, and David Bowie was there.

RH: David Bowie came, I remember. He talked to you and he actually talked to me for quite a while afterwards. I think because I had played so much, you know, I had played a lot of the parts. He was a very nice guy. So these days people say, "Oh, you know Steve Reich? Fine. Oh, you met David Bowie!" (*laughs*)

SR: I think he made a comment, he said, "I just came back from doing a tour with white shirts and black pants, and when I saw Steve Reich and Musicians, I knew they really had good taste." (*laughs*) Later he put it on a list of his fifteen all-time favorite recordings.

RH: Those were great experiences, great times.

SR: They were, and it's wonderful to be doing this with you now as you're preparing *Drumming at 50.*

RH: That's exciting. And interestingly enough, 2021 will be the fiftieth birthday for Nexus. So, it all happened around the same time. Like you say, there was something in the air back in the '70s, world music, my first time hearing African music and gamelan and Indian music, all these things.

SR: There absolutely was something in the air. As a matter of fact, I believe the best music always reflects that because it's honest and intensely felt—because it's really there. And it was definitely a change, it was a break from the Stockhausen, Boulez, and Cage mentality. It was definitely a very productive period.

RH: Well, it certainly changed my life, I think it made me realize that I could have a life playing contemporary music, or new music. Up to that point, I was playing all these other kinds of things. And it's not that I didn't like it, I just didn't know there was anything else. And the combination of your music and the non-Western stuff that I was learning at the same time really changed the whole direction of my musical life, for sure.

SR: We were all in the position of having to invent our lives. One of the most important things that just evolved was our ensemble. I was able to continue writing what I really wanted to write and rehearse it with musician friends who wanted to play it. And it was also a time, in the '60s and '70s, when there was a kind of confidence. I did whatever I had to do to pay $65-a-month rent.

RH: Well, you certainly had confidence. I was surprised when I first started coming to your rehearsals in the spring of '71, you'd already arranged concerts at three major venues in New York City. And the piece wasn't finished. Thinking back on it, you had a certain confidence that you were going to pull this off and this was going to work.

SR: I guess the quality of the rehearsals, and the reactions we were getting, as you mentioned, from the people who would come over, friends who were painters, sculptors, filmmakers, musicians, and dancers. It all seemed to say, "Just keep it going." Keep working and it's gonna work out. All I can say is "Thank you. Thank G-d."

RH: Exactly. Well, little did you know when you were practicing your stick control exercises with Roland Kohloff, that it would lead to all this.

SR: I've got to thank you in particular, Russell, because I often say to people you were the right arm of the ensemble. I've got to thank you for what you're doing right now, and for what you've done since the very beginning.

CHAPTER 7

ROBERT HURWITZ

Steve Reich: When did you first get involved in making recordings?

Robert Hurwitz: My first job out of college was at Columbia Records during its golden age. But even before I got there, I was already taken by what the company represented in terms of its creative choices.

I met a number of incredible musicians during my time there, including Ornette Coleman, Aaron Copland, Elliott Carter, Wayne Shorter, Bruce Springsteen, and most importantly, Glenn Gould, with whom I remained in touch long after I left the company. I also met and became friendly with John Hammond, their great A&R man; and Goddard Lieberson, the legendary label head. Both of them were important role models for me.

I look at those two years at Columbia as my graduate school experience, except it was in a record company rather than a university. I especially paid close attention to Lieberson's accomplishments in terms of the impact he made, not only in classical music but over all different genres. Columbia Records recorded Igor Stravinsky, Leonard Bernstein, Glenn Gould, but also Bob Dylan and Miles Davis. It was a kind of template that I hoped one day to possibly duplicate, although I didn't know it at the time. I was just paying attention to what was happening.

Early on I had lunch with Keith Jarrett, who had recently been signed to Columbia. Keith told me that he had started making records for this small company in Germany called ECM; it was the first I'd heard of them. I ran out the next day and bought the solo piano records he had made with Chick Corea. They were amazing. By coincidence, a few months later, Manfred Eicher, who ran the company, came to Columbia looking for a distribution deal. They sent him from office to office, no one was really interested in ECM. Eventually they sent him to the head of publicity, who said, "You should meet Bob Hurwitz. Bob loves your records." Manfred and I sat down and spoke for maybe half an hour; by the time he was ready to leave, he said, "One day I'm going to have a company in America, and I want you to run it." I was shocked. I was twenty-four years old. I couldn't believe it; I'd never heard of such a thing, but about a year later I was running ECM. And sometime after that, I became aware of your music when DG put out the *Drumming* record. I can't remember what year that was.

SR: '74, I think.

RH: You and I met in '76, actually. A wonderful man, Roland Kommerell, was the head of Polydor in Germany when Deutsche Grammophon recorded *Music for 18 Musicians*. Roland felt that Polydor really didn't have the capability to market the record. And so, he proposed to Manfred that ECM take over *Music for 18 Musicians*. Manfred then called me and told me about the record. Not long after, I heard a knock on my door, and it was you.

SR: Well, we had a very apocryphal first meeting, which neither one of us is probably entirely accurate about. But it was all for the good. I think you said something like "I don't like minimal music, but I love *Music for 18 Musicians.*"

RH: It sounds like the truth! But you know, that's only forty-five years ago, perhaps my memory has slipped a bit.

SR: Right. Well, when *Music for 18 Musicians* finally came out on ECM, I was dealing with you and the staff at ECM and at Warner's. I remember when the Deutsche Grammophon *Drumming, Six Pianos, Music for Mallet Instruments* box set came out back in '74, I had a meeting with a guy, very formal, head of DG USA, and he didn't want to release the box set. Finally it was released and placed in numerical order on the shelves. It didn't sell a lot, but people in the field definitely noticed. Anyway, when I met you, we quickly got into the actual details of what you were going to do. I think you said to me, "We want to get you out to talk to public radio stations and progressive rock stations." There were such things in those days. "And we want you to go to Los Angeles, to Houston, to San Francisco." And I just thought, "Are you serious?"

RH: Shall we not forget *Music for 18* at The Bottom Line?

SR: Ah, no. I do not forget that at all. That was the record release.

RH: The Bottom Line was one of the great rock clubs of New York; it's the place where Bruce Springsteen had his major breakthrough. The owners were pretty enlightened. I remember seeing, on a stage big enough for a five-piece band, Aaron Copland conducting the chamber version of *Appalachian Spring* and Tashi playing Messiaen's *Quartet for the End of Time.* What a perfect place for eighteen musicians crammed on a stage for your piece! It sent a very powerful message to the New York media regarding broadening an idea about breaking down boundaries. What had the most powerful impact was the fact that the music was that good! I am certain that even if I was not involved, it would have found its audience. It was unstoppable.

SR: Well, it's still going. I remember we were at the end of the concert at The Bottom Line and David Bowie came up to me and said some nice things.

What you did in those days, what ECM did in those days, was reach the audience that I wanted to reach, which was people who loved jazz, people who were into adventurous classical music, people who were interested in world music, which was just becoming an American reality in those days. ECM had that, and we used to joke, "What bin are they gonna put it in in the record store?" And the answer was "Well, three or four different bins."

Since that time, things have changed. And there are no more record stores.

RH: In other parts of the world, there still are record stores; the physical business over there has not yet disappeared like it has in America.

SR: The sales of *Music for 18* were kind of amazing to me. We toured the piece three times in Europe, and I believe that between the touring and the record sales, the piece really changed my life in terms of visibility and pressure to produce more. Then there's a jump, that was '76–'78, and then 1984 was a big year for both of us. I finished *The Desert Music* and you took over Nonesuch. How do you remember our beginning to work together at Nonesuch?

RH: I had told Manfred that I was leaving ECM and I gave him six months' notice at that time. He didn't think it was enough! You and I had lunch about a month before I began at Nonesuch, to talk about your next ECM recording of *The Desert Music*. I have an old journal entry from that day, which refers to the fact you and I did not speak about Nonesuch at all, our main topic of conversation was setting up the new recording. Although in the back of my mind I hoped we might work together one day, I just couldn't imagine how it could happen because you seemed so tied in with ECM. I wanted to be honorable. The line I would never cross—and never did cross—was going after and poaching an artist who I had worked with at ECM.

But… If an artist called *me*, well, that was another story.

And then you called me. In my first week at Nonesuch. You were really upset, Manfred had pulled the plug on the recording, after you had spent months raising money, getting the Brooklyn Academy of Music involved, scheduling Michael Tilson Thomas to conduct.

I know you were upset, but that was a great call! The best call! That moment really was the beginning of my time at Nonesuch. We had a chance to work with Steve Reich!

SR: That was a very fraught time because I had never dealt remotely before or since with about 100 musicians and singers. There were people, money, time, energy, and dates on the line. And so, it was a great relief, and amazingly a success. Do you remember the actual sessions when Michael Tilson Thomas was conducting?

RH: Absolutely. I was able, in short order, to put together the cash from our end needed to make the session possible. It was a

tight schedule. At the end of the sessions, I thought the record
was in the can, I think MTT thought it was in the can, but the
composer was not sure. Because it was still my first month on
the job, I didn't yet have the resources to go into overtime.

SR: I'll interject that what happened was that Paul Goodman,
that really wonderful engineer, looked at me and said, "Are we
going into overtime?" And I gulped. And I knew we should
musically, and I said, "Yes." My credit card would have been
rejected for sure...

The next day I called Karen Hopkins, who should get the credit
right here. She was the fundraiser and eventually the president of
Brooklyn Academy of Music, BAM, and she was a champion of
The Desert Music and of my work at BAM in general. She turned
to the funding sources that were over there, and that saved both
of us from financial disaster. So, credit where credit is due.

Now, jumping up a few years to another big record, which is
Electric Counterpoint with Pat Metheny, and I remember I was
on the phone with you and I said, in passing, "You know, Bob,
a lot of classical guitarists come up to me and ask, 'Why don't
you write for guitarists, because your music will sound great
that way.'" And I said to you, "Well, I feel the guitar of our time
is the electric guitar." And you said, without dropping a beat,
"Well, why don't you write for Pat Metheny?" And I said, "Do
you think he'd be interested?" And you said, "I don't know,
let's call him up." And you called, and five minutes later I was
talking to Pat about getting together to go over writing for the
guitar. And of course, *Different Trains*, the other part of that record, the first of our Grammy awards, was very important to me.
I wonder what your remembrances of that are.

RH: The piece floored me, from the very first takes you sent
me; they had such a dramatic impact before ever even hearing

Kronos play it. It is hard to equate "happiness" with the seriousness and even tragic aspect of *Different Trains*, but the album that came out made me especially happy because two artists with whom I had a very close relationship, Kronos and Pat, were both on this record.

I consider myself, as far as the music that I care about, to be an enthusiast, which means I probably had the right job. And so, one of the things I've always done is share music that I'm involved with, with other musicians, not to force them to listen to something they don't want to hear, but with the hope, on their own time, they might also care about it. I knew that Pat was already a big fan of yours from the ECM days, that he had already written music with his group that in a way was influenced by you, so that was a completely natural fit. Kronos, at that point, it was inevitable that the two of you would start working together. And so, the entire experience was something that I think has been very valuable for you, for Kronos, for Pat, for Nonesuch. It had a big impact on people.

SR: Yes, *Different Trains* is played by a lot of groups around the world. It's out there having a life of its own, and *Electric Counterpoint* has a life of its own.

RH: We even have two recordings at Nonesuch of it. Jonny Greenwood and Pat.

SR: I met Jonny Greenwood in the early 2000s. I got to talking with him and we immediately hit it off. His recording was with a solid-bodied guitar as opposed to Pat's hollow-bodied Gibson, and their two styles of playing are clearly different. It's great that both those recordings are out there.

A few years later, in 1998, we did *Music for 18* for Nonesuch in the Hit Factory. I remember, we were right off a tour from Japan and we were hot. We were into playing the piece. I remember that being a very positive recording experience.

That brings us up to the present with three records sitting in the can. We don't even know what's going to happen. The present state of the nonexistent record industry.

RH: In the time we've known one another, there have been a series of changes that have greatly affected the record business, sometimes for the better, in recent years, more for the worse.

When we met in the midseventies, the record business was as it had been for decades. The dominant format was the long-playing vinyl album. Then in '81, the CD format was introduced, and within five years, CDs completely dominated the industry. Around '98, Napster brought a nonphysical alternative for listeners (though not consumers). Things started happening faster and faster—in 2002, iTunes arrived, which again had a big impact on what the record business looked like. 2005, YouTube. All of Tower's stores—the place where most of your records were sold—were closed by 2008. And in 2010…streaming.

But in terms of the relationship between Steve Reich and Nonesuch, our focus has remained on the physical object, even with the knowledge that the business is moving away from it. Whether 1984 or 2020, we make a record, we put it out into the marketplace, we keep it in our catalog.

I always thought we were making recordings for the moment, and at the same time, for the future. I still feel that way. Right now, on September 22, 2020, as we speak, we have two projects waiting for release, and a third awaiting its recording. At whatever point they are released, they will be recordings you can hold in your hands, and future generations will hold in their hands.

SR: I've got to say just for the record that knowing that there was a record company that was just there...a record company with a great staff—David Bither, Peter Clancy, Karina Beznicki, Melissa Cusick, and others—has been a supportive stabilizing reality. We've lived in an age from the day we met where recordings reached more people than concerts. Even if you gave a lot of concerts. And this has only accelerated, for better and for worse, in the years that you've just recapped, with the physical recording slipping further and further away. In any event, the word is "Thank you."

RH: My pleasure, Steve, but I'd like to talk about one other thing, the idea of long-term relationships between artists and labels. That's one of the things I noticed about Columbia when I was younger—whether it was Copland or Stravinsky, Miles Davis or Dylan, Bernstein or Gould—there was a consistency to those relationships that evolved over time. By building something slowly over a long period of time, it was like a book publisher who believed in an author enough to publish everything they wrote, or a museum or art gallery, they would show the work of an artist as he or she evolved every few years.

In the early days, we began working with you, John Adams, Kronos, Philip Glass, and a few others. I don't know what it would have meant if we only put out one or two records of yours, or Kronos. But once making a decision that this was an artist I was willing to make a big commitment to, we built a catalog of your work—the whole, in this case, is every bit as important as any of its parts. We now have a catalog with practically every note you have written, starting in the '70s, that will live well into the future.

CHAPTER 8

STEPHEN SONDHEIM

This conversation, moderated by John Schaefer, was recorded at Lincoln Center in 2015.

John Schaefer: Stephen, when did you first hear Steve Reich's music?

Stephen Sondheim: It must have been, well, it was right after, I think it was right after he wrote the *Octet* because that's the first piece I ever heard, and I don't know what year that would be—

Steve Reich: Midseventies.

SS: Midseventies, yeah, and I think it was right after *Pacific Overtures*.

JS: And how did you come across his music? There was no internet to be trolling through then.

SS: No, no. Curiously enough, I subscribe to something called Records International, which is an importing organization in

California that imports records from every country in the world that we just don't get here. But they have some American records that are not that well-known, and this sounded interesting and I was knocked out. And I'll tell you something else; I take credit for this: I immediately went to Jerry Robbins and said, "You've got to make a ballet out of this." And he did.

JS: Wow. Were you aware, Steve, at the time that there was this guardian angel hanging over your shoulder distributing your records to important people?

SR: I've come to recognize Stephen Sondheim as my best PR agent on the planet.

(*laughter*)

But at the time, we met, in my memory, at a party given by Michael Tilson Thomas when Michael lived in New York City. I would say just before *Sunday in the Park* [*with George*] opened— you would maybe be in rehearsals. I had heard his name forever, but I didn't know the music, I'm ashamed to say. And we hit it off at a meeting and you said to me, "Would you like to come to a preview?" And I said, "I would be delighted to." And that was it. (*laughs*)

SS: That's before you came over to the house and we discussed your family when my jaw fell on the table.

SR: I think first my jaw fell on the table, then your jaw fell on the table. (*laughs*)

JS: Just so we can get people's jaws up off the table and back where they belong, your mom has a very intimate connection to the theater?

SR: Well, my mother's no longer with us, but her stage name and her married name was June Carroll. My parents were divorced when I was one year old. And she was in a series of shows called *New Faces*, which Stephen Sondheim is well aware of.

SS: And her brother was the producer, Leonard Sillman.

SR: Exactly, and the one, I guess it was in '52—

SS: That's the one I saw.

SR: —was the hit. And Eartha Kitt was in that one.

SS: And Maggie Smith.

SR: Yeah, and Alice Ghostley, and several other people.

SS: Yes, Alice Ghostley was a friend of mine. That's why I went.

SR: So, when Stephen invited my wife and I over for dinner with Hal Prince and they said, "Are you gonna write a show?" and I said, "No," they were terribly disappointed (*laughs*). And they said, "But your mother is June Carroll!" I said, "Yes." I didn't know anyone knew or was that aware of her, and I was very impressed, so thank you for that.

JS: So, this is part of the American Songbook series and at some point this evening I want to talk to you both about, you know, your relationship with the song form. It's actually kind of appropriate we're doing this today. January 31st is the birthday of Franz Schubert, who of course wrote—

SS: No longer with us.

(*laughter*)

SR: That's a good song!

(*laughter*)

JS: Wrote some 500 songs. Some of the great classical songs. Also, today, 100th birthday of Alan Lomax.

SS: Oh, my goodness.

(*light applause*)

JS: A folklorist who... That is the very definition of a smattering of applause.

(*laughter*)

SS: There are some people here who remember Alan Lomax. Isn't that nice?

JS: Who is responsible for many of us knowing some of the classic American folk songs and blues songs. So this is a great night to be talking about songs. In 2012, Steve, you got the gold medal for music from the American Academy of Arts and Letters.

SR: He was the one who preceded me! (*laughs*)

JS: And you, Stephen, wrote a kind of induction speech for the occasion in which you said, and I'm paraphrasing here but not by that much, "I've been ripping off Steve Reich for decades."

(*laughter*)

What form does this musical theft take?

SS: Well, the form is that what we're both interested in is vamps and that's what we spend our lives writing. And his vamps are the supersophisticated, most imaginative and inventive ones I've ever heard. You've got to get infected by that. But I've been writing them myself for a long time. It's his rhythmic verve, I'm being facetious here, it's the rhythmic verve and it's also his chords and my chords, I mean, we share a fondness for the same harmonic structures. For me, harmony is what makes music. I'm just exhilarated by everything he does, that's all. But it is true, when you hear things like that, you know, I can feel the influence.

(*musicians play Stephen Sondheim song*)

JS: Do you hear it, especially the opening piano part, that kind of rhythmic drive? That kind of restless [drive]?

SR: Yes, I just recognized somebody who was a music relative, unbeknownst to me, unconsciously derived. Things are in the air; people gravitate towards them in different ways. There we were gravitating towards them. I had an actual question.

SS: Sure.

SR: I was looking at *Sunday in the Park* on YouTube—

(*laughter*)

It was a very small proscenium.

(*laughter*)

And one of the first things George comes out and says is "I hate that tree!" And the tree, of course, just flies up into the flies, because we're in the theater. And I take it that what you're trying to make clear immediately to everybody is that this is not a park. This is the imagination of Georges Seurat projected so that you can see what's in his head. So obviously what was in his head at the time was "That was no good, I'm gonna change what I did." And he does instantly. So, I'm asking you, when I listen to what you do, it sounds like it just comes out in a stream of unstoppable... Do you ever change anything?

SS: Don't tell me that, I could ask you the same question.

(*laughter*)

As we both know, it takes an infinite amount of hard work to make something sound like it took no effort, like it's effortless. Also, I should mention this was written by James Lapine and his idea, the book, but that whole notion of George erasing a tree and the scenery disappears, it sets up the entire poetic idea of the evening. It says to the audience, "This is not real, enter this world." And what's brilliant about that is that it's done in a gesture in a moment in the first two minutes of the show. So, the audience knows where they are. That's called master playwriting. But the whole notion of living in your imagination, of course, is what it's about. But of course, I work very hard to make it sound effortless, and so do you!

(*laughter*)

Because I picture you sitting there, just going like that (*laughter*), and you've got your machine on and you go (*imitating sound effects*), and I can feel your body going, feel your hands going, you know?

SR: And a CD comes out the other side!

(laughter)

JS: But now this raises kind of an interesting question and I mentioned before wanting to talk to you both about songs. Stephen, your songs have to do double duty. I mean, you want them to be songs as songs, to stand up on their own, to be able to hear them on a stage like we're hearing them tonight. But they also have to serve the dramatic, narrative arc of the theater. At what point does that enter into the—

SS: It doesn't. I never think of them as being stand-alone songs. Forty years ago, the theater stopped supplying hits. In the days when I was a teenager, they were still trying to write hit songs. Well I remember when I was writing *Gypsy* with Jule Styne, he was so concerned that each song should not only serve the piece but [be] something that Sinatra could sing or that Peggy Lee could sing or whatever. We were all freed by that once the pop revolution came in and once the 1950s really took hold. It was a joy. We didn't have to worry about that at all. So, I've never thought about that at all.

JS: Have you ever written songs and thought, "Wow, where did that come from? What does that go to? What story is this a part of?" Or is there always a story first that's driving it?

SS: Oh, yeah, I only write for story. I don't write just for fun. I occasionally write birthday songs, that sort of stuff. But I don't see any reason to write unless you're telling a story.

JS: And, Steve, your relationship to the song as a form is almost a little more—

SR: Almost nonexistent.

(laughter)

JS: Well, here's the thing: we're about to hear *Electric Counterpoint*.

SR: Yes.

JS: Which, like many of your pieces, is in a fast-slow-fast form.

SR: Yes.

JS: Which, if not a literal A—B–A, at least kind of echoes the A—B–A.

SR: Well, fast-slow-fast has been around a long time.

JS: A long time.

SR: Since Scarlatti and before.

(laughter)

SS: He's mostly fast, though. He seems pretty fast.

SR: When he's fast, he's very fast.

SS: He's fast-fast-fast! Fast, very fast, fast!

(laughter)

SR: Let me tell you this, instead of using the word *song*, I believe, as I think a lot of composers do, melody is king. Melody can be achieved in very odd ways. I've got a piece called *Music* *for Pieces of Wood*, which is not being done here tonight. It's for interlocking, tuned claves. But the notes matter and how they interlock will form melodic patterns, and if they didn't, the piece would not be very good. So, if you divorce yourself from melody, you might as well leave, in my book.

SS: But there's a further thing, too, which maybe we can discuss later, which is the relationship of melody and speech.

SR: Yes.

SS: I mean, Steve takes many of his pieces from the inflections of the way people talk. And the fact is, as many people here must know, he has made pieces out of the way people talk. And I do the same thing. My melodic lines always reflect the character and what the character sounds like. And that is song. I consider what Steve writes songs when he's dealing with text. Particularly when he's dealing with the musicality of text, not when he's just setting a poem, but when he's dealing with the musicality of what I'm doing right now, what I'm doing right now, what I'm doing right now.

JS: And what we end up with is a song form that is extremely elastic in the right hands. Having said that, and I want to come back to the speech versus song because it turns out that border, if there ever was one, is very permeable. But, Steve, the counterpoint pieces, of which *Electric Counterpoint* is one, revolve around a certain kind of musical endeavor.

SR: Well, what happened was, in 1981 I think it was, I got a telephone call from the flutist Ransom Wilson and he said, "Would you write me a flute concerto?" And I said, "No."

(laughter)

"I don't really relate to the concerto form and I appreciate your asking." And that was the end of the conversation, and then I sat down and I thought, "You know, here's a world-class soloist who's calling me up and all I can say is no?" So, I began thinking about these pieces that I wrote in the 1960s, *Violin Phase*, where instrumentalists will play against a recording of themselves to make a contrapuntal, canonic relationship between tape and themselves, or it can be done with four live players. So I called Ransom back and said, "Look, Ransom, I don't know how you feel about this, but would you be interested in playing a piece where you prerecorded yourself on flute, on piccolo, and on alto flute to extend the range of the music? And then after you finish the prerecordings, would you play against it live as a kind of a recital piece?" He said, "I'd love to!" to my amazement. And, lo and behold, that's what happened. It was recorded at the Capitol Tower, I remember that, when Angel Records still existed. And it's done, I think Claire Chase just made a very outstanding recording of it recently.

JS: The piece is called *Vermont Counterpoint*.

SR: That's *Vermont Counterpoint*. And so that was okay, so much for that. Then Richard Stoltzman, the clarinetist, similar kind of story, similar kind of response. And that piece, I think, was extremely successful, called *New York Counterpoint*. And then I began hearing from guitar players that I would run into. You know, "Would you write for the guitar? We've got an attack and your music is so rhythmic, it would work very well." But they were mostly classical guitar players. So, I was talking to Bob Hurwitz, who is the president of Nonesuch Records, with whom I've been with quite a while, as has Mr. Sondheim. And Bob said, "Why don't you write for Pat Metheny?" And I thought, "That's great." I said, "Is he interested?" He said, "I

don't know, I'll call him up!" And in five minutes I was talking to Pat Metheny.

(*laughter*)

It's good to have a good record company. And so, we made a
date to get together and I said, "Look, I know how the guitar is
tuned and that's about it." He said, "Write single lines." I said,
"Aye, aye, sir!" And there are a couple of very simple triads in
the piece. And that's exactly what happened. And it became
Electric Counterpoint because the guitar in our day is, let's face
it, the electric guitar. And so, I felt the reality of that being the
idiomatic instrument of the day, I was drawn to that. And to
write for Metheny, I think the piece reflects somewhat his style.

JS: So now there are two ways a solo guitar player can do this.
They can use the Pat Metheny tracks, or they can make their
own.

SR: I would say that judging from the publisher Boosey and
Hawkes renting the piece out, they offer the tape, most people
say, "No, thank you very much." Because the good part of the
computer, after it destroyed the record industry, was that it made
it possible for you to make a really good recording in your living room if you wait until 2:30 and there's not too much traffic and you've got a lot of carpet and you can just overdub from
two to four in the morning, whatever. People do this, especially
when they're young.

(*laughter*)

JS: Stephen was talking before about the songs are always telling a story. Some of your works do tell a story.

SR: Yes.

JS: The piece that *Electric Counterpoint* was paired with on the Nonesuch record was *Different Trains*, which tells a very definite story. What about a piece like this? If there's not a story, this happened, then this happened, then this happened, is there at least some kind of a thread that, for you, takes you through the piece?

SR: Well, yes, the piece *Different Trains* refers first to the trains I took as a very young child between New York and Los Angeles between my divorced parents and then the trains that took Jews to concentration camps in Europe during those same years. The piece is made entirely of speech recordings of my nanny, a Black Pullman porter, and three Holocaust survivors. The melody of their speaking voices is doubled and harmonized by a string quartet. The piece is about the text. It literally gives voice to the people recorded through their speech melody and the nuance of their voices. That's my starting point, and everything comes out of that. On the other hand, *Electric Counterpoint*, or any purely musical piece, may have a melodic thread and a harmonic thread; the chords at the beginning give you a sense of "these are the harmonies we're going to use." But that's not a story. I mean, there are certain musicologists who say "da-da-da-dun" (*sings an excerpt of Beethoven's Fifth Symphony in C minor*) is fate knocking at the door. I think it's a great short motive, and it turns up in the timpani in the third movement going to the fourth movement, that's amazing! But fate knocking at the door? You think so? Fine.

(*laughter*)

That's just not my cup of tea. So, if I'm writing with a text, you bet, it's about something. It's about the text. But in a piece that doesn't have text, then the starting point is the music, is the harmony, is the notes, and it's about that. Enough said.

(*laughter*)

SS: It's about music.

JS: Some years ago, I asked John Adams, the Pulitzer Prize–winning composer of *Nixon in China*, *Death of Klinghoffer*, how affected he was as a composer by the rhythms of American, English speech. And he sputtered for a few seconds and then said, "It's so central to what I do, I can't even begin to answer that question." At the risk of getting the same reaction from you guys, I'm gonna throw the question to you. Stephen, the rhythms of American English, you know?

SS: The speech rhythm of every country, every country in the world, is what determines their music. You hear English music, you hear French music, you hear German music, sounds like the German language. That's why operas are so hard to translate, because the speech doesn't match the music. It's the music of the country, they're intertwined. It's very simple.

JS: And, Steve, both your earliest works and a lot of your most recent works have kind of existed in that gray area where speech becomes something more than speech, where those implied melodies and rhythms of speech become something really tuneful.

SR: Yes, well, there's Stephen's "And then another hundred people just got off of the train." I mean, when you say that you don't have to write much, I mean, it's finished already. If you just get the English right, hey! Okay, finished! Next case!

(*laughter*)

Yes, I completely agree. I mean, *opera*, *bel canto*, those Italian words accurately describe the music. And *rock 'n' roll* accurately describes itself, as well.

JS: And, Stephen, for you, there are moments in your songs where that boundary between speech and song, between speaking and singing, becomes a little blurry, as well. We're about to hear "Barcelona" in a couple of minutes.

SS: That's all speech.

(*laughter*)

JS: But it's also still—

SS: No, it's conversational. You're just talking about conversational songwriting, which I tend to do. I like conversational songwriting. But it's not really the same thing. One of the things I noticed when I was listening to, I guess it was *Come Out.* I noticed an interesting comparison. What you do quite often, particularly with the speech pieces, is that by looping them and working with them, sounds come out of them that aren't part of the actual language. And what happens is the listener's ear mixes the sound. That's exactly, of course, what Seurat was doing with color. He was making the eye mix the color instead of making it on the palette. I thought that's another thing you and I have in common, is you have the ear-mix and Seurat has the eye-mix.

SR: Well, I'm glad to join the club.

(*laughter*)

JS: For folks who maybe don't know *Come Out*, a quick…?

SR: *Come Out* was composed in 1966 after *It's Gonna Rain*, which is also a speech piece. And those were the first two pieces of mine that were recorded, by Columbia, and so I first became known for them. *Come Out* was premiered as part of a benefit for the retrial of the Harlem Six back in about 1967. The piece consists of the words of one of the six, a Black kid mistakenly arrested for murder. He was beaten in jail and wanted to be taken to the hospital to be cleaned up, and he explained, "I had to like open the bruise up and let some of the bruise blood come out to show them." And my ear went to "Come out to show them." The speech melody was very pronounced and in C minor. When we speak, we sometimes sing. We're not aware of it. Kids do it the most.

SS: It also happens when you're arguing with somebody.

SR: Oh, yeah.

SS: As soon as you're arguing with somebody, "Will you get out of here?!"

(*laughter*)

JS: Hellos and goodbyes, we tend to be very musical with our greetings and farewells.

SR: And "Thank you" sometimes if you want to be charming on your answering machine.

(*laughter*)

Anyway, re speech-melody; I gave a talk about *Different Trains* at Juilliard, and an elderly European gentleman in the back who I did not know asked, "Have you read the writings of Leoš

Janáček?" And I said, "No, I haven't." And he said, "Well, you should." So, I dutifully went out and bought the book, and sure enough, Janáček writes a very beautiful poetic statement, he says something like "Speech-melody is like a water lily on the surface, but the roots go down to the very bottom of the soul." And to prove his commitment, Janáček used to walk around Prague with a music notebook, writing down not what people sang but what they said. He even transcribed a railroad conductor announcing stations, first in Czech and then in German. And he'd say, "Ugh, see this German Major 7th and this beautiful triad in Czech." Because he was a Czech national.

SS: I'm not an opera fan, but one of the first operas I ever liked was Janáček, I think it was *Káťa Kabanová*, and I thought, "Jeez, I know what he's doing. He's imitating." And I can't understand the language. I knew what he was doing, he was imitating speech.

SR: But if it comes out right, it comes out right.

JS: And to go to your point, those operas are impossible to translate, which is why it took so long for them to really get traction on the opera scene, because they have to be sung in Czech. They don't work otherwise.

SS: I didn't even know he wrote about that. Incidentally, do you know Toch's "Geographical Fugue"? It's a fugue made entirely of speech.

SR: Ernst Toch? I know that name.

SS: Ernst Toch, he wrote "Geographical Fugue." Get it. It's really fun.

JS: It's all names and places.

SS: It's a fugue. It's just names but it's done as a fugue. It's really terrific.

SR: Okay, I'll do a Google later.

(*laughter*)

JS: Steve had taken this little tape of this guy being trotted out by police in front of the TV cameras and turned that into a piece which had a kind of political subtext to it. Stephen, *Company* doesn't have a political subtext to it, but it deals with the ambiguity that the characters feel.

SS: It's a social subtext.

JS: Yeah.

SS: It's the '70s.

(*laughter*)

JS: But it was the beginning of the '70s!

SS: Beginning of the '70s. The end of the "me" generation, so to speak.

JS: So, were people ready for *Company*? Were people sort of perplexed?

SS: (*sings*) They were not ready.

(*laughter*)

SS: It startled people. But it startled people mostly because it didn't have a plot. It wasn't a revue and it wasn't a plot musical, either, so that's what I think most baffled people. But it was well received.

JS: But the idea of a series of vignettes that revolved around the same people and yet not necessarily in chronological order.

SS: It's a series of sketches the way you would have in a revue, except it all revolved around one character, and that hadn't been done before. It was made from a series of very brief one-act plays by George Furth, and Hal Prince thought they might mash together and make a musical, so George and I did just that.

JS: But it really sort of changed—in the way that Steve's early pieces change what we think of music—this helped change the way we thought of the musical.

SS: Absolutely true. It opened up new avenues and led to things like *Chorus Line*, which is a series of vignettes that cohere. It freed people from a certain kind of storytelling.

JS: Right. And, Steve, as we come to the next piece of yours, called *Radio Rewrite*, we come back to the song because *Radio Rewrite* is, in fact, built on or based on two songs by the English band Radiohead. For whom, again, the song form is a very elastic thing. Tell us a little bit about the genesis of this piece and what it means for you to take [Stephen's] "Finishing the Hat" or "Everything in Its Right Place" by Radiohead and to make something of your own out of that.

SR: Well, the pieces couldn't be further apart in precisely that respect. I've commented to Stephen that the subtitle of *Finishing the Hat - 2 Pianos* is "Slavish Imitation in Changing Meters."

(laughter)

Because if he's in G-flat, I'm in G-flat. If you don't catch "Finishing the Hat" in my piece, you should see an ear doctor.

(*laughter*)

But just the contrary, for those of you who happen to know Radiohead or know "Everything in Its Right Place" or "Jigsaw Falling into Place," which are the two tunes alluded to in *Radio Rewrite*, you may not hear any of it, or you may. But the idea from the inception was this melody is interesting, this harmonic progression is interesting. What happened was, I went to Kraków for a music festival which was predominantly my own music, and one of the sort of superstar performers was Jonny Greenwood, who is the guitarist and keyboard player with Radiohead. And he is one of a number of interesting younger musicians emerging today who was trained as a violist and can read just fine. [He] is writing his own music, if you saw *There Will Be Blood*, he wrote the music. If you listen to that music, you think, the guy listened to Messiaen, which he does. And you'd never think, "Oh, this guy is a rocker." So that intrigued me before I even got there. Well, I got there, he played *Electric Counterpoint* beautifully, and he had made all the tracks himself, a completely different version. And we immediately hit it off; he's a very literate, very interesting, very open guy, and I thought to myself, "I've met this guy, I've heard of this famous band. But I haven't heard a note of their music." So, I came home, out came the computer, and I went to their site and listened to a number of songs, and two of them said, "I'm yours." (*laughs*) The first song's first word is "Everything," one-five-one, which of course is, in a sense, "everything." Whoever in the band wrote that line, I'm sure just sang it, but it really humorously encapsulates something. What could be more "everything" than the tonic and the dominant going back to the tonic? So that stuck with me. The other tune has a very attractive harmonic progression, which interested me. I didn't use it the way they did, but I certainly appropriated it. So that's really what happened, and I just let myself write my own piece, going where I felt I had to go. So if you're interested in Radiohead and you're looking to hear it, listen sharp and you might catch something.

(*laughter*)

SR: Stephen, do you still keep up with rock bands?

SS: No, I've listened to very little rock music. Probably Radiohead is one of the few bands I've ever heard that really interested me. Because it's a simple reason: as I said earlier, harmony is what music's about to me and most rock is not interested in harmony. They're interested in rhythm, they're interested in visceral reactions, they're interested in orchestration, in sonic experiments, but harmony doesn't interest them a lot. And that's what interests me. So, it's hard for me to listen to pop and rock more than once.

JS: Right, well, you know, Radiohead's Jonny Greenwood—you mentioned *There Will Be Blood*—he did the soundtrack for *The Master.*

SR: And many more.

JS: He's done quite a lot of that.

SS: The whole band, I mean, it's not just the forms but the harmonies are really fun.

JS: Steve, something you said earlier just kind of struck me. When you were talking about *Electric Counterpoint*, how all these classical guitarists were asking you to write pieces for them and you were like, "Nah. I don't think so." And it wasn't until you had the electric guitar that you could get that piece going. Look

what's happened to that piece since then. Now it's been performed by classical guitarists, percussionists, an electronic percussionist, and most improbably of all, an Italian group playing
ethnic world instruments, lutes and various. So, as composers,
you guys write the songs or the pieces, you put them out there,
and then they have a life of their own.

SR: They have a life of their own.

SS: If you're lucky.

(*laughter*)

SR: We've both been lucky. Especially with early pieces, if I
write all for guitar sounds, well then, the notes are there. So, all
you're changing is the timbre. And as long as the timbres match,
then you get this web of overlapping counterpoint. So, if you
had all harpsichords, that would probably work. Any instrument
that has a clear attack is going to achieve that. And so I welcome
that, I'm delighted to see it, and it's something I hope will happen with as many pieces as possible. And so do you.

(*laughter*)

JS: And obviously with the theater pieces, there've been very
different takes on some of your works.

SS: If a show has any strength at all, it's open to many interpre-
tations, which is what keeps theater alive. As opposed to movies.

(*laughter*)

Movies always give the same performance every time. Actor
never changes. They don't wait for the laughs. (*laughter*)

JS: It always shifts from black and white to color when she opens that door.

(*laughter*)

So *Pacific Overtures*, this is a piece that at moments is full of pentatonic scales, things we associate with, among other things, East Asian music. How much musicological research did you do?

SS: Hal Prince and I went… It was based on an idea of John Weidman and he was a sinologist, he was a lawyer but also a sinologist. But we went, Hal and I, to Japan for two weeks' research.

(*laughter*)

It meant Kabuki. And a lot of talk. But I also went and got some recordings of Japanese instruments and tried to learn something just by listening to them about the scales. It's pentatonic, but it's a minor pentatonic.

JS: It's not the blues.

SS: I made an odd association, which a number of musicians have sneered at me for, I associate it with the Spanish guitar and with de Falla's music. That was, at least for me, the way I got into it. And also, one evening I was having dinner at Leonard Bernstein's house, he had a long-distance phone call. I wandered into the living room and he had a harpsichord. And just experimentally, I put my forearms on the two manuals and very gently leant in and went (*imitates harpsichord pitches randomly*). I went home immediately and made a prepared piano à la John Cage, with thumbtacks and paper and that sort of thing. I played my next song for Hal Prince and he said, "It's so Japanese!"

(laughter)

JS: So we're going to hear two songs from *Pacific Overtures*.

SS: Right.

JS: The first is "Poems" and then, of course, "Someone in a Tree."

SS: Well, "Poems" is a song sung by the two main characters in *Pacific Overtures*. As some of you may know, it takes place in 1853 with the gunboat diplomacy, the incursion into Japan from the United States under the command of Admiral Perry. And the two main characters are Kayama, a minor samurai—these are based on real people—and a character named Manjiro, who is a Japanese who had left the island and sailed to the United States and gone to Boston and then returned to Japan. You weren't allowed to do that. He was under the threat of death, so he's put in the charge of Kayama. Kayama and Manjiro, in this song, are going back from the shogun's palace to Kayama's home and this long walking journey, and Kayama suggests that to pass the time, what the Japanese did in those days, they would exchange poems. One would make up a poem and then the other would make up a poem and then the first. And that would pass the time as they went.

JS: And to wrap things up, "Someone in a Tree."

SS: Okay, the Japanese didn't want the Americans contaminating their land, but they were forced to have a treaty meeting. And so, they built a treaty house with tatami mats that they planned to remove the minute the Americans were off the island, so the land would remain completely pristine. And so, this treaty house was built, and just to be on the safe side, they put a warrior underneath on the ground, so that if anything went wrong in the treaty house, he would spring up and slaughter all the Americans in the meeting. So many years later, we have no witnesses to what happened in the treaty house, it was never known exactly what happened. But the reciter of the evening, the narrator, encounters an old man who was there, not in the treaty house but outside the treaty house, who reminisces to the narrator about what happened. And the song is sung by the reciter and the old man, and the old man remembering what it was like when he was ten years old.

JS: "Someone in a Tree" from *Pacific Overtures*. That wraps things up for us here tonight, but let me thank all of the musicians who played for us so splendidly here on this stage.

(*applause*)

And of course, our composers: Stephen Sondheim and Steve Reich.

(*applause*)

CHAPTER 9

JONNY GREENWOOD

Steve Reich: A few years ago, I went to see *There Will Be Blood* because I heard you wrote the music and the film sounded interesting. I was watching the movie, and listening to the soundtrack, which was really cranked, the level of the music is really high in that movie and I thought, it sounds like Messiaen. I know who wrote the music, but I would never have guessed. I can't imagine anyone who watched this would say, "The musician who wrote this score is a rocker." I can't imagine that. So I guess you have at least two musical lives. How did that come to be?

Jonny Greenwood: Well, it came about just from being obsessed with music from a young age, I suppose. I remember stumbling on the octatonic scale when I was ten or eleven or something and thinking it was new. You know that thing where you find something fifty years out of date, 100 years even, and because you found it you think you have ownership. You have real pride in it. And it was only five years later I realized that was Messiaen…but I'd never heard his music. And I was the kind of kid who was excited to get a recorder and play the recorder really seriously and I just really loved music from a young age. I was obsessed with being able to make sounds and make music. And being in a rock band was just one part of that, in a way. I often think that the only reason I ended up as a guitar player is because I had to tour with Radiohead and I had to play every night, it was like practice. So, I got good at it. That's part of the reason, I think. But the other side of me was always a teenager playing in my Baroque recorder groups. The least rock 'n' roll thing you can be. But I took it really seriously. And that's what I'm secretly ashamed of, which is ridiculous. I should be ashamed... You know, it's funny, it's like you're in a band, you're meant to be ashamed of the rock 'n' roll lifestyle. But I've never had that. And instead I'm ashamed of being really into Purcell and all of this sort of Baroque music—when I should have been stealing cars and, you know, getting into fights and stuff.

SR: (*laughs*)

JG: I was in churches tooting away, so yeah.

SR: I heard you played the viola for a while?

JG: Yeah, exactly, and just didn't rehearse enough and found the guitar easier and fell into that. I'm lucky that I still play it and still use that knowledge in Radiohead stuff, so yeah.

SR: Well, if you're a string player, you've got good ears.

JG: It's true. It's really true.

SR: I remember, I was studying with Berio, I think it was, and somehow, I heard *Atmosphere* by Ligeti. And I saw the score and I thought, "Every string player in a whole orchestra has got their own part." And there's this massive, incredible sound because you've got over fifty different voices going on. Did that piece get to you, too?

JG: Yeah, it did. Especially seeing stuff like that live. Because I grew up, as everyone does, listening to recordings. And you're just led to believe that the recording is a good substitute for the real thing. But especially that really complex stuff like Penderecki and Ligeti, when you see it live, it's just so much more beautiful and colorful and softer and stranger and all of these wonderful things that the recordings never really get across. Penderecki suffers from that especially, his music is meant to be harsh. When you hear it live, it's so sort of strange and softer and more colorful than the recordings let on.

SR: I think any music... I've had people come up to me after we did *Music for 18* and say, "You know, I heard the record, but this is so much better!"

JG: So much better.

SR: But that's a general truth, no?

JG: Yeah, I think it is. I just think that complex stuff suffers even more. When there's that many voices going on, I think it just can't be recorded, you know? But having said that, and having seen *Music for 18* a few times live and it's always been a really emotional, amazing thing because, again, the difference between recording and live. I'm just thinking about what I'm about to say, which seems self-evident, which I suppose it is, but I find it really moving to see the effort being made. The fact that there's all that sinew up there, all that sweat and concentration, people moving to the next instrument. You've got all these people making an organism with all these limbs moving, and it's all this sort of collective sweat—and obviously that's not going to be on a recording. But you just come away realizing there's a real emotional impact to that kind of thing.

SR: Right.

JG: That's why live music will always have this, especially now in the age of not being able to see any or hear any.

SR: I was looking back online because I can't keep my years straight, I can't remember a lot of things in order, and I saw that we met in Kraków in 2011. You performed *Electric Counterpoint*, and you had recorded all the backing tracks before we ever got there. And I wonder, when did you decide to do that? And why? (*laughs*)

JG: (*laughs*) The Polish promoter invited me to play it. It was his idea. And I'd never read sheet music for a guitar ever, and so I spent the summer doing it, to the extent that my kids would walk around the house whistling some of the tunes, because they heard me playing it all day every day.

SR: (*laughs*)

JG: Which was great to hear, and they still know it and are still very fond of it as a result. And I just took it on. I suppose part of me was feeling that connection to being a teenager, when I did have to rehearse and read music and understand that stuff. It was a point when the two parts of what I do came together in a weird way for the first time. I've never played sheet music on a guitar. It was a moment when I thought I should really take this seriously. Not just playing *Electric Counterpoint* but what I'm lucky enough to be able to do. I'm still really grateful that I did that and got the invitation. It was amazing you were there to

CONVERSATIONS   173

see it, I was understandably nervous, but you just seemed really happy and excited to see it happen. So that was great.

SR: I was, absolutely. It was a great performance and it was the first on solid-body guitar that I heard. And again, as you say, when you see it live, you see all the effort and the nervousness and getting into it, that's what people who are listening to records miss out on, they miss out on all of that.

JG: I've got one embarrassing confession about *Electric Counterpoint*. I rehearsed it really hard, and then the more I listened to it, the more I thought this is a bit like African guitar bands, like what I used to listen to when I was a kid. It was really fashionable, this great DJ named John Peel was one of the first people in England to play African pop music. And I think when I met you, I said, "I think of this as sort of like an African thing." Thinking I'd made some sort of perceptive comment. And then I read the introduction to the score, where you say exactly that! And I'd just been too lazy to even read the first page of notes, where you'd said this is African influenced (*laughs*). I was very ashamed of that for a while.

SR: No, no, don't be. The first movement is. The others aren't. It came from a book by Simha Arom, who transcribed this unusual Central African one-note horn ensemble music. I wrote about that in the original CD notes and *Writings on Music*. I think the score note just has performance details.

JG: What I did struggle with was working out how you wanted it to be played in terms of feel. It's funny because when you record in Pro Tools, if you're ever so lazy, as I'm sure you know, you can get the computer to correct the timing of the notes by a percentage. But then you lose the feel.

SR: Absolutely—losing the feel is losing a lot. I want each musician to interpret it exactly how they hear it. Actually, it's impossible not to. You are who you are. Your recording is very different from Pat Metheny's recording, and there are others around and they all have a different feel.

JG: There's always going to be imperfections, which can make something beautiful—it reminds me [of] when I got my first commission to write for an orchestra and I'd read about Penderecki and the white noise effect. I thought, "Well, great. I can make the sound of a drum machine." And I had the bass drum with the double basses, which kind of worked. But the trouble with the high hats and the white noise thing is that they just couldn't be precise. They couldn't play it at exactly the same dynamic as each other for it to be pure white noise, because some notes would be poking out. So, that made me change my mind about the whole thing and realize that those imperfections are what's amazing, it's great when every performance and every chord has to be different because you can't contain it. You can't get that precision. So you start thinking about the individual player and what kind of day they're having and why they're playing slightly louder or whatever. I found that really kind of exciting and overwhelming, too, to start thinking like that, to start thinking: it's a room full of people with names, it's not just the violin 1, violin 2 section.

SR: Right. And that's an experience you have in Radiohead and I had in my own ensemble. I think, "Oh, that's Russ's part, that's Jim's part, that's Bob's part."

JG: That's the beautiful thing, though, isn't it, when you've got a player in mind when you're writing notes out and you kind of have their sound in your head and it changes how you work, I think.

SR: Actually, when I wrote *Electric Counterpoint*, I did have Metheny's sound in my head, and when he got it all together, it sounded just like him! And when you play it, it sounded just like you! (*laughs*) And if that's not there, there's something really wrong somewhere. That's life, that's music, that's the way it's been long before you and I were around, and I hope that's never lost to AI or whatever.

JG: It's interesting. What I came away with was thinking what a joyful piece of music it is, especially at the end. You have such a triumphant key change. It's such a sort of uplifting, positive thing. It's beautiful. And I think that's really hard to do for some reason, to have real joy in music. To write music that is joyful. It can be looked down on. And I find myself doing this. When I listened to Bach as a teenager, I would always skip past the major key movements and think, "It's a bit too *up*." I love the misery (*laughs*), I was just obsessed with that. But as I got older, I realized that joy and expressing joy is such an amazing thing to do, and people don't or people feel—not ashamed— but feel like it doesn't have the weight, I suppose. But now I've changed my mind completely and I think it completely does. It's what music has always been about: celebrating the harvest and celebrating the good points of life. That belongs in the concert hall, as well, I think.

SR: Well, it's been there whether we like it or not. (*laughs*)

JG: Well, that's true. (*laughs*)

SR: The opening of the Fifth Brandenburg (*imitates melody*), it's just great, you're there, "Hey! Wonderful! Go on!" And he does! An unbelievable harpsichord solo. You know, you don't want to be a Pollyanna, but I think that when there is joy that is obviously real, which is generated from the music itself, you get into it, you love what you're playing or hearing, and it has to do with the joy that comes from those notes and those rhythms and that particular piece of music.

JG: Yeah.

SR: What drew you to my piece *Pulse*?

JG: Well, again, it was such an intense period of obsession, listening and learning that. I think about it today and the fact that you managed to incorporate the bass guitar in such a way that solved a problem that I'm always finding in acoustic groups. Whenever you use acoustic bass in a small group, there's just no attack. There's never enough rhythm from it. It's always such a soft, warm sound. And having an electric bass pinning that all together, it was such a satisfying collection of colors. It felt like a real classic lineup for writing music, you know?

SR: I love the electric bass because it's so clear. In *Electric Counterpoint*, you can even have two of them interlocking. If you had two acoustic basses, you'd have mud. But you hadn't played much bass, that wasn't your instrument at all.

JG: No, which is why I really had to play it a bit like a guitar. But again, it felt like a lot of my frustration of wanting to be in a reggae band came out in that piece, actually. There are moments when you're climbing up and down and it's like good Jamaican reggae. And again, it was a question of feel. I remember we talked about it, and it's about the performance and the room. All the players loved it. We talked about *Pulse* the whole time when we were rehearsing it and getting into it. And I was excited, as well, for selfish reasons, that it's a brand-new piece of music. I've always been thrilled at the idea that something was only put on paper in the previous year or two years and suddenly it's in a room and people are hearing it. And that's exciting.

SR: It's a miracle (*laughs*). Happens a lot but it's still a miracle every time it happens.

JG: Well, I still find it weird that stuff is on paper. The idea that you can put a musical idea on paper and post it in an envelope. To me, that's still bizarre. I'm just used to other forms of spreading music.

We had a recording session yesterday with twelve string players all in masks and separated, and that was all horrible. But it was about hearing live music again for the first time this year. Is it happening out there? Are there any concerts going on?

SR: Well, what I've heard are all virtual—some people have been doing *Clapping Music*, others are doing the *Counterpoint* pieces, because you can do them by yourself in a room, which is nice on the one hand but kind of sad on the other.

JG: What are you writing now at the moment?

SR: I just finished a piece called *Traveler's Prayer*, which uses the text—not of the actual prayer you'd say when you get on an airplane that you'd find in a Hebrew prayer book—but some of the other verses that are connected with it that I've been drawn to over the years. There's no articulated beat. It's mostly in 2/4 but it doesn't get you to tap your foot.

JG: That's properly exciting to me because it's my opportunity to tell you how much I love *Tehillim*. It's just such a beautiful piece of music. I listen to that all the time.

SR: Well, your wife can understand the Hebrew!

JG: She can! She really can.

SR: Ask her if it's well set or not. She'll know better than we do. (*laughs*)

JG: It's funny, I can speak lots of Hebrew, but it's mostly from hearing her tell the kids off. So, I'm really good at sort of saying "Sit up straight!" and "Do your homework!" and that kind of thing. I can tell you off in perfect Hebrew.

It's funny. The only other thing I was going to tell you was that when we're working with Radiohead, it's still amazing to me how often when we're doing computer processing of sound, and it suddenly sounds like *Music for 18*.

SR: I remember people listening to *Music for 18* on a record, and they asked me, "What synth patch did you use for that frog-growling sound?" I said, "No, that's a bass clarinet." (*laughs*)

JG: Yeah, that's the lesson. There are so many colors and sounds, it still floors me how one player, let alone more than one instrument, can change their color and make so many sounds with it. It's great.

And in *Tehillim* the same—it sounds like it's been treated. It sounds like a lot of electronics are involved.

SR: Actually, the only electronics are microphones.

CHAPTER 10

DAVID HARRINGTON

David Harrington: You know, Steve, I've been thinking about this a lot and how to explain to people just how we began working together. You were in San Francisco, I can't remember which year it was, it might have been '82, '83, something like that. You and I had a cup of coffee downtown and later you sent me *Vermont Counterpoint* for Kronos to arrange. Do you remember that?

Steve Reich: Not really, but I'm finding this very interesting.

DH: Because at that point you were like, "Oh, it's string quartet, I don't write string quartets."

SR: Right.

DH: I don't think I've ever told you this, but I'm gonna tell it to you right now. You sent me *Vermont Counterpoint*, which I already knew. But what you didn't know was that the flute is my least favorite instrument in the universe.

SR: (*laughs*) I got a bull's-eye.

DH: It has to do with a high school girlfriend and the whole thing went completely nuts. She was a flute player, okay.

SR: Okay, got it.

DH: So, then I was thinking, "We've got to figure out a way." And so, then it was 1984, and as a matter of fact, we played the world premiere of Viktor Ullmann's Third String Quartet. That was written in Theresienstadt. It's the only string quartet that I know of, written in one of the camps, that survived. And Kronos, Joan, because she had the best penmanship, she copied the score from the manuscript at the Schoenberg Institute. I dug out the program recently, and on that program, we also played Shostakovich's Eighth Quartet, and we played your *Clapping Music*.

SR: (*laughs*) Well, that was definitely a contrast.

DH: It was a crazy program. We opened with the Shostakovich, then we did *Clapping*. No, no, no. We opened with *Clapping Music*. And I remember I wrote to you after that and I said, "Steve, we just premiered your first string quartet."

SR: And I almost ruined your hands for the Shostakovich. (*laughs*)

DH: And trying to play Shostakovich, my hand was all puffy! (*laughs*)

SR: First I hit you with the flute, then I hit you on the hand!

DH: And so, that began a conversation, right? And I don't know how many letters went back and forth or calls or whatever, but eventually Betty Freeman heard about it.

SR: Yes, yeah.

DH: Remember?

SR: Yes. Betty wrote to me and said, "You should write something for Kronos." And you were clearly becoming a very important ensemble in the world. And, you know, Betty's enthusiasm was very persuasive, and so I said, "Sure." And then I thought, "What am I going to do?" (*laughs*)

DH: And I remember there being, this could be totally wrong, you know how memory works. It transposes sometimes. But I remember there being some kind of a get-together in someone's home, after a concert or something. And you and Beryl were there. I talked to Beryl about Etty Hillesum's book *An Interrupted Life*.

SR: Right. Yeah.

DH: Now, what I don't know is, was that before *Different Trains* or after? That's what I can't remember.

SR: I don't remember, either, but now you've got my memory going. Go ahead.

DH: Well, there was this kind of conversation, and I think Beryl got the book and she made a painting.

SR: Yeah. *Etty's Rosetta*.

DH: Yes. But what I don't remember is whether that was before or after, but I do remember another thing that happened at Betty's house, and it might have been when she and I began our talk about working with you. Hoping to work with you. We played Morton Feldman's Piano and String Quartet piece.

SR: That's one of the most beautiful pieces Morty wrote that I'm aware of.

DH: We played it in her home.

SR: Aki Takahashi played piano.

DH: Yes, and then I'm pretty sure after that Betty and I just started talking and I think that's when we started talking about you. And all I remember is after you started *Different Trains* is that you sent me cassette tapes.

SR: Such things existed. (*laughs*)

DH: I know, I know. And I've got them still somewhere, I do have them. As a matter of fact, I'm trying to go through some of these things.

SR: Archive them.

DH: Yeah, but it wasn't the whole piece. It was part of one of the movements, but slowly over the composition time, you sent me the whole piece.

SR: Right. Now I remember after Betty approached me, the other thing that was in my head was the sampling keyboard. I'd just discovered that it existed. And I thought, "That's for me." I don't do "electronic" music, but speech—or any analog sound, but particularly speech—is something I've always loved to work with. And so, it became clear to me pretty fast that it would be Kronos and speech samples. But what was missing was "Who's speaking and what are they speaking about?" And I remember, I had candidates. The first one was, the voice of Béla Bartók.

DH: I remember that. Did I ever tell you that when I was growing up in Seattle, where the recording was made, I believe, was at the University of Washington.

SR: You mean the recording of Bartók?

DH: Yeah, he gave a talk at the University of Washington in 1944 or '45. And that was recorded, and I grew up listening to that as a teenager in the music library. So, I knew his voice.

SR: Well, I listened to the recording he made in '44 or '45 at WNYC in New York. Then I began to think, "Wait a minute. I'm going to write a string quartet—do I want Béla Bartók sitting on my shoulder? That just might be a bit inhibiting. Okay, I'll find the voice of Ludwig Wittgenstein," because I had studied Wittgenstein's philosophy at Cornell. And then I started to make inquiries. Wittgenstein was a recluse. The last thing in the world he would have been involved in would be a tape-recorded interview, and there were no tapes.

DH: Oh, right.

SR: So then, and who knows how these things work, those trips I took as a child between my divorced parents, my singer/lyricist mother in LA and my lawyer father in New York, popped into my head. Maybe because I was going out to Queens to see Virginia, my nanny, who was still alive and who I visited regularly. She was with me on all those trips. Suddenly the bell rang in my head, and maybe initially it was just about her and our trips together. But then at some point, I began thinking, "What was going on in the world when I was making those trips? I was

born in '36, so there was 1937, '38, '39, '40, '41—well, clearly
we know what was going on in the world in those days. Hitler
was trying to take over the world and sending Jews and Jewish
children to camps and then up the chimney."

I began thinking, what if I had been in Berlin? What if I was
in Paris? I might have been on very different trains. And then
it all clicked. I got to work pretty quick making the recordings
with Virginia and Mr. Davis down in Washington, DC. He had
been a Pullman porter most of his life riding those same trans-
continental trains. Then up to Yale to their archive of recordings of Holocaust survivors.

DH: I remember there being a call when you and I talked, and
I think maybe it was right after you had that idea. And I think
it's not like you were asking my permission or anything like
that, it wasn't that, it was just that you wanted to know, "Well,
what do you think?"

SR: I probably did.

DH: And I remember saying, and I say this to everybody, "It's
always the best thing to do something that's really personal. Always the best."

SR: A big virtual hug, David. (*laughs*)

DH: Well, if you look at the history of the string quartet, that
is its power, you know? From Haydn, Mozart, Beethoven,
Schubert, the founding four. Some of their music is the most
personal music and then you also carry that inside you. You
mentioned Bartók, we were talking about Feldman. That is
the history of this art form, I think. So, when you mentioned

that to me, and maybe this was before "Europe" and "After the War" became part of it. Maybe it was the early first movement.

SR: I think it was. I would have probably contacted you as soon as the light bulb began to clarify in my head and your enthusiasm was invaluable. If I'm writing for some particular group, if I don't feel that there's some energy there, it's doomed.

DH: Right, right, right.

SR: It's a doomed endeavor. So, your enthusiasm was just... "Go, go!" And that attitude that you have is not only nice, it's true, it's accurate. If you do something you're not really engaged in, the prospects are dim.

DH: For me, there are so many things that can be done in music, but the ones that I have to do are the ones that magnetize me.

SR: Right, perfect word. It's a magnetic attraction.

DH: And I'm always looking for composers who want to do the same thing, you know? They want to write their best piece. Just imagine, I remember growing up and reading about Beethoven after he wrote the cavatina, tears streaming down his face. Totally deaf and he's hearing this music and he's realizing that he did something amazing. Totally amazing. I wish for every composer in the world, that they find a personal sound, something that defines them. I don't know if I've told you this before, *Different Trains* totally changed Kronos. Maybe we've talked about this, but there's before *Different Trains* and there's after *Different Trains*. It not only has to do with the fact that we had to become an amplified ensemble in order to play *Different Trains*, but we ended up having to have our own sound engineer travel with us. So essentially, we became a quintet. And what happened is when we put *Different Trains* in a concert, this allowed other composers to begin thinking in new ways. So, it's like, there's what you accomplished artistically in *Different Trains* in your own life and your own work. To me, it's so definitive as a piece. Every time we start that opening, it's so American, it's so cool (*laughs*). I just love it. I just love it.

SR: Paradiddle and crossing bells, what more do you want? (*laughs*)

DH: But also, the voices, you know?

SR: "From Chicago."

DH: Yeah, yeah. And I'm not so young that I didn't hear a Pullman porter when I was a kid. I used to take the train from Seattle to Portland to visit my grandparents, and I remember hearing that texture of voice.

SR: Mr. Davis had a beautiful voice.

DH: Did I ever tell you that two of the survivors from *Different Trains* came to our concerts at different points?

SR: One in Miami, right?

DH: I think that's right, and there was one...

SR: And one was the West Coast, that was Rachella from Holland. "On my birthday the Germans walked into Holland."

DH: "On my birthday." Yes.

SR: I heard from her and I think I heard from you that you had seen her or met her. I talked with her; I never had a chance to actually see her. In Miami, apparently you spoke to the son or daughter of Rachel, who said, "No more school."

DH: "No more school."

SR: "You must go away." And her son or daughter came up and said, I think to you, that they were so glad they had come and that their mother would have loved it but she had just passed away.

DH: Yes, yes, now I'm remembering. Yeah. I don't think I ever told you this, but somebody wanted us to play *Different Trains* and film it in Auschwitz. But I had been there. I went there about two years after my son Adam died. And there was no way I could play music there. I couldn't do it. I had to tell them, I can't, there's simply no music in me there. I can't do it.

SR: We went there in I think it was 2011. There was the big chamber where the gas was turned on. And I just felt like there was a force field repelling me from even going in there.

DH: Yeah. Did you happen to see the film that they showed at the information center before leaving? It's like an eight-, nine-minute film about one boy.

SR: A film that they showed at Auschwitz?

DH: Yes, there's like a little center that you can go to, and when I was there, it was very cold, it was November. And I had tennis shoes on. And my feet got really cold, really cold. And then we went to this little room and they showed a film and it was about one person, this is after you see the thousands of eyeglasses, and the hair, and the suitcases. The film then focuses on one person. Over the span of those eight, nine minutes, my feet began to warm up, and you know what happens? You start to tingle?

SR: Right, life returns.

DH: Yeah, I will never, ever, ever forget that. It was so powerful. And having *Different Trains* as part of my life allowed me to—I've never tried to express this before—but it allowed me to go there somehow. I really, really appreciate that because it was an impossible thing to do. Even in safety, it was impossible to be there. But experiencing that sense of one young little boy who tried to help other people by sharing a piece of bread. And the Nazis made him stand out in the cold, barefoot, for a whole day. It's just...

SR: Right.

Well, going over to a musical thing, I remember we spent about four days at Russian Hill Studio just preparing the prerecorded tape. And then when we got to the actual recording, it seemed to me that the most important problem was for Hank [Dutt] and Joan [Jeanrenaud], who had to double the voices. Their question was, "Do we play the notation or do we play the voices?" And the fast answer is "Play the voices." But the notation will help, it won't hurt. And then there was a lot of discussion about bowing. I don't know if you got involved in that, but there was a lot of it.

DH: Oh, yeah.

SR: And they would try this and that, and we went back and forth. But it all paid off.

DH: And that's been true of *Triple Quartet* and *WTC 9/11*, too. It's true of any music we play, the bowings are so important. It's very idiosyncratic for each person, too. Somebody else could do an entirely different bowing maybe and make it sound great. But with me, for example, the way I play, I need to feel a certain connection with the bowing itself. It's like breathing, enunciating words with the bow.

SR: Working with Hank and Joan was like a dream. This is the way it's supposed to be. They ask questions and together we go on to work out the best bowing.

DH: Well, I think one thing we've always tried to do is ask, what are we really using as the score? In the case of *Different Trains*, there are the printed pitches, but then as you're saying, a good part of the score is actually what you're hearing the voices say and how they say it.

SR: Right.

DH: And that's the same with *WTC 9/11*. You have let the voice lead, and this is where the bow comes in, you know what I mean? The lilt of the bow, what it can offer us for diction, things like that.

SR: Exactly, exactly. Diction and punctuation are all done with the bow. Precisely.

Well, now, *Triple Quartet* is a whole different cup of tea. I remember, I guess it was in '98 and the first thought in my mind was "I'm gonna go back to the Bartók Fourth, the last movement." Hammer and tongs. I want to get that kind of energy. And I started the piece and I was in the first movement, moving along, and Betty Freeman sent me a copy of your recording of Schnittke's quartets. And I thought, "There is some kind of message here, I better check it out." I only knew a little about

Schnittke, I knew he played on Pärt's recording of *Tabula Rasa*, but I hadn't heard his own music. So, I put it on, and I thought, "Wow, this is pretty abrasive stuff." This is more abrasive than Bartók by a long shot. But then I got to the Third Quartet and there he's got [Orlandus] Lassus. A very calm and meditative sixteenth-century world, but then he goes on to his take on Beethoven, and then to Shostakovich.

And I just went back to working on what I was doing, but every once in a while, I would hear what I imagined to be Schnittke's voice saying to me something like *"Wo ist die schmutz?"* (*laughs*), Where is the dirt? And I thought, "Okay, you've got a point." And I consciously introduced dissonances at points in the score where I felt, "Yeah, you're right." It's a little too easy going here. It was strange. I wrote the piece in 1998, the year Schnittke died. In any event, between Bartók on the one side and Schnittke on the other and you and Betty Freeman, that was kind of the engine that was getting me going.

DH: You know, it's interesting. There are two composers that I have encountered. I can't say that I met Stravinsky, but I walked by him once when I was sixteen years old in Seattle. And then there was Alfred Schnittke in a hotel dining room in Warsaw, Poland. Those two composers actually had auras, in my opinion. I mean, that's all I can tell you. It's like, do I believe in this stuff? I don't know, but Schnittke had an aura. I had breakfast with Alfred and the wonderful pianist, his wife Irina. And then I started corresponding with him a little bit. Actually, he was going to write a quartet for us and then he died, but for our *Early Music* album, where we recorded Pérotin, I think I told you once that I heard about Pérotin from an interview that I read of yours.

SR: I spread the good word.

DH: You were talking about, I think it was Miles Davis and Coltrane and Pérotin.

SR: Right, what's he doing there?

DH: And I knew Miles Davis's music and Coltrane, but Pérotin, who's this? So, I went and got some recordings and it blew me away. Absolutely blew me away.

SR: Glad to hear it.

DH: And do you remember when Notre Dame burned?

SR: Yes. Very weird, very weird.

DH: That's where Pérotin was the music director.

SR: Back in the twelfth century.

DH: The fire seemed impossible.

SR: Right, imagine that.

DH: And so, the second movement of *Triple Quartet*—there is this Notre Dame–like sense of space as in Pérotin. Getting back to the first movement, I actually asked you one time, I don't know if you remember this, but I said, "Steve, is there any Klezmer influence in the first movement of *Triple Quartet*?" Do you remember me asking you that?

SR: Vaguely. What did I say? No?

DH: No, you didn't say no. You said, "I'm not sure, there might be. I don't know." (*laughs*) If you check the first violin part, there's this one really high part, and every time we play it, I think, "Steve is channeling Klezmer music here."

SR: If I'm channeling it, I'm just the channel, I just work here! (*laughs*) Well, actually, I do remember something else, were we at Skywalker [Sound] for *Triple Quartet*?

DH: Yes. We were.

SR: I remember, but I think it was in rehearsals. We had some rehearsals in town before we went up there?

DH: Yeah, that's right.

SR: And I remember hearing you guys, and particularly you, playing something with the typical Harrington-like "Take that!" down bow (*laughs*). And I thought, "That's exactly what I heard in my head! He just did exactly what I heard in my head!"

DH: Oh, wow!

SR: So that was another thing.

DH: I just want to say that the last movement of *Triple Quartet* is so much fun to play.

SR: Oh, that's important!

DH: It really is fun. I remember telling some audiences… Bryce Dessner wrote a piece that has a…

SR: *Aheym*. I love that piece and you guys play it to a turn!

DH: *Aheym*. I remember saying to the audience one time after *Aheym*, "You know, I like quartet music that makes you out of

TOP: *Pendulum Music* at the Whitney, 1969.
Left to right: Richard Serra, James Tenney, Steve Reich, Bruce Nauman, Michael Snow.
Photo: Richard Landry

BOTTOM: Steve Reich in the studio, 1971.
Photo: Richard Landry

Clapping Music,
1972.

Left to right:
Russell
Hartenberger,
Steve Reich.

Photo: Steve Reich

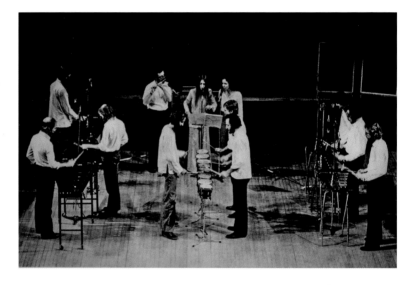

Drumming,
performed at
Loeb Center
NYU, 1973.

Steve Reich
and musicians.

Photo:
Gianfranco Gorgoni.
© Maya Gorgoni

Pieces of Wood,
performed
in 1975.

Left to right:
Bob Becker,
Russell
Hartenberger,
Glen Velez,
Steve Reich, and
James Preiss.

Photo:
Mary Lucier

Steve Reich at
Music for 18 Musicians
rehearsal, 1976.

Photo: Betty Freeman

After completion of *The Desert Music* recording, 1984.
Left to right: Steve Reich, Michael Tilson Thomas, Robert Hurwitz.

Photo: Deborah Feingold

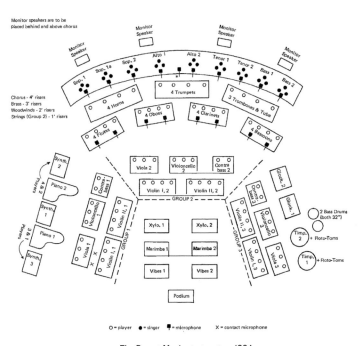

Monitor speakers are to be
placed behind and above chorus

Chorus - 4' risers
Brass - 3' risers
Woodwinds - 2' risers
Strings (Group 2) - 1' risers

O = player   ● = singer   ▼ = microphone   X = contact microphone

The Desert Music stage setup, 1984.

...eich and Beryl Korot (left to right) setting up for
...w in Hebron in 1990 or 1991.

...Trilling

Music for 18 Musicians performed at
Saitama Arts Theater near Tokyo, 1996.

Steve Reich and musicians.

Photo: Keizo Maeda

1. *The Cave* Act III, at London's South Bank Centre, around 1993

Photo: Andrew Pothecary

2. *Three Tales*, act 2, Bikini, Vienna, May 12, 2002.

Photo: Wonge Bergmann

3. *Daniel Variations* rehearsal by Los Angeles Master Chorale, 2006.

Left to right: Grant Gershon, Gloria Cheng, Steve Reich.

Photo: Courtesy of Los Angeles Master Chorale

4. *Four Organs* at Brooklyn Academy of Music, 2014.

Left to right: Philip Glass, Nico Muhly, David Cossin, Timo Andres, Steve Reich.

Photo: © Stephanie Berger. Courtesy BAM Hamm Archives

TOP: Left to right: Steve Reich, Justin Peck, and dancers after performance of "New Blood," choreographed by Peck to Reich's *Variations for Vibes, Pianos and Strings* at New York City Ballet, Lincoln Center, 2015.
Photo: Paul Kolnik. Courtesy of New York City Ballet

BOTTOM: Reich / Richter at The Shed, 2019. Performed by Ensemble Signal and conducted by Brad Lubman.
Photo: Courtesy of The Shed

breath." (*laughs*) I'm panting! I just want to tell you that it has a similar quality to the final movement of *Triple Quartet*. The physicality of that is so great and you really feel like you're just giving it, you have to give it everything you've got, you know?

SR: So here we are going into *WTC 9/11*, which was, in a sense, something old, and something definitely new. I think we recorded that in downtown San Francisco after recording studios had been collapsing all over the place.

DH: Yeah, that's right, it was downtown San Francisco.

SR: I remember the premiere performance; I remember we were at Duke. And there was this Japanese film crew.

DH: Film crew, right.

SR: And they came over once and then they came back, I think the day of the concert, after they had had that huge tsunami off the coast of Japan. And I remember going up to one of the crew and I said, "I want to thank you. It's really extraordinary that you're able to be here." And he looked me right in the eye and he said, "9-11 changed the world," and he went back in to plugging in his stuff.

DH: Wow.

SR: And I thought, "Well, that's interesting because these people have had some pretty heavy historical things happen." I thought it was very moving that they took it that seriously.

DH: That was after Fukushima, wasn't it?

SR: Yeah, it was the one that had the radioactive flood. It was affecting Tokyo, too, it wasn't just on the coast.

DH: Right, yeah.

SR: I don't remember if it was in *WTC 9/11* or *Triple Quartet*, I think it was in *WTC* where the cello is Jeffrey Zeigler?

DH: Yeah.

SR: I saw something where I thought, "Oh, I goofed!" There's something in the viola that should be in the cello and something in the cello that ought to be in the viola. And you were all inside, I was in the control room, and I said, "Excuse me." And I walked in. I said, "I feel terrible." I went over to Hank and to Jeffrey and I said, "Look, you should change parts here, I should have done this, and I feel like an idiot." And everybody just did it, you know? Like, okay. "You got a pencil?" Yeah, sure, yeah (*laughs*). And I thought, "Wow, you don't have to hide anything. You can just be a human being who makes errors, too." And then it went on and was a really amazing recording. I don't remember anyone having the lengthy discussions about doubling the voices as we had in *Different Trains*. It was kind of like, "We've seen this before." But when you got to the last movement and Maya Beiser was singing in Hebrew the ending of the 121st psalm.

DH: I forgot it was Maya who sang that!

SR: It was Maya. She's got a good voice. Then this cantor in New York, who is no longer with us, chanting what it is appropriate to chant over a body. And neither one of them is singing in a really fixed rhythm. And it's a canon, I think it's a three-voice canon for Maya and two-voice canon for the cantor. And there were a lot of takes. And then it was like, "Well, we've got the notation, but would you turn up the voices?" (*laughs*) And after a while, there it was. Again, it was that tension between, "There is notation, it'll sort of get the job done." But we don't want to just sort of get the job done, we want to really get inside of it. And you took the time and you did.

DH: You know, one thing we've learned from our work with many, many different composers is every person who writes notation has a different idea of what notation represents. You could write a half-note D natural, and your idea of it and XYZ's ideas of it will be different. There's just no question about it, you know? And one thing we like to do is we like to get composers to sing.

SR: Oh, absolutely. Singing the parts is essential. If you can't do that, then whose piece is it?

DH: But from our standpoint, hearing the composer do that is like it kind of reveals the story behind the ink.

SR: Right. Beautifully put.

DH: And each person who writes a piece of music is the very first person to have had that musical experience, a personal inner musical experience. And we're always hoping it's the most unbelievable experience humanity has ever discovered and then eventually it gets delivered to us. Okay, now what do we do with it? Well, we need to get as much information as we can. And the first person to talk to is the composer, you know? What can he or she give us in terms of knowledge, in terms of ideas? I just did a talk for composers in Tehran. It was really cool. And one of the things—you might not like me for this but I'm going to say it anyway—one of the things that I said to these young composers, I said, "It's important for a composer to allow the performer to take the music away from you, the composer."

SR: Absolutely. I've talked about that a lot with musicians and conductors.

DH: We need to take the piece out there for the audience. There is this fine line of respect and tradition and knowledge. I think all of us that are involved in creating musical work have to find the balance that will allow us the broadest range of possibilities to focus on whatever music it is we're playing.

SR: The older I get, the more I think—the pieces are out there in the world. I made them at one point but now they're literally in someone else's hands. Thinking back, let's say to the 1970s and early '80s, it was impossible for me to get a performance in Europe that didn't sound stiff and staccato. Now there are really idiomatic performances of all sorts all over the world. Why? Because time has passed, records were made, other people performed it, their teacher showed them something. If the music is not amenable to that, there's something deeply wrong with the music. It's some kind of frozen gimmick. That's why, very early on, in 1967, I had to stop making tape pieces. In that sense, one of the most important pieces I ever did in my life was *Piano Phase*. Look, ma, no tape!

That was back in '67 and here we are now.

DH: So tell me, what are you working on right now?

SR: I recently finished a piece called *Traveler's Prayer*. It's scored for two tenors, two sopranos, two string quartets or string orchestra, two vibes, and one piano, which comes in every so often as a very low, deep tolling bell. It uses three texts, two of which you know from the last movement of *WTC 9/11*. It's mostly in 2/4 but there's no noticeable pulse. Also, though I've known about retrogrades and inversions most of my life, I've never actually used them. This time I did.

The idea probably came from reading Stravinsky's *Conversation* books, which also suggested the format for this book. Stravinsky sometimes used a series of less than twelve tones, like in the Cantata and Septet, and created a tonal serial technique. In *Traveler's Prayer*, I'm taking diatonic or modal melodies and applying retrogrades and so on as composers have done since the thirteenth century.

Back in 1955 my mother arranged for me to take a trip to Europe and it was the summer that Stravinsky premiered his *Canticum Sacrum* inside Saint Mark's Cathedral in Venice. I made it a point to be there. Before the premiere Robert Craft conducted antiphonal brass choir music by Gabrieli and Schütz right in their original setting.

DH: Oh, wow, I love that music.

SR: Then Stravinsky conducted the premiere of *Canticum Sacrum* and I just stood up for the whole thing. After intermission, *Canticum Sacrum* was repeated. They did important premieres that way back then. For me, *Canticum Sacrum* and *Agon* are the high points of his late period. He miraculously combines serial technique and still maintains some continuity with his characteristic harmonic language, albeit more complex.

DH: I didn't get to tell you my Stravinsky story. Here I am sixteen years old and Stravinsky had just conducted *The Soldier's Tale*.

SR: Oh, wow! (*imitates the opening*)

DH: I felt, I gotta meet this guy. So I go backstage in the Seattle Opera House. It's all dark, and there's this light in the corner and a figure seated in a wheelchair I can just see out of the corner of my eye. I'm walking along and I literally was pushed out of the way by the force field of his powerful personality. So I just moved out of the way.

CHAPTER II

ELIZABETH LIM-DUTTON

Steve Reich: So, Liz, you were at Juilliard—and you studied with Dorothy DeLay?

Elizabeth Lim-Dutton: Yes.

SR: She was almost mythic.

EL: Without question, she was one of the most important and influential violin pedagogues of the twentieth century.

SR: Well, after that you were a freelancer in New York City. You'd come out of Juilliard and you had a lot of different experiences as a performer. When you got into our ensemble, how did that strike you in terms of "I'm performing now in this new ensemble, what's that ensemble like?"

EL: Well, let's start with my first piece, *Different Trains*. That was the first piece of chamber music I had ever learned where I had to play with musicians on prerecorded tracks. It was a totally different kind of learning curve for me because of time and rhythm. I thought I had a decent sense of time, but starting with *DT*, I realized I actually had very little understanding of the space between beats. After playing with your group for so many years, and thanks to Russ [Hartenberger] and Bob [Becker], my rhythm was always better after coming back from a tour. Larry [Dutton] used to notice and say, "Wow, your rhythm is even better."

Larry watched me learning *Different Trains*, and he would tease me and say, "You're practicing that more than the Sibelius Violin Concerto." And seriously, before the first time I played *DT* for you in the concert that was my "audition," I did work harder on that piece than probably any other piece. I had to learn how to adjust to playing with a tape, pitch-wise and how I feel time. If you base it on the metronome, you're way off. You have to feel the time. Learning *Different Trains* really stretched the boundaries for me in terms of getting me out of my comfort zone in a good way.

SR: In *Different Trains*, the viola and cello were doubling the pre-recorded voices while the violins were sometimes doubling the train whistles. In all cases you had to make subtle adjustments between following the notation versus following the speech or sound fragments. How did you work that out yourself and how did you notice that being done in the lower strings?

EL: A lot of the integration of seeing what was written on the page and hearing what was on the tape was done by paying attention to every detail. I loved the challenge of trying to capture the inflection of a word, and imitate it. In *Different Trains*, sometimes you first hear the viola, then you hear the woman's voice. It's like "Who's speaking?" The person or the instrument? We wanted to be synonymous with that voice because the recorded voice imparts who that person is. So, we're not just playing notes now, we're playing *who* the person is. For example, one of the resonant moments for me in *Trains* is "Are you sure?" because you're not only trying to play the notes, you're trying to play the hope *and* fear that's in that voice, "Are you sure?" The person speaking is not sure if the war is over. Matching spoken words, literally and figuratively was something I had never been taught in Ms. DeLay's studio. It was a new musical language to learn. You follow the notation, but then you try to go to that other level of sensing the timing, even of a breath before the person starts a word, so that you're breathing in with the start of the word. When Mr. Davis says the sentence "But today they're all gone," you wrote an A-flat augmented chord, the harmony you used in that section informed me about how I wanted to play it. Your use of the minor seconds, down a half step, up a half step for the first violin when one hears Rachella say a fragment of her sentence, "And they loved to listen to the singing, the Germans," guided me about what kind of a sharper-edged articulation that I wanted to use for that phrase. One of the most resonant emotional moments in *Trains* is always at the very end where it's Rachella who says, "There was one girl, who had a beautiful voice, and they loved to listen to the singing, the Germans, and when she stopped singing they said 'More, more!' and they applauded." For me, always, in that section communicating what is positive, even in the midst of the negative. We could talk about that aspect, as well, in *The Cave*, because that infuses the music there, as well.

SR: Do you want to talk about *The Cave* since both pieces use prerecorded voices?

EL: Yes. But may I inject a bit of personal prehistory to illustrate what a family affair it was? I had the audition concert for you in New York and then here we are going to Vienna for three weeks and after that to Berlin and Amsterdam. This was just the first five weeks with *The Cave*. Larry and I knew we were going to try to plan a family. We were not sure if we would be blessed or not. So, I mentioned to you, "You know, I might be coming with a baby and my mom." And you were fine with me doing that. Memorably, the Vienna run of *The Cave* did turn out to be a big family affair. I came with my mom and my five-month-old baby, Luke, as did a lot of others with their families.

In *The Cave*, you and Beryl go into the world of opera in a way that nobody has ever envisioned it before, bringing it into this century, the blending of both the notated singing of the voices onstage and the recorded voices that imparted each speaker's personality. For me, *The Cave* is a musical note-in-a-bottle for future generations. When we were in Vienna for those weeks of rehearsals, many times, we were sitting there so that the lighting, staging, etc., could be tweaked, we were hearing and absorbing the text many, many, many times over. I remember I was really taken with the very first person, Ephraim Isaac, when he would say, "Abraham, for me, is my ancestor, my very own personal ancestor." And then he lists eighteen generations from Abraham, and then lists twenty more to himself, *all by memory.* Then Itaf Ziad, in the second act, says, "I mention his name, (Ibrahim), sixteen times a day when I pray." And I was thinking, "Do I even pray once a day?" And then you go to act 3, where Abraham is asked to sacrifice Isaac, and I think it's Valerie Steele who says, "Very difficult for modern people to conceive of," and then she goes on, speaking about Isaac, saying, "I wonder why he wouldn't fight his father?" How far removed do I feel as a Westerner from that, both culturally and in terms of faith? It was really astonishing to me. And yet another powerful moment playing *The Cave* was at the very end when Daniel Berrigan says, "Entertaining angels unawares" and Francis Peters says, "Three strangers come and Abraham, without asking questions, offers them hospitality," and you write this beautiful melody for us to play, this beautiful music, and I feel like, here he is, Abraham, the father of Jews and Muslims, and he is simply showing kindness and hospitality. I just loved the piece and playing it.

SR: Any thoughts about *Daniel Variations*? I think you know Daniel Pearl was a fiddle player, and particularly in the second movement of the piece, for me personally, that is maybe the best string writing I've ever done. Your quartet playing was so great that when we got to record the piece out in LA with the ensemble out there, we thought, "No, let's bring in the New York quartet, they really know what's going on." And somehow for me, that string playing feels like "Daniel, this is for you." How did that strike you?

EL: Well, you know, in the first movement you took the text from the book of Daniel, and Daniel is interpreting Nebuchadnezzar's dreams, right?

SR: Right.

EL: And here you're writing E minor, G minor, B-flat minor, C-sharp minor. Like you do in *Triple Quartet*, right? But then we go in movement two to G major. And here Daniel Pearl is saying the words that were on the tape from when he was kidnapped by Islamic fundamentalists in Pakistan. Here he is, and you lay the groundwork with movement one, harmonically. You lay this intense harmonic landscape. But then Daniel Pearl emerges in movement two in G major, vibrant and hopeful, it's not negative. I don't know if this is how you're thinking while you're composing it, but that's how I felt it while playing the music. Despite knowing where his words are coming from, what you write for the violin, the key you utilize, the musical topography you create is not one of despair. It's one of hope. You reflected Daniel Pearl's vibrancy and life. Additionally, I love in the last movement that you quote the tune title, "I hope Gabriel likes my music." And I always wondered...didn't you add the line at the end "when the day is done"?

SR: I did, yeah. The original line, "I hope Gabriel likes my music," is the name of a tune that was played in the '30s by Stuff

Smith, the jazz violinist who was someone that Daniel Pearl really admired. After he was murdered, a friend of his was asked by Daniel Pearl's parents, "Please go over to Danny's place, and clean it up." And he started going through the record collection that Daniel had, and he finds this Stuff Smith record and he sees the first tune is "I Hope Gabriel Likes My Music," but the fact of the matter is that he discovered that after Daniel Pearl was gone. So, I added "when the day is done," maybe as some kind of personal farewell or remembrance.

EL: Well, when I was playing it, I took it that that's *your* question that you're asking? "I sure hope Gabriel likes my music when the day is done."

SR: You're right, yes, it was also a question for me.

EL: The way you did it musically made it work, but also the fact that, for me, just knowing you personally, especially those two movements, two and four, when playing them, did have a powerful impact on me.

SR: Right, right.

And you were also involved in *Music for 18 Musicians*.

EL: Well, *Music for 18*...

SR: That's a piece where you are surrounded by percussion and keyboards vastly outnumbering the two musicians playing strings. It's a very different kind of ensemble and yet you always struck me as being intensely... I mean, everybody seems to get into it, but you were sitting in the customary position of a concertmaster and you hold that organically, very easily. I was talking to Russell and he didn't remember which section, I think it was section five, he said, "When Liz and I are playing,

I'm playing marimba and she's playing the repeated pattern on violin. Anyway, we just look at each other every time. It's like there's some kind of...let's ride with this."

EL: Right, right. Well, honestly, *Music for 18...* What pieces of music would I want on that desert island of eternity? I would pick the Bach "Chaconne," from the D-minor *Partita*. And I would pick *Music for 18*. I was trying to figure out why that piece means so much to me, in a cogent way. One thought that comes to mind is that there's two words in ancient Greek for *time*, one is Chronos (man-made time) and one is Kairos, that's G-d's time. You find the most opportune time to say something, it has to do with how you pull an arrow and how it hits the bull's-eye. How one finds that perfect moment. For me, *18* is that. It is the most perfect, opportune time while one is playing it. It's many minutes long on a clock but you're out-of-time while embedded in it. I have so many great memories of Jim Preiss as the gate-keeper. He'd have his arms crossed, and he'd look, and he'd lis-ten, and then he'd bring us through the next door. He'd signal the changes on the vibraphone and we would move on through. I don't know if you remember that we also recorded it right after we got back from Japan? We had just gotten off the plane and the thinking was that we would be less jet-lagged than during the subsequent days? So, we went into the recording studio in the middle of the night in New York, middle of the day Japan time. I'm just wondering if we were either jet-lagged or we were also just enjoying it because the starting tempo is not that much different but the recording was longer than other record-ings of the piece. For example, the ECM recording, which is actually my favorite, that was 56'31". Our recording was eleven minutes longer. 67'42". So, talk about fluidity and differences. I did a nerd thing where I went through each section to find out where the longer sections were between the two recordings. It really was in the pulses. But that's also a tribute to your piece, you give that freedom to the players.

SR: Well, I think there are two things here that come to mind. One is that, as you say, there's a flexibility in terms of the number of repeats. I unquestioningly accept the judgment of the people in the ensemble who have a particular decision to make, or Jim Preiss playing the vibes, as you say, that he knows when the right time is. That would suffer from being notated. That would not clarify matters, it would rob the players of their freedom and responsibilities. The other explanation is much more mundane. Les Scott and everybody else who had played the piece back in the '70s had aged, this was in the '90s. In the early days, they could play those pulses on the bass clarinet (*imitates taking a fast breath*). Twenty years later, (*imitates much longer breath*). But that works, it's still coming from the gut, literally. That is how they play it now, that breath pacing has literally aged—and the piece accommodates it.

EL: I also remember that when I started learning *18* there were only the handwritten parts, and at one point we got printed parts, right? When I first started playing *18* you would hand out the manuscript parts when we would get to the venue. Even after printed parts were published, Jeanne [LeBlanc] and I both went back to the handwritten parts. We wanted less to look at. We wanted less page turns. A lot of the sections we'd just have them memorized and that was part of the joy of playing the piece, not being tied to the page and notation, but being able to really enter into the ebb and flow of what was going on, that mystery that is part of *18*. The shifting of the landscape, rhythmically and harmonically, it's always just the perfect place to be.

SR: Well, on that note. I was going to say, *Music for 18* is still a large piece of chamber music.

EL: Yes, that is perfect in its architecture.

SR: I remember back when I was at Juilliard, there were sort of two branches of the musical community. There was the orchestral mentality and there was the chamber mentality. One of them is to follow the leader, and great conductors are wonderful, and in *Tehillim* we actually needed one and we had several. But the chamber mentality was what I gravitated towards and the musicians I gravitated towards. Not only are you closely reacting to other musicians in performance, you have to actually invent your own life.

EL: Right.

SR: That mentality, I think, has a very positive effect. I've seen videos of groups whom I've never met, don't know them, no personal connection, didn't go to rehearsals, and they perform *18*. And I still see they're enjoying performing with each other in that same chamber music climate. Does that ring a bell for you?

EL: Definitely! You mentioned section five when I would look over at Russ and lock in. That was always so joyful, to pass through that door to the next section and to collectively arrive and feel, "Yeah, now we are HERE!" And then different times when you would enter on the piano. I'd look over at you and you'd nod your head and we'd go on from that section. All of the different resulting patterns that came out. They would emerge out of the fabric of the music, it was just incredible, like (*demonstrates melody*), but each time it was always a little bit different depending on the acoustic of the hall. I remember once we performed *18* at Seiji Ozawa Hall at Tanglewood and we had trouble with that hall because it was something with the way the sound was bouncing off the walls where onstage we couldn't hear well what was coming out of the monitors. Another hall that comes to mind is the Krannert Center in Champaign, Illinois, which is also shaped like a rectangle. I think it had the same architect who did what is now David Geffen Hall, formerly known as Avery Fisher Hall. For some reason, the Krannert works, and Avery Fisher, before improvements were made, had a lot of issues acoustically. So, where is the logic in that, right? Whenever we'd go to different places, sometimes depending on the acoustic of the hall it would change how we would react to each other. Especially in this time of COVID, what I really remember and miss are the audiences and how much they were a part of the atmosphere of the performance. I don't know if you remember this one but I'll never forget when we went to Vilnius, Lithuania, where people traveled from hundreds of miles around to get to this concert to hear *18* there. The feeling in that audience was incredible. You sensed everyone listening, you felt everybody being so much a part of that performance, and so many of the performances were like being in a rock concert in terms of the response at the end of the performances. The audiences were so invested.

SR: That makes a big difference.

EL: That's right.

But, by the way, I would also love to talk about *City Life*.

SR: Sure!

EL: I'd love to talk about *WTC 9/11*, as well.

SR: Okay, both of them.

EL: So, what I want to say about *City Life* is that we did the New York premiere in 1996 at Tully Hall and then we recorded it soon after that. We only did the one performance and the recording. What stays with me is the first movement, a kind of love letter to New York City, and then the fifth movement where you used recordings of field communications from the NYC Fire Department from the bombing of WTC in 1993. Eight years prior to 9/11. What has struck me especially about *City Life* was that we do the performance, then the recording, and the next time that I really get into the fabric of it is ten years later because of the workshop "Reich on Reich at 70" held by Carnegie Hall. So, we go in for about six days in 2006, now ten years later, to coach a talented group of students. It was really fascinating for me because in the '70s when hip-hop and rap came into being, that was not on my radar at all, in terms of having even heard it. In general, I didn't listen much to rap music, but in that ten-year period from '96 to 2006 after I came back to *City Life*, rap music was now on my aural radar. I can't help but wonder what your influence has been on rap music. The acronym RAP stands for "rhythm-and-poetry," right? So, I'm sure your music has influenced all sorts of musicians outside of the realm of classical music.

SR: Seems so.

EL: That was so interesting to me on a musical level.

SR: Well, you just linked *City Life*, which ends with the first bombing of the World Trade Center in '93, with *WTC 9/11*, which was in 2010.

EL: Yes, we played *WTC* for the 13th anniversary of 9/11 in 2014 at BAM for the Next Wave Festival. What struck me was that in the second movement a young woman says, "I was sitting in class." And it reminded me of *Different Trains*, "I was in second grade, no more school." For me personally, this always resonated with me, as my mother was enrolled at Ewha Womans University in Seoul when the Korean War broke out. She was sitting on the lawn in front of the school with friends and, as she's told us many, many times when hearing about our family history, basically "school was over." Somebody came outside, said school was over, and that was it. That was the end of her education and life in Korea. Then she came to California and went to Mills College. Also, what was interesting to me—I don't know if this was something you changed notationally, but it's actually the only time in the ten pieces I've played of your music that I saw *sforzandi* written in. Was that a musical notation that you decided to use specifically for *WTC 9/11*? There are so many dramatic moments in all of your music, such as in *The Cave* when Abraham is about to sacrifice Isaac, but this is the first time I saw a *sforzando*? I didn't see it in *The Cave* but I did see it in *WTC 9/11*, so that's actually a question I'd like to ask you. In all of your pieces that I've played, I've never seen you use that marking before?

SR: I have no fast answer for that. I generally don't use *sforzandi*. The first time *sforzandi* entered my music was when Michael Tilson Thomas was conducting *The Desert Music*. In one of the sections which is full of changing meters, there's a lot of brass going. It's a natural place for an accent. And he suggested it and I said to him, "Michael, pretend I'm dead." (*laughs*) And he put in the *sforzandi* and I said, "Thank you! That's great!" Because I really want to get input from other musicians about my music that I don't necessarily see because eventually it may happen anyway, so it's a pleasure to hear it while I'm still alive... Now, whether that had any carry-over so many years later, I doubt. *WTC 9/11* is a particularly emotional piece in that it's something that happened to me and my family in a direct way. We lived four blocks from ground zero. That may account for the *sforzandi*. It's interesting that you picked that out. It happens in the second movement right after David Lang says, "Run for your life!" because he was walking his kids *to* school when the first plane hit. It was intensely emotional for him and for me, as well.

EL: Wow. What also was so moving for me about *WTC 9/11* was the singing of the traveler's prayer and the woman who says, "I would sit there and recite psalms all night, simply sitting." What a beautiful thing to do.

CHAPTER 12

DAVID ROBERTSON

Steve Reich: So, let's see. It's 1996.

David Robertson: Right.

SR: We're in London at the Barbican with the LSO, and Synergy Vocals, who don't even have that name yet.

DR: Yes.

SR: And this brilliant young conductor, who you know very well (*laughs*). And the concert begins, and I think to myself, "Oh, no. This is way too fast. It's going to spin out completely." Then, miraculously, it doesn't! It's absolutely fabulous. It was you. How did that concert come about?

DR: I'd done *Tehillim* in Paris with the Ensemble Intercontemporain, when I was first with the ensemble, my second season. What was really important to me for the LSO concert was to have vocalists who could really nail the parts of *Tehillim* because the piece is demanding, and it is absolutely beautiful. You need people with pure voices who can hit the intervals and hold them with enormous control so that the organs and the woodwinds, who are doubling them at any given time, make the proper blend. I had chosen four individual voices when I did the concert in Paris. I taught it to them, and I thought, "This is ridiculous. I need to get a group of people who actually always sing together." And as luck would have it, I had worked on a couple of productions with the Swingle Singers. At the time I worked with them, there were four ladies, and I thought, "These are the people we should get." I got in touch with Micaela Haslam and Sarah Eyden and said, "I'd love you to do this." And they said, "We're not Swingle Singers any longer, but we'd love to do it." So, we got those people together. There was Rachel Weston, Heather Cairncross, and they all said, "We've never done this piece before." And I said, "That's fine, we'll work in some time where we can practice it." And so, in fact, because of the London Symphony Orchestra being split between two different projects, they actually gave us five rehearsals, which, in London and with a group of the quality of the LSO, meant the sky's the limit. What was interesting, right from the start, was that having this group of four singers who knew each other intimately meant that the change of the group from one day to the next was just astounding in terms of the solidity that they gained over three days. Everyone was listening in such a way that by the time we got to the performance, it was this fantastically well-engineered, high performance racing car! I thought, "Okay, let's open up the throttle on this baby and see what a Hallelujah in D major can really sound like!" (*laughs*)

For me, the performance was a huge moment, because I'd come up through the whole contemporary music scene, while also doing bel canto operas and things like that. I'd been very interested in contemporary composers who had ideas about tempo and ideas about rhythm and ideas about rhythmic scales, I'm thinking of Messiaen and Stockhausen as two of them. Either scales in tempo with someone like Stockhausen, or even in duration with Messiaen's work in the early '50s. The interesting thing for me with *Tehillim* was it just sort of jumped out at me when I first heard the work, it was that ECM recording from 1981, I believe, which was such a discovery. Because here all of a sudden was a rhythmic structure that was forming the basis of the music, and had this melodic scale made out of intervals of the same type as the rhythmic scales, so that the X and Y coordinates for me in *Tehillim* suddenly had this parallel quality. And that was something that I just found incredibly fascinating in the musical language, because the melodies were easy to remember, they fit the words beautifully, and they seemed to come out of the incantation of these religious songs. But at the same time, because of the way that the rhythm worked underneath, you hear Part 1, and then you arrive at Part 2, and while the melody seems similar, suddenly this melody is one that can be elongated, so that the whole sense of the musical phrase has an upbeat feel. The augmentation is not simply that the note is longer, but that— Okay, here's where I'm going to put my cards on the table:

I grew up for the first eighteen years of my life watching Pacific Ocean breakers. So, this sense of a 15/8 bar or an 18/8 bar, where it has a couple of notes moving and then a long note which actually is just like this wave pulling back and then crashing on the downbeat of the next bar. This is among the most enjoyable conducting experiences that I have ever had.

SR: I'm really glad to hear you find conducting *Tehillim* enjoyable. Isn't conducting it a challenge with all those meter changes?

DR: Well, in fact, I think this is a misnomer. One of the things I learned during *Tehillim* for the first time with Ensemble Intercontemporain was that, in fact, much of it is going by at a speed and in a groove that means, unlike the nineteenth-century and early twentieth-century conception of a conductor, you can't influence the rhythm. All you do is confirm what it is that people hear. So, in a sense, it's not like you're using twos and threes to push people into a rhythmic space. The drums, the claps, that's happening all by itself. It's happening because of the rhythmic heartbeat that's in the piece. In fact, what ends up happening for you as the conductor is that your gestures do something that no one else in the ensemble can do, which is to shape where the phrase is going. Because of the voices, it seems absolutely natural to take the phrase to the last note. While it's not necessarily the same in all pieces, that sense of "I'm responsible for people understanding the long-term trajectory of this phrase" is actually how I approach conducting any of your pieces.

SR: That's great. When I finished composing *Tehillim*, I began wondering if it would be better to re-bar it, never getting longer than a 7/8 bar? You could have 5/8, 7/8, but no 21/8, forget that. But as you said, even with the challenge of performing such meters, that is the way the piece goes. If you want to see how the piece goes, I'm writing these long meters, not to give you a hard time but to show you, yes, there are these small chunks, but this is all one long phrase made of groups of twos and threes.

DR: Right. Exactly. I remember when we were doing the premiere of *City Life* in Paris, it was kind of like the World Series of ensembles because it was done by Ensemble Modern afterwards and done by the London Sinfonietta right after that. Who's going to do it the best? For me, the interesting thing about the piece, right from the start, is that you present this chorale, and I've heard the chorale played in such a way that each chord is "what you see is what you get." It's neutral and there isn't a clear of a sense of which of the chords is more important than another. It's not like a tonic-dominant relationship, or here we go to the subdominant. They are chords that, in a sense, kind of float and set up a frame. My take on that has never been to play them with neutrality. A chorale like the one you wrote at the beginning of *City Life* feels to me like a huge question asking "We are social creatures; how does that work when we all get together?" The interesting thing is that those chords, in an altered state and in an almost slightly distended way, come back at the very end of the piece. So, for me, your whole approach to them is as a question that, while not answered in the end, is continued, is now asked in a different way because we've heard the different movements in between. The pile drivers, the car horns, "It's been a honeymoon." All these different passages that have informed what makes *City Life* expressive and moving, going on to the prequel of the World Trade Center attack. This means that when you get to the end, there has to be a kind of timelessness that we know from the end of Mahler's *Lied von der Erde*. And that is something I call the fragile part, because that's not something you can put down in a score. That's only something that an interpreter can read and pick up from a score. And it's one of the things that has continually impressed me about the depth of every one of your pieces, even the ones that are not necessarily connected up with major events like *Different Trains* or grave subjects like *Desert Music*, but all of them have this sense of trying to articulate or trying to grasp something that is just beyond words. Does that make sense?

SR: Well, the opening chorale for me is just the kind of calm, contemplative slow-paced music that has no place in the noise of New York. For me, it vaguely connects to Stravinsky's *Symphonies of Wind Instruments*. The chorale comes back at the end of the first movement all banged up with street noises and, as you noted, it comes back at the end of the whole piece covered with warnings and smoke.

DR: Yes.

SR: You revised on the spot, or suggested revision which became part of the piece, in the last movement. We went back and forth on it; it wasn't an easy sell. (*laughs*)

DR: Yes.

SR: But you won me over! You saw things that I didn't see in the piece. And I thought, "This is great. He has something to say, I want to hear it." I mean, sometimes people will ask, "Your music is very rhythmic, it's very fixed, is there any room for expression?"

DR: (*laughs*)

SR: And I say, "Well, the short answer is yes."

DR: Yeah.

SR: But some people have a really deep view of the possibilities of "interpretation," which can even go to the point of rewriting, as in your case. That's priceless. That shows a level of engagement and a musical intelligence which is just terribly welcome. So, thank you yet again.

DR: Well, it's one of the things that... Let's see... I think it's when you start to work on a piece, what ends up becoming clear is that you are learning something that has already been formed and that a creator has let go.

SR: Right.

DR: I once had to translate in Cologne when West German radio was doing a whole thing about John Cage. And one of the questions came in German. "What does he think about this piece?" And I translated this to John, and he said, "I'm more interested in what I'm working on now." Which is very much how creators work. Once you've actually let go of the piece, yes, you might make some revisions to it, but essentially, you're moving on to something else.

SR: Exactly.

DR: And the thing that's interesting for us as interpreters is that we have this set of instructions, and no matter how accurate those instructions are, you will come back and find that there are things that still reveal themselves to you even after years of study. When we did *Desert Music*, I'd done it in the small version a couple of times. And all of a sudden, we were doing it in the full orchestral version.

SR: In Sydney?

DR: Well, in Sydney, but even before in Munich. It was in the Herkulessaal in Munich with the Bavarian Radio Orchestra where aspects of the orchestration I thought I knew, heard in that particular acoustic, revealed different sonorities for the very first time. And I think that's the thing which is surprising, and where one has to keep an almost biblical sense of awe in front of these works because they will suddenly light up something just by the sheer nature of the number of relationships they have. So, for us as interpreters, the idea is to try and find those relationships, to articulate them as much as possible, and allow them to come forward. It doesn't surprise me that the creator themself often says after the fact, "You know, I hadn't heard that" or "I didn't know that."

SR: Exactly.

DR: Not because they aren't in total control of making it happen, but when they're listening to it afterwards it is as though a different part of their creative personality is involved in that experience, rather than the one that's writing it down. *Pulse* is a great example of this because I think that when you write a work that has vibraphones, which have a very long resonance, and you have pianos, which also have a long resonance, you will often use those resonances compositionally. And so you are working with their natural decay, a decay that is a contrast to a marimba decay and certainly to a membrane decay, which is much quicker. So, the danger is, I think, to look at something that may have a long decay on a vibraphone, and when a similar type of phrase is suddenly given to a flute, a clarinet, or a voice, to think that when you get to that note, it has the same relation when that pitch is on a vibraphone that it would on a voice or an instrument that sustains. This is where the danger is, I think, if you're doing something like *Pulse*, is to land on a note and think "Okay, I've arrived on this note." Whereas, in fact, the phrases are really long. You need to have these tendrils of sound, almost as though there is this whole procession that is going up some hillside path. There are switchbacks in different places, so we become aware of the line moving in a certain place, but no one, even if they are resting for a moment on a particular part of the hill, is stopped. No one goes static. If I were to contrast it with something in the same time period like *Quartet*, *Quartet* works with the fact that you set something down and we just hear the resonance expand. That's a completely different way of approaching the music than what many people tend to do. I think there's often this idea that what's on the page is what I do, and so there isn't much interpretation. But in fact, the possibility for shadings and for colors that you get out of the music is without end.

So, in the full orchestral version of *The Desert Music* there are sounds that are amazingly specific and well done, but they don't have any real precedent in terms of the way the orchestra sounds in earlier works. And it has always surprised me that when people ask a composer to do something and then they come up with something unusual that people haven't heard before, there's the criticism of "Well, that's not standard." Although that's what you actually want them to do in the first place!

SR: I have to ask you, and I alluded to it earlier, in Sydney you programmed *The Desert Music* full version, and *The Rite of Spring* as the second half. I got feedback from you and I saw the review in *The Australian*, and I thought it was amazing to see both pieces got rave reviews. And I thought, When I was fourteen years old and I discovered *The Rite of Spring*, which changed my life, that almost seventy years later I would be on a program like that with a piece that could stand up to such a challenge.

DR: Yeah, yeah.

SR: How did you experience that performance in Sydney?

DR: It was fascinating. I've often seen in orchestral concerts that if you program pieces the orchestra hasn't necessarily played in that combination, a dialogue between the pieces ensues in the minds and ears of the players. So, there was something about really having to lock into a tempo that flows in the way it does in *The Desert Music.* In a sense, without gravity, you sort of joined this flowing rhythm without stopping it or changing it, this meant that there were certain passages in *The Rite of Spring* which were so much easier for me to bring about because of this whole exercise. You have a group of twelve eighth notes going on, and when you come in, you enter at precisely the right time or you start and fade your notes in and they must be at exactly the same speed, even if you're in *piano.* There are so many passages in the Stravinsky where, while they might resemble ruptures—because he's putting irregular bar lengths all over the place, in fact, the eighth-note pulse, quarter-note pulse, sixteenth-note pulse, is absolutely inviolable. And this goes the whole time. Yet what ends up happening for me is I often hear a kind of start and stop feeling to *The Rite of Spring* because it almost feels like a new driver learning to drive stick *(laughs).* So, they do get it into second gear but, man, everybody feels a little bit of whiplash as they go… Whereas, I think Sydney was particularly sensitive to this, being a very malleable and quick-on-their-feet orchestra, so all sorts of passages where I've usually had to insist, "Actually, you know, we're not keeping time." You know, like when it goes from 6/8 to 3/4, there's an accent and so it looks like it's the same bar but, in fact, they have to feel quite differently. We can't take on any extra rhythmic cabin baggage and shove it into the overhead compartments. This was so much easier to do after the work on *The Desert Music*! It was such a self-evident thing, this idea of "We have this ongoing pulse, and this ongoing pulse is the determinant of everything that happens above it melodically, harmonically, and rhythmically." And so, from that point of view, it was a fascinating experience. The other thing, somewhat below the surface, which the Synergy Vocals brought out so well in your piece, is that neither it nor *The Rite of Spring* is a nice story.

SR: No.

DR: We are not going to have a happy ending here. And there are moments of eerie harmonies that are really rather chilling, but we've gotten used to them. In fact, in *Star Wars*, John Williams was asked to use one of them to describe the atmosphere of Tatooine. But the main feeling should be that these harmonies get under your skin, and in a reverse way, having *Rite* on the program meant that when we played your passage "Man has survived hitherto because he was too ignorant to know how to realize his wishes" it spoke to the Stravinsky. When that passage comes back the second time, your harmonies have quite a bit of existential spice to them. And being able to pull that out, or to pull out the very slow process building into that with (*demonstrates rhythm*) the whole violin melody, as it gradually shifts through the harmonies and goes darker and darker until we come to that verbal kernel, was something that was easier to have everyone understand with the *Rite of Spring* on the program than when I've done it in Lucerne or Munich or other places where it's just been an all-Reich concert.

SR: Right. So, I was able to help Igor and he certainly has helped me.

DR: Yeah.

SR: That's by far the best news I've heard today. So, jumping to the more or less immediate present, back in Sydney you also did the premiere there of *Music for Ensemble and Orchestra*. How did it go?

DR: When you were writing it, we were talking about it, and you said, "I think I've found my way of handling the orchestra, which is one that goes back to the Baroque idea of the *con-*

certante group and the *grosso*." And the interesting thing is that
the stage setup in all of your pieces, I think it's actually crucial.
If you don't get the instruments that really need to be heard by
everyone *heard* by everyone, you're in trouble. Whether it's the
percussion instruments in *Desert Music*, the pianos in *Three Movements*, or whether it's the maracas, the small drums, and the claps
in *Tehillim*, that you set this acoustic ensemble up is essential.
And so, the way we were able to do it, where you have a circle
of strings with all of the string soloists at the center, makes perfect sense within the normal orchestral mindset. Right behind
them are their cohorts of the string tutti who make up the rest
of the string group for the orchestra. And then the two pianos
are nestled together in the center behind the strings, with the
two vibraphone players each behind the keyboards of the pianists
on the left and right sides. And then right up against the nested
pianos, you've got the woodwinds in a single raised line. And
then behind them, the trumpets still higher up, to embrace the
whole group. This means that when you perform the music, the
dialogues are constantly shifting back and forth, not only side
to side for the canons, but also back and forth when it's woodwinds, when it's strings, and when it's the combination of the
two. All of this means that the work really does have kind of a
symphonic scope. It doesn't so much feel like a Baroque concerto, per se, but rather as though the main discourse, provided
by the ensemble, allows the orchestra to make this frame or halo
for the whole group. And that's been really fun to do. Although
you could say, "Well, there's no room for interpretation in the
score because you're going to keep the same pulse, you can't play
around with the rhythmic underpinning of these interlocking
canons and groups of eighth-note figures." At the same time, I
have to tell you that doing it with the Czech Philharmonic Orchestra in their hall was just revelatory. It reinforced the whole
experience that I've had where I've performed your works as
much as I possibly can on non-all-Reich concerts. Where, in

fact, what happened is after playing the Reich, the Bartók had a kind of inevitability about it because of the use of similar types of intervals, and the use of folk music, and the use of things that you don't think about and yet the universal structure of it becomes completely evident to the ear. I've loved doing *Triple Quartet* with Haydn symphonies. My favorite is to have *Triple Quartet* and Haydn 103. Both because of the restrictive way that Haydn is using the material, which takes this idea of minimal and blows it wide open. On top of that is the Croatian folk song that he uses in the second movement, it is modally so close to the middle section of *Triple Quartet* that this universal grammar of musical expression just becomes really obvious to any audience member, whether they thought of themselves as a "Reichhead" or not. (*laughs*)

SR: Well, I'm glad to hear it. I wish I had been in Prague, that sounds like a really interesting concert. We've covered a lot of ground here. I'm fresh out of questions.

DR: I was thinking I should be the one that questions you!

SR: If you have a question, I'm here.

DR: One of the things that I have thought about time and time again, which you said kind of laughing as you told me, was when Peter Eötvös did a premiere, I guess it was West German radio, or was it in Stuttgart?

SR: Actually Peter Eötvös did two things. He did *The Desert Music* with WDR, which was catastrophic. Peter was great, as usual, but the orchestra and chorus were just totally out of touch with my music. He also did the first two movements of *Tehillim* with the Süddeutscher Rundfunk. I don't remember much about it. It wasn't a catastrophe and it wasn't a triumph, it was just an in progress performance. But the interesting thing about that experience is that Peter and I were driving down from Paris to Stuttgart, and he had very little English and I had very poor French and no German, which he would have preferred to speak. Somehow he asked me, since both the first two movements of *Tehillim* are fast, he said kind of sheepishly, "So, you'll continue in the same tempo?" And I just immediately sort of wilted and thought, "Oh, you're right. I've got to change." And it was in that moment that I knew I had to write a slow movement, which I hadn't done since my student days. And now I think the slow movement of *Tehillim* is exactly what the piece needed. I have to thank Peter for sort of forcing me to do that.

CHAPTER 13

MICAELA HASLAM

Micaela Haslam: We've worked together for over twenty-five years now. This is amazing!

Steve Reich: Right, and I don't think anybody thinks of me as a "vocal composer," but look at all these pieces we've done together!

MH: I know, I've got them all in a big pile next to me on my desk.

SR: And it all started in an incredible performance of *Tehillim* by yourself—was it Synergy in those days?

MH: Well, we didn't have a name. That was the beginning of Synergy Vocals.

SR: Right. And it was the London Symphony Orchestra, the LSO, and the incredible David Robertson. It was in 1996, almost twenty-five years ago.

MH: David is an amazing conductor. It was funny how so many things in the world came together to make that particular moment happen. That concert changed my life. I didn't really know your music in 1996, and had just left the Swingle Singers to join the BBC Singers. We had recently performed Berio's *Sinfonia* with David Robertson in Italy, so when he needed singers for this concert of *Tehillim*, he approached the Swingles and the gig ended up coming to me. The LSO called me up and asked, "Can you do this piece *Tehillim*? Do you know it? And can you organize the other singers?" So, I said, "Yeah, yeah, I know this piece." I had never heard of it.

SR: *(laughs)*

MH: That's the kind of thing you do when you're young, right?

SR: Right.

MH: So, I got the score of *Tehillim*, I opened it, and I read Voice 2, which is the voice that begins first and then continues throughout. And I just thought, "Someone has written this for me." It was the most incredible thing. Apart from the Hebrew (a language I had never sung in before), everything made sense to me, the rhythms, the notes, the melody, and everything about it. I just thought, "I know how to do this." I'd never come across your music, and this was just one of those fortuitous moments. It's strange now to think that when I was at university studying music, your name didn't come up at all. Now students all over the world are writing dissertations about your music. Anyway, fortunately, the other three women, who were still in the Swingles, were free to do that concert. So the four of us did it, and we became Synergy.

SR: And you sounded great! But when you first read the score and got to the four-part canons, didn't you think, "Hmm? Might be a bit of a challenge."

MH: Strangely enough, when I was quite young I read a book called *The Rhythmic Structure of Music*, which I really enjoyed, so when I saw all those triangles and lines, I thought, "I know how this goes." My introduction to your music was an extraordinary combination of factors...and also, let's not forget, *Tehillim* is on microphone, and I'd just spent four years in the Swingle Singers singing exclusively on close microphone.

SR: You just brought up the microphone, which is very important. How would you describe how you studied nonoperatic vocal production when you were in school? You must have done a lot of early music?

MH: Sure. Actually, my background was as an instrumentalist. I first studied bassoon and piano at university. And I played the guitar and recorder. I loved the clarity of the recorder and used to play a lot of Brandenburg Concertos and Bach cantatas, that kind of stuff. I also sang a lot of early music in university choirs. I never had an operatic voice. It just was not how my voice worked. To be honest, I loved pop music. That's the kind of music I would sing at the piano as a kid. I would sit for hours writing down pop songs from records and tapes. That's what I really loved. But my whole family was very classically based. My mum was a music teacher; my dad was a composer, a flute player, and a conductor. So, right from the start, I was led down the classical path. But I would keep jumping over to the Stevie Wonder side at the end of my piano practice! My mum is a big opera fan. My name, Micaela, is from *Carmen* by Bizet. That's where she got it from. Sorry, Mum, I'm never going to sing that role! She took me to the opera many times as a kid, bless her, obviously to try and inspire me, but it just left me cold. I just couldn't relate to those weighty voices with lots of vibrato, and I often couldn't understand what they were singing about, even if it was in English. It didn't appeal to me. So, as I said, I sang a lot of early and contemporary music with small chamber groups at university. Then, in my early twenties, I sang in various choirs, including with early music legends such as Gustav Leonhardt, Trevor Pinnock, and Peter Phillips. I also sang with the Deller Consort and in The Sixteen Choir. I thought that early music was my destiny, but then I got the Swingles job and everything got thrown in the air.

SR: When you were studying, were you studying voice or was it only instrumental?

MH: I switched to singing in the final year of my music degree because I knew I didn't want to be a professional bassoonist. Initially, I studied singing with Honor Sheppard, who had been in the Deller Consort. I sang lots of Dowland, Purcell, and Handel, et cetera, with her. Then I went to the Royal Academy as a postgraduate to study with Rae Woodland. I remember going to a class where the tutor played recordings of various famous opera singers. She'd say, "You all know whose voice this is," and I'd be thinking, "I have absolutely no idea—and I don't really like it." I used to hang out with the instrumentalists who were playing Baroque music. If they were having lessons on obbligato passages in Bach cantatas, for example, I'd go and sing the arias. That's what I enjoyed. I don't think my voice would ever have become operatic, however much I practiced. Maybe it's because I sang too much pop music in my spare time! Most of the singers in Synergy have sung jazz, pop, and/or early music, so they can sing with real clarity and without vibrato—in an instrumental way, if you like. And also have a great feel for rhythm—something I think is often lacking in vocal training. Things are probably better in colleges these days, and there are certainly far more singers tackling your music now than when we started. In '96, '97, there really weren't many at all. For me, I think of the difference between what we do and what an opera singer does in sports terms. The opera singer is the bodybuilder, the power lifter, whereas we're the high jumpers, sprinters, and hurdlers. We have more vocal agility because we're not having to worry about producing volume and weight of sound.

SR: That's extremely well put, particularly about rhythm and clarity. It's exactly what I look for in a singer. I've never had to ask you, or anybody in Synergy, anything about performance style or about clearer diction, even transliterated Hebrew—you always got it. The diction had to be clear. If you've got the diction right, you'll get the rhythm right, as well.

MH: Yeah, for sure. The voices need to sound "natural" and somewhat untrained, but you do need a good technique to produce the diction effectively and get that precision of sound. I think you actually need quite a lot of pressure behind the consonants, whilst being careful that they don't "pop" on microphone. And the vowel needs to go on the beat. There's generally no room to take your time over the text, the way choral singers or soloists might use long consonants to be more expressive. When a choir is singing "Kyrie," the K might last for half a second. If they did that in your music, we'd be on to the next bar by the time they finished their K!

SR: (laughs)

MH: I need people to sing "now" so that "ow" is on the beat. But we still need a strong N. For me, it's about the energy behind the sound. I often talk about surfing when I describe singing your music. The pulse is the unstoppable wave, and you need to stay on the front of it. The minute you lean back a bit, you're in the water!

SR: You brought up something very, very interesting because it applies to actually three other important pieces that you did.

You said you basically wanted to sound a bit like an instrument. The record producer and former singer Judy Sherman, whom I worked with for years, when we were doing the mixing of either *Drumming* or *18*, said to me, "What you want is a voice-strument."

MH: (*laughs*)

SR: So, that gets us to what I guess in vocal terms is vocalese, which is what you sing in *Drumming*, in *Music for Mallet Instruments, Voices, and Organ*, and *Music for 18 Musicians*. Now, we began working together with *Tehillim*, written in 1981, which, with all its peculiarities, is singing words. It's "normal singing." Pretty soon thereafter you started doing these earlier pieces, *Drumming* is 1971, *Mallets* is '73, and *18* is '76, but you took to them like a duck to water, so what gives?

MH: Well, again, it was as though this was meant to be. Synergy Vocals was created at that *Tehillim* performance in '96, just before the new modular score for *Music for 18* appeared. In 1997, you, Russ [Hartenberger], and Bob [Becker] headed to Frankfurt to teach the piece to Ensemble Modern, and I guess because we had been associated with your music quite recently, we came on board to provide the vocals. Singing scat "do, do, do," et cetera, was second nature to us, having sung for years in the Swingles. We had the luxury of a whole week with you and Russ and Bob teaching us how the piece worked. What amazing timing for us in the history of this piece. *Music for 18* had obviously been in existence for a long time in 1997, but until that point, no ensemble—perhaps with one exception—had performed the piece apart from your own.

SR: Right.

MH: No one knew how to make it work, and this modular score suddenly made it transferable.

SR: It was the handoff between my ensemble and Ensemble Modern and Synergy precisely as you've explained it. It was Russell Hartenberger, Bob Becker, and myself, sitting in and coaching the performances of *Music for 18* which were eventually recorded. It was that moment, in the late '90s, that was literally the handoff from three Americans to the UK and Germany saying, "Now, you've really got it, congratulations and thank you."

MH: Ensemble Modern was the perfect ensemble for the hand-over, as they don't have a conductor or leader as such, and there is room for everyone to discuss and work out exactly how things go.

SR: Basically, you could say, it's the chamber music mentality.

MH: Absolutely, and for me, that's the joy of making music— being in an ensemble. I never wanted to be the soloist standing out in front, it's just not me. Maybe that's due to my instrumental background, playing in orchestras. I'd rather be in the band. Even for *Tehillim*, where the voices are the main feature, we usually stand at the back with the mallet players, and for *Desert Music*, too. For all your vocal pieces, apart from *Proverb*, we are literally in the band with the instrumentalists. Most singers are either in a choir, a cappella or accompanied, or they are soloists. Having the singers in the band was kind of a new thing. Of course, we'd already performed *Sinfonia* by Berio, that iconic piece of the 1960s in which the singers are seated in the orchestra, but that's a whole different kettle of fish.

SR: You know Berio was one of my teachers?

MH: I know! Again, what an amazing coincidence. We had some hilarious times with him… How did you get on with him?

SR: I always thought he was a brilliant composer and very easy to get along with. You also mentioned *Proverb*, which happened fairly recently when we did it in Paris with Colin Currie. That piece is not as well-known as the pieces we're talking about, but for me it's one of my favorites. What was your take on *Proverb*?

MH: It's the most beautiful piece and, as you say, it's not really like anything else that you've written. It's an "early music" piece.

SR: Exactly. It's an homage to Pérotin and his *Viderunt Omnes* was on the piano. I was looking at his four-part organum as I was writing the piece. Of course, he never wrote augmentation canons that make up my piece, but I never would have done it in the first place if I didn't know Pérotin. I wouldn't have done a lot of things without Pérotin. Did you ever study any Notre Dame organum?

MH: I did at university. We had a professor who was a massive Josquin and Machaut fan, but most of the early music I sang was sixteenth/seventeenth century, like Thomas Tallis, John Dowland and William Byrd. Dowland songs are so beautiful and like folk songs. They really suited my voice. *Proverb* resonated a lot with me. It's a beautiful melody and so expressive in its simplest form at the beginning and the end of the piece. Here, there is time to sing long consonants and really deliver the text, "How small a thought it takes to fill a whole life." Then, after the opening, the words for me become color. We've established what the text is and now the soprano lines are just part of the texture. They are more instrumental. In the middle of the piece, there's that wonderful moment where you invert the melody.

SR: Do you remember doing *Daniel Variations*?

MH: Yes, we did the premiere. I think it was 2006 at the Barbican, it was your seventieth, I guess? It's funny, every time your birthday ends in a zero or a five, everything goes crazy.

SR: That's part of the music business. (*laughs*)

MH: (*laughs*) 2006 was indeed crazy! Yes, *Daniel Variations* is in four distinct sections, and the changing moods and characters from one movement to the next make it fun to sing. In the second movement, the tenors sing only "My name is Daniel Pearl," which calls for a beautiful, easy sound, though it's not easy at all because they're singing top As and B-flats. I think that's the key word for the vocals in your music, whether it's the sort of scat vocalese of the early stuff, or the text of the later music, it has to be easy—or at least it needs to sound easy. I've heard some singers say they can "take the vibrato off," but that often results in a hard, laser-like sound, because their voice is being clamped, and that's not the right sound. "My name is Daniel Pearl" is heartbreaking. It's simple, it's beautiful, it's fragile, and it's very high!—but tenors like Andy Busher and Gerry O'Beirne just smile through it (*laughs*). It's difficult, isn't it, finding tenors, because if you say, "We need good top As and top Bs for a 'classical music' concert," most people think of strident operatic tenors and that's not what we need at all for your music. That said, you do need a strength of sound. The voices should never sound flimsy. Quite often you have to sustain quite high, straight notes, and that is hard work. With the high soprano parts and the high tenor parts in *Desert Music*, for example, I believe you can either do it or you can't. Singers need to be handpicked. There is no such thing as "a tenor" or "a soprano"—every voice is unique. Some singers sound great on one piece but maybe not so great on another, and you don't want to ask someone to do something that is really uncomfortable. At the end of the day, you can either sing repeated top As for ten seconds, or you can't.

SR: The nice thing in *Music for 18* with those high pulsed notes, it's always "if you can reach it, fine, if not, sing the lower tone." Also, as you mentioned earlier, time is on our side. As the years pass, more singers are singing my music really well.

MH: That's true.

SR: I remember you sang in *You Are (Variations)*. What was your take on that?

MH: For me, *You Are (Variations)* and *The Desert Music* are your rock 'n' roll pieces. They appeal to my James Brown, Stevie Wonder, Earth, Wind, and Fire side (*laughs*). In the first movement of *You Are*, the vocals are like Big Band chords, the winds versus the voices, and you get a lot of that in *Desert Music*, too. The chords are just so deliciously scrunchy, and so well voiced. It's the kind of music that makes you want to throw your hands in the air! Again, the contrast between the four movements of *You Are* is a joy. In the second movement, "Shiviti," there are some tricky canons. As in *Tehillim*, if you're the second or third or fourth voice in the canon, the conductor's beat patterns can be off-putting, but it's imperative that you know how they fit with your own part. I've heard some singers say, "Oh, it's okay, I'll just feel the melody and start a beat later." Good luck. (*laughs*)

SR: Hasta la vista. (*laughs*)

MH: Sit back and wait for the car crash! It doesn't work. You need to know and feel where the conductor's beat is. Once you've done that, you can unpick it and then sing your part with the correct phrasing. Even in *Desert Music*, with a massive orchestra and twenty-seven singers, you have to feel the rhythm, not just think it. With all due respect to conductors, I'm not always watching (*laughs*), I'm listening to the percussionists because they're usually the driving force. And in *You Are (Variations)*, the piano parts in the first movement are pure James Brown.

SR: So, have you had a chance to listen or look at *Traveler's Prayer* yet?

MH: Yes, it has the feel of a slow movement, with a kind of poise and tranquility. It's meditative. Interestingly, and very unusually for you, it also has a distinct lack of pulse. I love the way the harmony is suspended in a slightly ambiguous way, until the very low piano spells out where we are. And I like the sparsity and quiet of it. How did you come up with the melody? Is that a melody of something you've written? Is it part of something else?

SR: It's traditional Jewish chanting. The first text is sung in the standard American-European Ashkenazic style of chanting the Torah. I don't know if you've heard *WTC 9/11*, but there's a recording of a cantor in the background of the last movement, and the strings double him. I took that melody from the recording. In the second movement, I worked with a different cantor who chants in Sephardic Middle Eastern style, but, interestingly enough, we ended up using a recording of an Italian cantor as the model. Now, all chanting of the Torah follows a notation found in printed editions of the text. The notation is called Ta'amim or Biblical Accents. They are also the punctuation marks of the text. They don't give you the notes. They're neumes, meaning they are short motives that may be for opening, continuing, half cadence, full cadence—actually, twenty-two varieties. The actual notes used to realize those neumes come from different traditions depending on where you come from geographically. And the Italian-Jewish community was very separate. It wasn't like the Arabic-Jewish community, nor was it like the European one. The second movement is taken from that tradition. The last movement is a psalm, actually the last line of Psalm 121, which also appears at the end of *WTC 9/11*, and no one, except Jews from Yemen, has a living tradition for how to chant psalms. So I composed that melody, just as I did with the psalm texts in *Tehillim*, which has no Jewish chanting in it at all.

When I was first working on *Traveler's Prayer*, I had sort of pauses, stops, at the end of each musical sentence, and Beryl kept saying, "Why did you do that? I was in something beautiful and then you broke it—just keep it going." It was such a natural response that I sensed she was right.

MH: Interesting. I think she is right. It has a beautiful stasis. The music sort of hovers and you lose yourself in the long vocal and string lines, with just the piano quietly reminding you of where you are.

SR: The lines, the melodies I described to you are always there in one of the voices. Then these extremely free canons begin where rhythmically the two voices can be very different. When they begin, both voices are the original notes of the melody, but as each section goes along, the second voice will either be an inversion, or retrograde, or retrograde inversion. Now, I've known all about those forms since I was a student, but I've never sat down and just written them out.

I was recently watching a film of a Stravinsky/Craft conversation, and when asked about a new piece, Stravinsky says something like "Well, the series is…" As is known, Stravinsky didn't always work with a twelve-note series but often with less than twelve. Once you get away from twelve, you can write all kinds

of tonal/modal music using those techniques that were originally medieval and Renaissance techniques. In *Traveler's Prayer*
first movement I'm in one flat. I wanted that constancy, but I
needed some harmonic variety and retrogrades, inversions and
retrograde inversions did just that by subtly varying the inter-
vallic harmony.

MH: But the second movement is slightly more juicy, isn't it?
A lovely harmonic change. And I find the second movement
more expressive, a little more pleading. The piece is unusual for
you, though, because you very often have a clear fast-slow-fast
structure.

SR: The tempo doesn't really change. It was a surprise to me.

MH: And, I'll tell you what, the tenors will be thrilled. (*laughs*)

SR: They finally get to star!

CHAPTER 14

ANNE TERESA DE KEERSMAEKER

This conversation took place by email in 2008.

Anne Teresa De Keersmaeker: I feel that there is a similarity between your work and mine. One could say that we both—especially at the beginning of our careers—used very extreme processes, like the early phase shifting pieces which I used in *Fase, Four Movements to the Music of Steve Reich*. Processes that are almost like algorithms! Twenty-five years later, our work has become more fluent. We have reached multiplicity and heterogeneity. But for my part, I feel that I accomplished this by expanding polyphony: more layers, more voices, more superimposed constraints—like in *Rain*. For you, I think it is partially different: the narrative aspect of the music played an important role in untying you from such processes. When I listen to *City Life*, for example, it sounds like a "symphonic poem." Your music tells stories now. Do you agree with this interpretation?

Steve Reich: You're right about our early work. We both started with extreme forms of organization that focused on one aspect of music or dance to show how that one aspect could create a whole work. In my case, the early phase pieces like *Piano Phase* and *Violin Phase* were based on slight changes in rhythmic relationship while pitch stayed constant (in *Violin Phase*) or changed slightly only after several minutes (in *Piano Phase*). Timbre never changed as only identical instruments were playing. As for my later work, starting with *Music for 18 Musicians*, I would say that all of it changes at a faster pace than the early work, though still more slowly than in most classical music. Beyond rate of change, it depends very largely on whether you look at my vocal pieces like *Tehillim, The Desert Music, Proverb, You Are (Variations)*, and *Daniel Variations*, or instrumental pieces like *Six Marimbas, Eight Lines, Sextet*, the four *Counterpoint* pieces, the orchestral pieces, *Triple Quartet, Variations for Vibes, Pianos and Strings*, or *Double Sextet*. In the vocal pieces no stories are told, but there is certainly subject matter, though always treated somewhat abstractly. There is yet a third category of pieces that use prerecorded voices and sounds of life around us, including machines. These pieces would include *Different Trains* (which began my return to prerecorded voices from *It's Gonna Rain* and *Come Out*), *The Cave, City Life*, and *Three Tales*. Again, no stories are ever told, but real documentary subject matter is presented with differing implications the audience must sort out for themselves. The essence of these pieces is that they are rooted in documentary material.

ATDK: At the beginning of your career, you were an underground composer and kind of a rebel. Today we get the impression that things are different, you are calmer. You explore the world in depth, but you avoid high drama and scandal. However, it is crystal clear that you will never write music that is merely made to entertain and that takes a just for fun approach, creating a world that is not yours. What would you call that? More precisely, what do you refuse when you are sitting in front of your music sheet? Do you think that the aesthetic aspect influences morals? When do you say no?

SR: Back in the 1960s, I was known mostly by other artists who were generally painters, sculptors, choreographers, and filmmakers. I was, in that respect, underground. I never set out to be a rebel. I just did what I really wanted to do musically, knowing full well that most of the musical establishment would dismiss it and dislike it since they were totally absorbed in serial or aleatoric music that forbade repetition, periodic rhythm, and tonality of any sort. As to what I would call what I do, I have no name for it other than "music." As to what I refuse while sitting in front of my music sheet, I refuse anything that does not seem to work musically and my ear is the final judge. While composing, I am constantly rejecting material and trying to improve the piece. When I'm done, I'm done and rarely change anything. As to aesthetics and morals, I believe they are essentially not connected—though we dearly, naively, would like them to be. We have only to think of Wagner, a proto-Nazi and simultaneously a musical genius.

ATDK: With *Tehillim*, we unexpectedly discovered your interest in spirituality. This appears to become more and more important to you. Yet at first sight, this seems a paradox: minimalism was a "cold school," a renunciation of intimate expression, and the development of formal mechanisms contemplated for the sake of it. But is it really a paradox? Didn't this rejection of the expression of the ego, the signature of minimalism, plant the seeds for mysticism? Is there a connection between forgetting yourself in the artistic process and an out-of-body experience in a state of ecstasy? Would you describe yourself as an "anti-romantic mystic"?

SR: With *Tehillim* (1981), my return to Judaism became apparent, but I was actively studying and beginning to practice it while composing *Music for 18 Musicians* (1976). Different aspects of this return became clearer in *Different Trains, The Cave, Three*

Tales, You Are (Variations), and *Daniel Variations*. We clearly live in a world of secular artists, intellectuals, and major media, but interestingly we find religion alive in several significant composers today, including Arvo Pärt, Gorecki, Philip Glass, Michael Gordon, Giya Kancheli, among others, not to mention Igor Stravinsky (or J. S. Bach). Music and religion seem to be intimately tied together. Every society has always had religious music. I am merely part of a long tradition that is still alive.

ATDK: You could say that authentic American music started with Ives, and took shape with Cage... But we could still hear echoes of European music in their work. With you, that is over, really over: there isn't a drop of Vienna in your music. The cord has been cut. How do you manage without Mahler, without melancholy, without that morbid, decadent touch to which we, Europeans, are so attached? Do you secretly listen to Mahler?

SR: You speak of me cutting the tie to Vienna and that was true of me even as a student. I found myself intuitively attracted to music written before 1750 and after Debussy. The classical period I sometimes enjoyed, especially, say, Beethoven Quartet 132 or the Fifth Symphony, but German/Austrian/Central European music after that held out no intuitive appeal to me. I acknowledge the genius of Schubert, Schumann, Brahms, Bruckner, Mahler, Sibelius, Schoenberg, Berg, Webern, et al., but I prefer not to listen to their music. I am often moved to tears by Stravinsky, J. S. Bach, Bartók, and many others from before 1750 and after Debussy, so my emotional musical life is complete without "romantic" music.

ATDK: De Machaut, Stravinsky, Coltrane, those were the composers that influenced you most, I read. Is that still so today, and if yes, which aspects of them specifically?

SR: Machaut's isorhythms are of real interest to me, but my heart belongs to earlier music by Pérotin at Notre Dame in Paris in the late twelfth century. You are certainly right about Stravinsky and Coltrane and don't forget Bartók, whose Fourth Quartet you choreographed and that same piece inspired my own *Triple Quartet*. You ask which aspects specifically: for Pérotin it is the idea of taking a line of Gregorian chant and augmenting its duration enormously so that instead of a melody it becomes a series of long drones. He (and Leonin) originate what we would call today very slow harmonic rhythm. For Stravinsky it is hard to point to specific points of influence. Suffice it to say, I might not have been inspired to be a composer if I had not heard *The Rite of Spring*. As to Coltrane, I would single out his *Africa/Brass* album in particular. Sixteen minutes on E, the low E of the double bass. Many notes, even noises become possible when the harmony is static. Don't leave out Ghanaian drumming, where repeating patterns are superimposed so their downbeats do not coincide, or Balinese gamelan, where different strands of counterpoint move at drastically different speeds. Finally, with Béla Bartók, I learned about the modes and canons from his *Mikrokosmos*. As you may know, canons are the backbone of almost everything I've done. Phasing is merely a small variation on canonic technique where the subject is usually short and the rhythmic distance between voices is constantly, slowly, changing.

ATDK: You are regarded as a composer whose early career was more influenced by artists such as Sol LeWitt than by professional mainstream composers. What about now? How do you relate to the new generation of visual artists in New York?

SR: As to being influenced by my friend, the late Sol LeWitt, I finished *It's Gonna Rain* in San Francisco in 1965 and then moved back to New York, where I finished *Come Out* in early

1966. I did not meet Sol until about 1968, although I saw his work before that, in late 1966. I just explained my musical influences above and they go back to my student days in the 1950s. What I found in Sol LeWitt and later in Richard Serra and the film *Wavelength* of Michael Snow were kindred spirits whose work all related to mine and to each other. There were things "in the air" as there always are in any given historical period and that was what we shared. I have kept up some of my relationships with those artists still living, but I have not been "on the scene" with newer generations of visual artists. I have noticed that even younger composers in New York do not seem to have the close relationship to their visual artist contemporaries that my generation did. I have no explanations for this.

ATDK: How do you cope with success? Do you find it hard to question yourself when everybody is watching? Do you have certain strategies to concentrate or to hide?

SR: Success can be a problem. I often joke that one can only survive if they know the magic word. The magic word is—"no." I found out many years ago that I got more music composed in rural Vermont than I did in New York City. I also found I genuinely loved being surrounded by trees and birds more than cement and noise. After thirty years of only going on the streets of New York with earplugs, I felt it was time to live outside the city. In 2006, Beryl Korot and I moved fifty miles north where we live now. I have recently been in Rome, Tokyo, and Ojai, California, so I am not exactly hidden—but it is a step in that direction and it's better for health and for composing music.

ATDK: With *The Cave*, you did not only take up religious and philosophical issues, you also struck a political chord. How would you evaluate that experience? Should an artist keep a certain distance from the world's problems?

SR: I believe an artist should work with whatever material they find of intense interest. If you are not deeply involved in what you are doing, how on earth can anyone else be interested? Contrary to contemporary, temporary concerns, subject matter ultimately means absolutely nothing. If the work of art is great it will survive—regardless of its content. Take, for example, the hundreds of great settings of the Catholic Mass which find interested ears today among people who are neither Catholic nor even religious. Or those who know nothing whatsoever about Nordic mythology but are swept away by Wagner's operas. Or those who still can't understand a word he's singing but love Dylan's "Subterranean Homesick Blues"? These people love the music they hear. Since they love it, perhaps they will cast a glance at the Mass text, or read up on Nordic mythology, or get Dylan's lyrics—but first the music must draw them in. Then the words, the subject matter, may follow. Finally, an artist should have no illusions about how their work will change the world. The best example I know is Picasso's *Guernica*. Guernica was a small town in Spain where Franco bombed civilians for the first time during the Spanish Civil War. Picasso was in Paris and read about it in a newspaper, hence his painting is in a kind of black and white. It is clearly one of his greatest masterpieces, but did it stop civilian bombing for a millisecond? Not exactly. What followed was Coventry, Dresden, Hiroshima, Nagasaki, and then 9/11. Judged as a political force, Picasso is an abject and total failure. Yet his masterpiece does serve a modest purpose beyond its mastery. The name of Guernica and its fate is at least remembered as a result of this great artist's work.

CHAPTER 15

JULIA WOLFE

Julia Wolfe: I was in a dance class in Ann Arbor. I was laying on my back, stretching, and this music came on. I was like, "Wow! What kind of music is that?" It was *Music for 18 Musicians*. I was collaborating with this fantastic dance company, a collective of four women, writing music for them. I was just stunned by this music. I had never heard anything like it before. This was while I was an undergrad at the University of Michigan. I was listening to things like the Talking Heads, and some Ligeti, some George Crumb. But I hadn't heard any Reich. Why hadn't I heard it before? The music school shunned it at the time.

Steve Reich: What year was that?

JW: I was there in the late '70s, early '80s.

SR: They definitely wouldn't have been playing it, no way.

JW: But the dancers were super hip to your music. They had discovered it, were totally into it, and were dancing to it.

SR: The dancers were ahead of the music department?

JW: Oh, yeah.

SR: So, I heard a lot of your pieces. As you know, *Lick* was a big favorite, and *Early That Summer*, a string quartet with an incredible slow movement/fade out. Is it an ending or is it a movement? What would you say?

JW: It's an ending. A very long ending (*laughs*). I think of it as a kind of an after-resonance.

SR: All right, jumping way ahead, we get to the piece for which you won the Pulitzer Prize, *Anthracite Fields*. I was very, very moved. I heard it in…

JW: In Zankel, I think.

SR: In Zankel Hall, right. And Beryl mentioned to me that it was much stronger there because of the scale and intimacy of the hall in relationship to the visuals.

JW: Yeah.

SR: I remember telling you about it and you said something about how the autobiographical documentary material was somehow tied into my own work. I wonder, what did you mean by that?

JW: There are so many connections, so many elements in your work that inspired this new direction for me—starting with early works like *Come Out*, *It's Gonna Rain*, up to *Different Trains* and into the video-opera pieces with Beryl. First of all, I became fascinated by texts. The beauty of using everyday speech, someone talking and saying something off the cuff, or saying something personal...so different from poetry or from most librettos written by writers. You were finding the beauty in ordinary speech. That was really striking to me. This became full-blown when you began to incorporate interviews in the large-scale works with Beryl—*The Cave* and *Three Tales*. Embracing natural everyday speech was one thing. But also, the unique way you found to tell history, to tell stories—I was really fascinated by that. It's a very personal telling. People were telling you their stories, their opinions. There was something very direct in that—a way of understanding an issue from different perspectives, of understanding our time. Those are the first two things that come to mind. But also, how you use the voice. That you want to hear the words. That you wanted the natural voice, a pure sound. In classical music that sound is generally associated with early music, but of course it's the voice of folk and rock music. Maybe not always in rock. When you want to hear the words you need a voice that has clarity, a voice that is speaking to you. That was huge—a huge realization for me. I have a strong background in folk music, but welcoming this into classical music was a breath of fresh air. Also, it was interesting to me how in large ensemble pieces you used the voice like an instrument. Again, with a pure and natural sound. Well, there are so many things I took away from listening to your music, but these are the first things that come to mind with this question—the use of the voice, the kind of text, and how to tell a history. This is all very different from contemporary opera where singers play roles, become characters—this person is Moses, and that singer is Cleopatra. You were telling stories in a very different way.

SR: It's funny, I just had a long talk with Micaela Haslam, who is a singer in London I've worked with a lot. We were discussing her training as a singer and we were discussing vocal style and how she felt that opera just didn't suit her voice, that kind of vocal production. When you were dealing with the chorus in *Anthracite Fields*, were there solo voices? I don't remember. Were there solo voices in *Anthracite Fields* or is it all chorus?

JW: The only solo moments are sung by the instrumentalists—the Bang on a Can All-Stars. Mark Stewart (guitarist) sings the John L. Lewis speech in kind of call-and-response with the men in the choir. They are all representing Lewis's words—but Mark leads the way.

SR: Well, I know *he* wasn't operatically trained!

JW: No, he's pretty rock 'n' roll in that movement. And the other solo in the piece is sung by the cellist. In the performance you saw, that was Ashley Bathgate, who was singing and playing. Ashley had this wonderful impish way of singing. Actually, the first time I heard Ashley sing was on tour in a karaoke bar in the Midwest. She got up and sang "These Boots Are Made for Walkin'." I was like, "Oh, she can sing! She's sassy." And that second movement of *Anthracite Fields*, "Breaker Boys," is sassy. These are the only two solos in the piece.

SR: Did you have to discuss vocal style with the choir, or was what they did naturally what you wanted?

JW: Well, choirs these days are so exciting. The choirs I have worked with can, and generally do, sing with a clear sound. Also, they function as a collective—which means that the singers' aim isn't to make a big individual sound. A choir is about singing together, about blending. There is a wonderful sense of community. I've had great experiences working with choirs. It's a whole new era—choirs are game to take on challenging work. The musicianship, the counting, are on such a high level. I first worked with the Mendelssohn Club choir, Trinity Wall

Street, LA Master Chorale, great choruses in Europe, and then more recently with The Crossing. All of these singers are very comfortable singing with the natural voice. Once in a while I might need to say, "Can we pull back on the vibrato." But then there are times when a warm vibrato is welcome. I'll write in the score "Like a folk song," or I'll have certain indications that ask for nonclassical sound—and no rolled *R*s, for sure. I really want to hear those words. In almost every rehearsal, the main feedback I give is about understandability—"Can I hear more consonants? Can I hear the words more clearly?" You can't miss a word of Joni Mitchell. (I know all the words to her songs.) So, why not ask to hear the words in the music I write?

SR: With *Fire in my mouth,* you had a whole different cup of tea because you had to deal with the orchestra. Was that the first time you'd dealt with orchestra?

JW: I have written for orchestra periodically over the years. But this was definitely a huge challenge, and these are hotshot players! Well, I've worked with many great players, but there is something about the experience of stepping into a major orchestra that feels different. This was the first time working on that scale—a large in-depth work, with lots of moving parts. There's a chorus of thirty-six women (The Crossing), and a chorus of 110 teenage girls (The Young People's Chorus of New York), visual projections by Jeff Sugg, director Anne Kauffman, and scissors. A lot going on.

SR: Yes.

JW: It was a big ask.

SR: And you got it.

JW: I got it, somehow, I got it (*laughs*). I had to go in and say, "You know, this piece would be really cool if 110 girls came down the aisles." The young women of the girls' chorus were roughly the same age as many of the young women who perished in the factory fire. It really was just incredible that they said yes (*laughs*). Better to plan for these forces more ahead of time, I've learned that. I had so much support for the project. Deborah Borda jumped right in and got behind it. I was truly gratified that it all came together.

SR: So, *Anthracite* is basically the Bang on a Can All-Stars. You knew them personally and musically. The orchestra is a whole different thing.

JW: With the orchestra, one can have the experience that the musicians need to "clock in." My experience was that the musicians didn't simply "clock in." They responded to the subject. They understood why I would ask for a special extended technique to make a certain sound that was a part of painting the history, of conveying the power of the tragedy. I also think that they responded to the expertise of the women's choir, and to the amazing teenage girls singing. Actually, it was very interesting, you wouldn't think this would happen in New York City, but there was a musician in the orchestra whose daughter sang in the girls' choir. I would imagine this being more likely to happen in a small town. That was great. The women of The Crossing are so top-notch. They totally devoured the piece. And they were completely open to movement, costume, theater. I think the orchestra players observed this and the vibe I got was "We're making this theatrical experience together." There were some humorous moments. The score asks for the string players to whip their bows in the air (*imitates swift air sound*). Well, those bows are very expensive, but I'm sure they brought an extra bow with them because there's also a bit of *col legno* in the piece. Not always the most popular thing to put in a piece. At first, the bow whipping in the air was done very gently (*imitates gentle sound*). I said to Jaap [van Zweden], "It's not this, it's like (*imitates a loud swift sound*)." And he responded, "Well, the bows, you know." (*laughs*) And then he said, "All right, I'll give them that note." And I said, "Actually, can I hear it now?" And then they did it. There are certain sounds I use in the piece that aren't typical for the instruments. I only use extended technique when I need to—for special meaning and purpose. In one section, the instruments emulate the sound of hundreds of sewing machines. The string players take the bow and press down hard as they drag it across the strings, while muting the pitch with the left hand. The result is (*imitates short, crisp, repeated K sound*). I don't know why, but it creates this repeated machine sound. The percussionists roll on the rims of drums to create clackity waves of sound. I had fun creating some very literal associations to the factory sound. The performers were game. They understood what I was doing.

SR: Right. When the New York Philharmonic just did *Music for Ensemble and Orchestra*, I had the same feeling. I'm getting older but they're getting younger.

JW: (*laughs*) That's true.

SR: And the attitude is entirely different now. I guess I completely relate to what you were saying. In other words, you were asking something reasonable that had to do with the matter at hand, and it wasn't gratuitous or something weird that no one would really care about or even know what it was. Once you used the scissors, I mean the scissors was like the big sound, right?

JW: I love a good pair of scissors.

SR: But that was the chorus?

JW: Yes, the women's chorus played the scissors. This use of "real" sounds also relates to what I heard in *Different Trains*, in *The Cave*, and in *Three Tales*. In these pieces you're using samples. But just the idea that a real-world sound belongs in the music, that was beautiful to me. This idea is not entirely new, but the way you integrate the sound and pitch was ear-opening. One of my favorite things in *Different Trains* are the train whistles. What a powerful and beautiful sound.

SR: Yeah.

JW: Every time the train whistle comes in, I think, "Oh, yeah, there it is again." Why is it so moving? I don't know if it's associative, or it's the harmony of the whistle. I just love it. Maybe this was in the back of my consciousness when I thought to use scissors.

SR: There's no other way to get a train sound than a train sound and there's no other way to get scissors than with scissors. (*laughs*)

JW: (*laughs*) Right.

SR: I remember going, when there used to be record stores, there was a big record store in my neighborhood right down on Broadway near City Hall called J&R. You probably remember that.

JW: Oh, yeah. J&R, sure.

SR: Would you believe I walked in there when I was looking for this kind of stuff and they had a bin called "train sounds" and there were a few hundred records in there!

JW: That's amazing.

And I also have to say that *Tehillim* has been a really important piece for me. For a lot of reasons. Again, the voices are clear. The music is so joyful—the counterpoint is so joyful, and the rhythmic singing really struck me. Over the years, people have joked that singers can't count. Well, guess what! In *Tehillim* they are counting and it's spectacular. On a more personal note, when I was a young composer living in Ann Arbor, there were moments when self-doubt crept in and I would wonder, "Why am I doing this? Can I do this?" I would literally put *Tehillim* on the turntable and listen to it. Am I saying it was my therapy? It kind of was. I would listen to it, and I would think, "Of course I want to write music. Music is amazing!" I did that whenever I felt blue about composing.

CHAPTER 16

NICO MUHLY

Nico Muhly: So, we're talking about three things: *The Cave,
Ensemble and Orchestra* and *Traveler's Prayer*. I have the most questions about *The Cave*.

Steve Reich: Great. But first let me preface by saying that *The Cave*
is a total collaboration with Beryl Korot, who did all the video,
and together we made the decisions about the libretto, and everything else from our first discussions of the piece to its very end.

NM: What I wanted to ask you about is something that I never
really noticed before but it's the way that you introduce the language of the piece, which is to say that it starts with pure percussion, right? Relatively unpitched, doubling the typing. And
then we get pure speaking voice with no music, and then we get
the sung scriptures, and we add more and more layers.

SR: That's true as to what happens, but we weren't trying to
introduce the language of the piece. We were introducing the
story itself, from Genesis, and typing it out rhythmically seemed
the best way to do that right in the very first scene. Our techni-

cal designer, Ben Rubin from the MIT Media Lab, wrote software so that if musicians tapped computer keyboards, that would trigger a prerecorded syllable on each tap. So, *The Cave* begins: "Now Sar-ai A-bram's wife bore him no child-ren," German translation, French translation, "and she had a hand-maid an E-gyp-tian and her name was Ha-gar" and it goes on to Ishmael and Isaac. First it's just the sound of typing, then typing and clapping, then typing, clapping, and claves, and finally add kick drums when we get to the Angel announcing, "And he will be a man of the wild" and so on.

Scene 2 is Ephraim Isaac, who is a half-Ethiopian, half-Yemenite Jew currently teaching Semitic languages at Princeton. And he begins speaking, with no musical accompaniment, "Who is Abraham? Abraham for me is my ancestor, my very own personal ancestor." He goes on to quote from memory all the generations from Adam to Noah to Abraham to Isaac to Jacob to the twelve tribes and then from his great-great-great-grandfather to himself. This is a way of introducing the basic material in *The Cave*. What cave? The Cave of Machpelah in the town of Hebron about thirty miles south of Jerusalem. Most Westerners have never heard of it. It is described in Genesis and is the burial place for Abraham and Sarah, Isaac and Rebecca, Jacob and Leah, and according to the mystical tradition, Adam and Eve.

NM: I guess what I found so interesting about *The Cave* was that if you pretend that we're all focused and we're all going to get to the non-sacrifice of Isaac, get to the mountaintop, and that that movement has the most different kind of techniques in it, and the tempo ratchets up and up and up. I found that structure really quite operatic in the traditional, old-fashioned sense. All the things are focused on the heart of the drama. But I like knowing you didn't plan it out that way.

SR: Well, you're certainly right that the most dramatic part of the piece is the non-sacrifice of Isaac in act 3. But, as you know, *The Cave* is structured on five questions: Who for you is Abraham? Who for you is Sarah? Hagar, Ishmael, and Isaac. In act 1 we ask Israeli Jews, in act 2 Palestinian Muslims, and in act 3 Americans. The real focus of the piece, from beginning to end, is the answers given by these three groups of interviewees to those same five questions. What you find is, both Israelis and Palestinians know very well who these biblical and Koranic figures are. Abraham, Sarah, Hagar, Ishmael, and Isaac are part of their cultural life whether they're religious or not. However, many Americans either do not know who they are or have only a very vague idea about their existence. They've lost touch with or rejected the biblical tradition in our civilization.

So, at one point in act 3, the fashion writer Valerie Steele quite accurately observes, "Very difficult for modern people to conceive of."

NM: It's so radical, both hearing you talk about it but also through my own experience. The character of Abraham is such a strange and radical person and that version from the Midrash where Isaac says, "You should bind me." I had never heard that in my childhood experience, I just remember being so struck by the inclusion of that, and when I was preparing for this, I found myself deep in various Midrashim which include that very intense detail. I'm wondering if you can talk about that.

SR: Well, in the Torah, Isaac says, "Behold the flint and the wood, but where is the lamb for the burnt offering," and Abraham replies, "G-d will see to the lamb for the burnt offering, my son," and the text continues, "and the two of them walked on together." The implication being that they both understand what's about to happen. As one of the interviewees, Saul Rosenberg, comments, "Isaac asks, says look, father, I'm a young man, when I see that knife, I don't know what I'll do. Why don't you bind me." Saul is just retelling the Midrash you mentioned.

NM: Where is the lamb, right.

SR: When Abraham says, "G-d will see to the lamb," I think Isaac gets it. He gets it but he doesn't leave or freak out, he absorbs that. I couldn't absorb it, you couldn't absorb it, but he absorbs it. That puts an extremely different light on the whole story.

NM: For you, it seems to ratchet up the intensity of that moment, which is one of the great thrills for me, just as a listener of that piece. That movement is so exciting, and it feels like a countdown to that moment. It kind of reminds me of *Three Tales*, which has that countdown at the end of "Bikini." A very, very dramatic treatment of the text. I'm obsessed with that part.

SR: You're right about "Bikini," and the binding of Isaac in act 3, it's extremely intense, more than anything else in *The Cave*— but we didn't set it as the destination we were driving at, at all. The direction both thematic and harmonic in the first two acts is the physical Cave itself, actually the Mosque built above the Cave of Machpelah and the A-minor drone one hears from the quiet conversations and random little noises in that large space, which is the result of the architecture of the room. I knew that the first and second acts, video and sound, would end inside that space. Then comes the third act, where there is no Cave. We're in America, where no one knows about the Cave. No more destination of A minor, either. So, the real end is not the binding of Isaac, dramatic as that may be, but rather where Abraham serves food to the three angels who appear as wanderers in the desert. For me, that's certainly the best music in the piece. It's very calm and simply melodic, now in C minor, ending with the words, "And he stood by them, under the tree, as they ate."

Now, I know you see things differently. You've written operas because that particular dramatic impetus is part of who you are, but it isn't in me to do that. That's why Beryl and I had to work out a different kind of music theater. The documentary nature of *The Cave*, the interviews being the source of the libretto, each interviewee's speech melody being the source of the music, is what gets to me. That's what gets my juices going. Every time you see one of the interviewees, they are set within an aural and visual portrait of themselves taken completely from the interview situation in which they were placed.

NM: Right, I see what you mean. Documentary creates the drama. So, listen, going back to what the voices do in *The Cave*, I noticed that they basically imitate the speakers for most of it. But then you get to Khalil and that poet says, "We call," and he goes down a descending third, and then the voices, for the first time, I think, go up. They go the opposite direction of the speaker, who had preceded them. And that clicks for me as a turning point in the piece, but I'm wondering if you planned that.

SR: Definitely spontaneous. Araid Naim is explaining what Ibrahim is called, which is translated "friend of G-d." My rising D-E "We call," is a call! Calling out for help, guidance. It's not a turning point in the piece, as I see it. Just a spontaneous response to what Naim said.

In terms of the singing voices, in the first act the singers can sing the Torah. You can debate that, I debated it in my own mind because it can be said that the real melodies of the Torah are only the cantillations found within different cultures. In the second act, you are not permitted to sing the Koran, and since that is enforced rigorously, I didn't set it. So, as you noticed, in the second act the singing voices comment on the spoken voices but not on the text.

NM: I'm now going to change tactics and get nerdy for a second. Let me ask the really technical thing: keeping the pulse together is something… I've listened to this piece like twelve times in the last week to get ready. Keeping the pulse together must have been a big…

SR: Deal.

NM: Deal and obstacle and question.

SR: Absolutely. The idea of following the speakers and letting the speakers determine the tempo began in *Different Trains*. Because there I'm dealing with the Holocaust and Virginia, my nanny, who basically served the role of my mother.

NM: Right.

SR: So, there's a reverential tone there of "Don't mess with this, I know you could put it into the computer and do XYZ, but don't." In other words, let it tell you rather than you tell it. And that mentality carried over to *The Cave* because the subject matter is really intense, religious, and thousands of years old.

NM: Exactly. I see what you mean, if you treat it as sacred text, with *Different Trains*, too. Speaking as a composer who's set a lot of found text—from the newspaper, from TV, from transcripts of trials—I know the feeling of coming across a piece of text where immediately you know what you're going to do with it. With you, you must have heard some sentences, some utterances, in those interviews that must have been such a gift to you. To me, still, I feel like one of the high-water marks of expressivity is the last couple minutes of *Different Trains*, "And when she stopped singing, they said, 'more, more,'" and the gift is the specific way that she says it. It's so musical and you could never touch it.

SR: Right.

NM: Let's go back to the pulse in *The Cave* for a second. With this, again, when I'm listening back to it, there's a way in which the ear forgets about it, you know, the violin that's always going. But there's also the constantness of the pulse and when it's in the clave versus the violin versus whatever, is that something that arose out of a technical need to have it or was there...? Do you know what I'm asking?

SR: Well, first off, there is no audible pulse in *The Cave*. There is a click track that only the conductor and sometimes the percussion hears, but the audience hears only the sometimes prerecorded sampler string sound doubling the first entrance of a new speaking voice, so as to establish the new tempo. That was one of the primary technical challenges of the piece. We solved it one way in *Different Trains*, and in *The Cave* it's similar. Basically, you have one speaker following another in the sections where you have the "talking heads." So how can a musician go on a dime from one tempo to an unrelated tempo accurately and comfortably? The answer is: they can't. And don't pretend they can.

NM: Right. (*laughs*)

SR: So, what can you do? Well, you can have them all tacit and prerecord a sampled violin, cello, or claves for that, doubling the new speaking voice long enough for them to hear the new tempo. The conductor and musicians all feel the new tempo, and then two, three, or four bars later, they're in. In the last scenes of acts 1 and 2, inside the Cave Mosque, there is a very quiet pulsing violin throughout the mysterious scene. That's all in the score.

NM: Yeah, the count off.

SR: In *Different Trains*, sections are fairly long staying in one speaker's tempo. In *The Cave*, because it's much more discursive, there are rapid changes. So, it's more difficult to play. And you're absolutely right. It's the primary rehearsal problem to be solved and why you need several rehearsals to feel comfortable with the piece.

NM: I guess my other question about choosing the sentences in *Different Trains, The Cave, WTC 9/11, Three Tales*, can you remember what proportion of stuff got left on the cutting-room floor? In terms of how many hours and hours and hours of interviews you conducted versus how much is in? Are we talking a fraction of a percent or...?

SR: I think you're about right. Probably a fraction of a percent. Beryl made the first cut discarding probably about 95% of the total. Then I went through that. What I did first was play it a couple times so I could write down in my music notebook the basic pitch structure and then record it on a floppy disk. I only picked the ones that really caught my ear. So again, I was doing a rough cut and at the end of the day there were a couple of pages of musical fragments in my music notebook and a pile of floppy disks, because that was the age of floppy disks. (*laughs*)

NM: It was the past, right? (*laughs*)

SR: Hey, you weren't even around! (*laughs*)

NM: I was nine years old when this was happening.

SR: In any event, I had to then figure out a way to knit together these short spoken melodies so they made both musical and verbal sense.

NM: Now I'm addressing the reader, but it's easy to gloss over how much work this must have taken before notes were even involved. What an incredible technical feat it is just to get to that point that you were just describing, the end of the day with the basic musical structures. There's an incredible amount below the tip of the iceberg, which I think is really important to acknowledge with a project like this. It's not something that composers deal with often, because we're so concerned with making something new, making something original, and the precompositional exercises can be purely musical, or mathematical, which we all do to a certain extent—but with these works, you and Beryl really become the caretakers of other people's stories, and archivists, which requires an unreal amount of sensitivity and even more time and work.

SR: I appreciate you bringing that out, but I don't want a medal for that, because, in the end, all that matters is the final result. But as a matter of history, yes, it was an enormous amount of work because first of all there were three separate field trips for three separate acts. Each of which was its own kettle of fish with its own problems.

NM: Did you write them split out, or did you write them 1–2–3 very quickly? Was there any lag between the compositions?

SR: I don't think we finished the first act by the time we made the trip to record the Palestinians. The same with working on act 2. Before being done, we took the trip to Austin to record Americans for act 3.

NM: I first heard this piece in 1993 or whenever the CD came out and I was twelve years old. I remember, when you get to that Carl Sagan part, that is an act of such crazy virtuosity of just the transcription of this thing. It's an amazing feat. I remember laughing, and when I teach the piece now, I am always sure to point out how funny it is because his delivery is funny, and it's such a technical victory.

SR: It is funny. He was a master public speaker.

NM: It's hysterically funny and it's so well transcribed.

SR: Thank you.

NM: When you heard him utter that, when he said that near you, were you already thinking, "Okay, I'm definitely going to keep this," or did you wait again?

SR: No, I mean, I'm the interviewer. So psychologically I'm engaged with the person I'm talking with, like I'm engaged with you now, only more so because then we were in the same room. I didn't have another part of my brain analyzing what was going to make the final edit. It was only when we went back that I listened through what we recorded and found "Aha! This is a prize response."

NM: The other one I felt was a gift—you know what I mean by a gift, it's an amazing piece of fish or meat that you got at the grocery store.

SR: Yes, but a gift is a better idea, because you can look at it as either chance occurrences, or you can say it's a providential gift. It's happening all the time, it's normal, and it's a question of how you understand the normal.

NM: Right. If you acknowledge it, exactly.

SR: You're not changing anything out there, it's all science (*laughs*). But it's also a gift at the same time.

NM: Taking you back however many years, thinking about act 2, the end of scene 1, the first Muslim thing. He says, "Peace upon him, peace upon him," and then you write this amazing chorale almost (*demonstrates chords*). All those reactions to it in the strings and then the four-part singers doing it. That is such a magical moment, I'm wondering if you could talk about that.

What I'm thinking of is the end of that scene where he says, "Abraham is our father, peace upon him," and then the choir says, "Peace." I'm just curious, if you could tell me about those chords. It felt like an exciting harmonic change.

SR: Well, they're all built around the dominant eleventh chord I used way back in 1970 for *Four Organs*, only now we're in B-flat major instead of A. The synth plays that exact cluster E-flat, F, G, A, B-flat with either E-flat or F in the bass. The strings and voices are not voiced as a cluster at all, but are fairly wide with two chords on E-flat and one on F. Simply put, it's just subdominant to dominant and finally to tonic, only tonic is now B-flat minor.

NM: I guess what I want to ask you about is that the music feels like a benediction. It starts to feel more like sacred music at this moment to me. Of course, I think much of your music is secretly sacred music, but this in particular feels like the harmonic language opens up in this incredibly generous way to Abraham. I don't know if there's any comment you need to make on it (*laughs*), I just think it's really great!

SR: Well, clusters with an octave on the bottom are very typical, as you may have noticed (*laughs*). But setting the word *peace* in this context obviously creates some intensity.

NM: The chords the choir sings felt special to me in a way that, again, I'm rewinding to thirteen-year-old me. This whole area, from there until the end of the scene.

SR: The common thread here is that there's a reverence for Abraham, and when a line is said which resonates with Jews, Muslims, and the Christians, it's particularly strong.

NM: It just feels like the music really respects that. At that specific moment it feels like a bigger light has come on, if that makes sense. I was thinking about the line towards the end where it says, "The stakes are pretty high in a place like that," right?

SR: That was Francis Peters from NYU, I think. Now we're talking act 3?

NM: Now we're talking act 3, which leads me again to this kind of reverence, there's this kind of expansion. I'm really curious about how you wrote this melody at the end from "The Lord appeared to Abraham…"

SR: I think that's the best music in the piece.

NM: Absolutely. And what's so exciting for me is that, inadvertently or not, you've started with this highly stylized percussion music, all eighths and quarters. Then, as we discussed, the voices imitate that, and then they start extending the lengths of their notes. Then they imitate the voices, and then they start commenting on the voices. Then you start combining all those techniques, which brings us up to the near sacrifice. After that, you get to the end, and all that secco material from the top has vanished and we're left with this delicious melody. It's a proper tune. "And he raised his eyes and looked and behold three men standing by him." For me, you had had three men standing by him in act 1, right?

SR: Exactly, that's directly from Genesis in act 1 and it's brought back at the end.

NM: And then here we have it again (*plays melody*), radically transformed. It's so great. When you were writing that, were you like, "Okay, I got the melody."

SR: Yes. You know the feeling very well. When I was writing that, I knew I had what I needed, and I had to keep it going, and finally it was right. It was the right thing. This is at the end of this very long piece and here is this very simple music. Abraham runs to the three men who are actually angels in human form. He does this on the day that he circumcises himself and he's ninety-nine years old. He's in pain but he lives to do kindness and hospitality for others. That's all that matters to him. So, G-d sends three strangers/angels so that Abraham can do this. "And he stood by them, under the tree, as they ate." It seemed the perfect ending.

NM: At this point, all the technological information has kind of vanished, the melody is what's guiding us, and then you check back into the real world. "All I remember is a long, thin grate in the ground."

SR: Yes, exactly.

NM: The camera move is so big here. It really feels like you're zoomed out and you're looking at this beautiful image of the tree and this beautiful image of the physicality.

SR: Actually, there is no image of a tree. While this music is being played and sung throughout, what you're actually looking at is five screens. What Beryl does, when there's a talking head, is, she zooms in on a part of a tie, or a dress or a floral vase that's sitting next to the person speaking. That's then multiplied to two, three or more screens so that the speaker is embedded visually in a landscape of themselves. You don't see Abraham and you certainly don't see the three strangers. In this case, she intercuts the text from Genesis with an American, Saul Rosenberg, speaking about his visit to Hebron. He says, "I expected a Cave. All I remember is a narrow, thin grate in the ground and I was pointed by the guide, who said, 'Here, underneath is, uh, Abraham, there's Sarah, there's Adam and Eve, so the tradition goes.'" The tension between the present documented reality in the video and the ancient text from Genesis generates energy. Abraham, Sarah, Isaac, all these biblical figures, they're only alive if they're alive in the minds of those we spoke to, or anybody else, for that matter. Otherwise, they really aren't around, they're gone. They've truly perished. In the first two acts they are very much alive, very much in conflict, very much being reinterpreted differently. And in the third act, "Abraham Lincoln High School. High on a hilltop 'mid sand and sea." (laughs)

NM: Exactly. Or like "Call me Ishmael" from Moby Dick, right?

SR: Exactly, because that's the truth about how they survive, and Melville, of course, is a very biblical author. Moby Dick would be inconceivable without his knowledge of the Bible.

NM: And he's not called Ishmael for nothing.

SR: That's right, and Ahab's not Ahab for nothing, either.

NM: Exactly. Well now, just speaking very personally, my religious upbringing was complicated. I went to the JCC when I was little, but I was also a chorister, which brings with it its own resonances.

SR: Right, I've gathered that in our getting to know each other.

NM: When I say that a lot of your music registers to me as sacred music, I think that's something I stole from you pretty explicitly, where there's a way to keep this one thing always in sight. And what was interesting for me when I first got to know this piece, but also as I know it now quite intimately, is that there's a way to treat it as sacred music in which the piece itself is this vessel that contains, as you say, the living memory of the biblical figures. And that it invites you to learn more, as I did in 1994 and as I did two weeks ago. We've talked about this in *Three Tales*, too, where certain Midrashim offer entirely new ways to think about and meditate on the stories we thought we knew. And that's what's fascinating about it. It doesn't say, "This is the version of the story that we're telling," but invites you to really peel the onion and take the detours necessary to deepen your knowledge. It's almost like you can finally reconnect your umbilical cord as an American listening to it.

SR: Yes. You can become engaged. One of the qualities of *The Cave* is that many points of view are given by numerous, very diverse people. So, it's a very different way to present "religious subject matter." Of course, I admire great contemporary settings of Christian Latin texts like Passio by Arvo Pärt. In music like that, one can focus on the music, text and the quality of performance. In *The Cave*, those same possibilities are there and the video helps you also engage with the subject matter in a very different way. Your attention flickers back and forth between what's down the block and what's thousands of miles away, what happened yesterday and what happened thousands of years ago. I wish it was up and running more often. Hopefully, as technology moves along, it will become easier and easier to present the piece.

NM: I think it's a tragedy that it's not done more, obviously. I think it's such an important work, and just to connect back to Arvo Pärt, something that I try to do in my own sacred music is, as you say, to not insist that this is a story. I say that my mission statement is to create a musical space that encourages people to look upwards. And that's the job. Even with *Different Trains* that's the case because it ends with such a poetic and oblique vision of the thing. It invites you to think about it more, and every time you hear that piece, you're never being told anything, but you're invited to think about it in a way that, I think, is very hard to achieve. Which is why I think *The Cave* should be performed every five minutes! (*laughs*) The only other examples I can think of might be *The Death of Klinghoffer*, which is an opera that seems like it has a much more pointed message, or possible messages. I'm just thinking of things that take place within the Israel–Palestinian context. The only other thing I can think of is Philip [Glass's] *Akhenaten*, where it ends with a tour guide being like, "There it is, it's all ruins." You've tapped into this thing that's incredibly dramatic without being dramatic. I think about it a lot. It's some kind of magic trick that you did.

SR: I'm glad you like it. Now, you proposed we next discuss *Music for Ensemble and Orchestra*, but I thought we might first talk a bit about your piece *No Uncertain Terms*.

NM: Well, it explicitly borrows from you (*laughs*) in the sense of a cycle of harmonies like in *Music for 18 Musicians* and it was for a concert that you were curating, so I thought I would just lean into that and figure out a pleasing cycle of chords that flow into one another but then deploy them very, very quickly. Unlike *Music for 18 Musicians*.

SR: When I listened to it, *chaconne* seemed like a possible description. Of course, chaconnes are usually very short harmonic cycles and you had fourteen chords, but, as you say, because you pace them quickly you can hear the whole as a repeating cycle. They're very beautiful harmonies, and when I heard it I thought, "Why didn't I write that?" (*laughs*)

NM: (*laughs*) Well, thank you.

SR: Years ago I heard Alvin Lucier's *I Am Sitting in a Room* and I thought, "Why didn't I think of that?" And Alvin had heard *Come Out*. Cross-pollination is actually a wonderful thing.

NM: It is, yeah. I feel the same way often. It's cross-pollination intergenerationally, and that's really interesting, too. You inherit traits from the people who came before you but you then process it in your own way. With that piece, I had designed it for a team of my friends, which is something that you've been doing for years. The core of it was a pair of pianos, which allowed me to do a lot of canons and things that made exploring the cycle really exciting. Something I was thinking about when I was writing it was that I have a chord, right, and of course I can space it differently, but there are always a couple more notes I can add to it that shade it. That changes the emotional content of the chord slightly.

SR: Absolutely.

NM: And this is something that you do all the time. One of the things that I also did was I built it around many homages, to your music, but also around this motet by William Byrd. What I was trying to figure out how to do—and at this point, I thought this is actually a really difficult compositional challenge, right? To fuse these universes inside this harmonic structure that I had already created and inside this ensemble that's very not choral (*laughs*). I was thinking about ways that this one melody from the Byrd could become a sort of ritornello but pop up in different ways. Super displaced and hidden but also very explicitly delivered.

SR: You really discovered Byrd when you were a chorister as a kid, right? So your whole experience with early music is like second nature to you and has a lot to do with the way you write.

NM: It really does. The idea that you could make music that has, not just a social function, but is made for worship. It's not done for applause. It's done at really weird times of day. That piece of music is not something that you would ever hear at eight p.m. in a concert hall, right? You hear it at 11:45 on a Sunday or four on a Tuesday afternoon or something. There's something very moving to me about that, that you're moving through this cycle of music-making as a child and it's all kind of functional and very, very beautiful. It's quite athletic, actually, because you're learning one thing for Tuesday, and then on Tuesday night, you're singing the thing you're learning for Sunday. It's a real kind of racehorse activity.

SR: Work to do. Work to do. I always think about Bach writing the cantatas like that. It's due, you know, it's got to be on the stands on Sunday. And I think that's supremely healthy, I mean, isn't that a marvelous thing where religion isn't foisted on you. It's something that means a great deal to you personally and to those who live around you and so you accept the discipline which demands that you produce music. It seems that attitude was somewhat lost somewhere after 1750. I don't think we can quite understand the period of Bach and earlier if we don't factor in the fact that their lives were not like the lives we lead at all.

NM: There was a huge hole in my musical education, which was that in the Anglican tradition, you're learning things from 1502 until basically the death of Bach. And even that's a little later than a lot of people go. And then you pick back up with Howells and Britten and people who lived well into the second part of the twentieth century. There's a big hole with the Romantics and one of the things I found so difficult when I was studying at Juilliard was this constant connection between the biography of the Romantic composer and the music. And that we were encouraged to suffer along (*laughs*) along with the composer. We were encouraged to really think about Brahms's unrequited love and how crazy Beethoven must have been. With Bach it's the most ravishing music but it had to be on the music stands. A bassoonist needed to look at his part.

SR: Right. And if you read the Bach Reader, it's requests for money, requests for firewood, requests for better musicians. And that's it, you know? That's the story.

NM: (*laughs*) Exactly. I think in my music-making now, I still write a lot of music for use, in a sacred context or for another context. But also, it kind of chilled me out from worrying too much about reception in terms of a concert hall. It's easy as a composer to get really anxious, like, "Did they like it? Were people clapping?" And thinking about some of the most moving moments that I've had as a composer, like sure there are big things, like it's great to have written an opera or whatever, but walking into a chapel somewhere like in Cambridge or some-

thing and hearing people rehearsing your music and not knowing that you're even there. That to me has a magic to it.

SR: Do we have time left for *Music for Ensemble and Orchestra*?

NM: I actually have a good segue. Something you said to me
once, "You have to find what your band is"? And *The Cave* obviously is your band, right? Looking at *Music for Ensemble and
Orchestra*, you put your band in the orchestra.

SR: *(laughs)* Exactly, yes.

NM: So, it's sort of a concerto grosso, in a sense.

SR: Absolutely a concerto grosso. If we go fishing around for
predecessors, we go no further than the Brandenburg Concertos.

NM: Yes, exactly. I listened again to the Brandenburg Concertos when I was preparing, just thinking of other concerti grossi.
Here's a kind of provocative question, and I did an informal poll:
How many orchestra players do you think have your music in
their hands? Just out of curiosity, what's your sense of that?

SR: Well, one thing I can say for sure is that it is a great deal
more than in 1980. I was personally at performances of *Music
for Ensemble and Orchestra* by the LA Philharmonic, the New
York Philharmonic and the San Francisco Orchestra. Even the
concertmasters were all uniformly asking direct matter-of-fact
questions, I didn't feel any "What am I doing here?" kind of
mumblings or unspoken expressions of that, the way I definitely did feel, for example, when *Tehillim* was done in 1986
by the New York Philharmonic. So, I'm eighty-four, but most
orchestral musicians are somewhere between their thirties and
their seventies. So, that means most everyone in the orchestra is

younger than I am. All of the percussionists, a lot of the wood-wind players and some of the string players would be familiar with something of mine along the way.

NM: Exactly. So, I called a bunch of my friends who are in orchestras, and it is really interesting because every percussionist has played your music, that's not even a question. String players, not so much. Some woodwind players may have played *Tehillim*.

SR: Or *New York Counterpoint*.

NM: Exactly. Solo wind players.

SR: Well, basically my whole life I've mostly written for ensembles. And therefore, there's a wide variety of ensembles around the world who are all pretty much in touch with my music in one way or another. My orchestral output has been slim because I wasn't drawn to it intuitively. I don't listen to a great deal of it, outside of Stravinsky and some Ravel. Basically, my musical bookends are before 1750 and after Debussy. The orchestra basically didn't exist before 1750. So, writing for orchestra wasn't something I was dying to do until *Music for Ensemble and Orchestra*, and *Desert Music*, as well, though that was not to write for orchestra. It was to set the poems of William Carlos Williams in a very large way. Now, the piece that preceded *Music for Ensemble and Orchestra* was called *Runner*, and it was scored for an ensemble of nineteen musicians, exactly the same as the ensemble in *Ensemble and Orchestra*. Beryl and I were in LA last winter to visit our son, and we went to the LA Phil for I don't remember what, and I'm looking at the setup, and there is the conductor, and there are the principal strings spread out around him, and right in back of them are the principal winds. And I thought to myself, all you have to do is bring up the pianos which are not too far away and a couple of vibes and that's my ensemble! And

I don't have to special seat them, except for the vibes. If you're going to write for orchestra, write something they can do with a minimum of reseating.

NM: Right.

SR: It felt like "Aha! This is the way I'm supposed to go at it." The rest of the orchestra is basically there to support the ensemble. It's ensemble first, and orchestra, and I believe it succeeds. You're a good judge of orchestral music, and you single out this one.

NM: No, it's great. It has a couple of things that I think, for you, are really exciting. I think the electric bass, the first bass drop where that comes in is thrilling.

SR: By the way, David Lang was there when it was played in New York, and he said, "I learned something." I asked, "What did you learn?" He said, "If I double electric bass and double bass, I'll be able to do all kinds of rhythmic things I can't do now."

NM: Exactly, and I also like that you put it in a weird place in the bar, too. It was exciting. Going back to the orchestral player question, was it the concertmasters playing the solo parts? I assume, right?

SR: It was exactly as they sit. The ensemble strings were the first stand strings. The concertmaster, assistant concertmaster, and then the principal second, etc. And all those first stand players are the ones who get the solo parts in any piece, they're used to doing that. They're all set up so they can easily hear each other and play intricate interlocking parts which for the full orchestra would never work.

NM: Did you find, and again, we don't have to name ensembles or names or where anybody sat, but did you find that any of them had trouble? For instance, this rhythm (*demonstrates on piano*) is a very "you" rhythm, and it's built into my hard drive and any percussionist could read it. I feel like there are a lot of orchestra string players who would not know their way through that rhythm.

SR: Well, I didn't go to first rehearsals. I was trying to minimize my time in travel. The fact is no, I don't remember thinking, "When are they going to get this thing right?" Not at all. Everybody just got it.

NM: Just figured it out, right.

SR: Maybe because of their youth, it's more expressive of the times. In other words, what I was writing was now something that was in the air, i.e., either like something in pop music, or in other music they may have played or heard. So, it's not like they have to only go from Mahler to (*demonstrates melody*).

NM: I ask this because we have this generational divide, but when I work with younger musicians in London, I don't think I could name a single younger musician in London who hasn't played a piece of yours. I'm really interested in what future generation...

SR: Yes, I am, too, Nico. You can bet I am. But if my music is played, and if the musicians who play it love it, and if the audiences love it, then I've succeeded, and whatever amount that happens, I accept that and feel fortunate.

NM: I like knowing that the amount of people who used to play *Music for 18 Musicians* was eighteen people and now it's...a lot more! At the beginning, that's how many people knew that music. And now there's generations of people who could play it from memory. I called Russell Hartenberger, who said that it took a million rehearsals to put *Drumming* together, and that now he can teach it to a group of college students in a weekend. That's such a cool thing. It was nice to see the hybrid thing work in the orchestra.

Another quick question about this thing, you now have a couple pieces that have this deliquescence at the end, that just fades off into the atmosphere. It feels kind of French to me. You were saying Ravel before.

SR: I see what you're saying. Basically, the idea of a fade-out began with *Runner*. It's a five-movement form that I've been addicted to since I was studying the Fourth and Fifth Quartets of Béla Bartók. So, you have ABCBA. And when I got to the fifth movement of *Runner*, I was going back and looking at what I had done, and suddenly it came into my mind (*sings two-note oscillation*), to hell with that, this is what I need.

NM: It's cool! I don't want to say it's a new thing, but I like hearing it dissolve. So, basically, you're saying you had an intuitive sense that this is how it needed to work.

SR: I would have to say, and excuse the use of the word, I had an inspiration. It literally came upon me because I had a plan, and this overrode the plan. Now, *Music for Ensemble and Orchestra* is, in a sense, *Runner: 2*, and that's why we're trying to get them on the same record now, if COVID ever allows that to happen. *Music for Ensemble and Orchestra* is already recorded.

NM: Yes, Bob sent me the master version, it sounds great. Is that the LA Phil doing it?

SR: Yeah, it's LA.

NM: The band sounds good.

So, thinking about resolutions, can we talk about *Traveler's Prayer* for a sec?

SR: Absolutely.

NM: I have a bunch of questions about this piece. How would you describe it, because it feels like it belongs to that kind of Pérotin extended universe of taking melodies...

SR: It's more Renaissance in terms of the lines, no?

NM: The lines themselves, right, exactly. It's got that kind of Renaissance-y motion. But it's incredibly simple and very restrained. And I'm wondering, how would you describe the shape of this thing?

SR: (*laughs*) I think I'll describe it as "A." The essential feeling was, keep the motion going, the same calmness, all the way to the end.

NM: Right, interesting. This is a more sacred music question, *Traveler's Prayer* is something that one utters before any kind of trip, right?

SR: The fine points of the law would be something that's at least three miles away from where you start. But my text is not the actual prayer.

NM: No, exactly, I printed out the prayer, this is a different thing.

SR: This is three ancillary verses frequently attached to the prayer. In other words, you've said the prayer and now you add these thoughts that feel attached to the basic prayer. Actually, the first text, "Behold, I send an angel before you to guard you on the way and to lead you to the place that I have prepared," appears in the last movement of *WTC 9/11*. Similarly with the last text, "The Eternal will guard your departure and your arrival from now till the end of time," which also appears in the last movement of *WTC 9/11*. The second movement is different. It takes a single line and permutes it: "To your lifeline I cling, Eternal, I cling, Eternal to your lifeline, Eternal, to your lifeline I cling." Like drawing a protective band around yourself.

NM: Right.

Oh, I have one more question that I wrote down about *Traveler's Prayer*. I listened first without looking at the score. How did you generate, how did you decide the length of the line when things get longer and longer and longer? Was that completely intuitive or are you adding up seconds?

SR: Completely intuitive. I wanted to have the vertical relationships working at all times. I wanted the intervals, the harmonic world to stay exactly right to my ear, and I extended whatever note was in question, to harmonize with the new one I was bringing in. There's no math there.

NM: I've coached a couple of your pieces with ensembles and, yes, the rhythm is obviously so important. But the tunes have to be tunes. You have to treat it like melodic information, which I think is again so nice to have it exposed in *Traveler's Prayer*, where the rhythm is not part of it. It's about the line. I think that's worth touching on.

SR: In *Traveler's Prayer*, it stands or falls on the interlocking of the melodies themselves. Even when the vibes come in, they're just color, they're not timekeepers at all.

NM: Right, exactly. There's something so satisfying about how long you wait to have the female voices come in, too.

SR: Well, part of it was a religious consideration. When the Torah is chanted in the synagogue, it's traditionally one man's voice, so that definitely encouraged me to write just for the two tenors throughout the long first movement. The women enter near the end of the second movement, and the last movement text is a psalm for which we have no traditions about singing, so there the women and men sing throughout. It's interesting since, as you know, I often write for women's voices alone. I more or less kept all voices in a comfortable range on the staff to maintain the calm focus of the piece.

NM: Yeah, that's right. I was just very moved by it. It felt like a really interesting meditative piece. I'm sure that people are going to find it a very useful piece of music, in a way. In the same way that I found *Proverb* when I was a kid—really inviting to think about, just thinking about what actually is a melody and what does it mean and what can it mean? Elongation is meaningful. You don't need to do a Brahmsian development section. You can do these other permutations and transformations that will still have an emotional effect, as you do here.

By the way, with this piece I'm wondering, for my own curiosity, when does it premiere? After there's a vaccine?

SR: I think the vaccine is definitely part of it.

NM: All right, so good to see you!

SR: I appreciate all the time you put into preparing this.

NM: It's my pleasure. Great to get back in the thick of it. Love to Beryl, see you soon.

CHAPTER 17

BERYL KOROT

Steve Reich: When did our very first thoughts about *The Cave* start?

Beryl Korot: Well, I remember driving along Route 100 with you in Vermont. I don't know, 1987 or something like that.

SR: Yeah, that sounds right.

BK: You'd been very excited about getting a commission from Betty Freeman for the Kronos Quartet. You had never worked with them before, and you were excited about it—but at the same time, you didn't really want to write a string quartet.

SR: Right.

BK: So, you were angsting about it, and I remember you had been talking to me about wanting to use the sampler, so I said, "Why wait? Why not use it for the Kronos piece?" And you did. And, in a sense, *Different Trains*, which was the piece that you wrote for Kronos, became a study for *The Cave*.

SR: Right, that's exactly right. I had no idea what to do. I didn't want to write a string quartet. The sampler enabled me to use recorded speech. I was thinking about my early tape pieces *It's Gonna Rain* and *Come Out* and the speech melody there. And I thought, what if I were to record some as yet undetermined speakers and have live musicians playing along with them? And since we were talking about it, what if we had videotape and you could see the prerecorded people speaking and you could see the live musicians doubling them? That kind of thinking led me to my part of *The Cave* for sure. The idea of opera, which was being done by my contemporaries, was not something that I wanted to do. I felt very uncomfortable with the operatic voice. I was much more comfortable with the early music or jazz voice. I had used those kinds of singers in *Drumming*, *Music for 18 Musicians* and *Tehillim*, so that pulled me more and more towards some kind of collaboration where we could use video-taped speakers, live musicians and singers.

BK: I remember when we would go to BAM, because that's where we saw these new operas, we would scratch our heads afterwards and think about the fact that sometimes there was contemporary subject matter. But there were actors onstage play-ing these still-living historical figures who had been filmed hundreds of times. Their recorded voices and faces were eas-ily available. Since you had done your early tape pieces and I had done my multiple-channel works *Dachau 1974* and *Text and Commentary*, we began to think that if we did an opera we would want to use what we thought of as the folk tools of our time—in this case, video and audio recordings.

SR: But how did we come up with *The Cave* itself?

BK: Actually, once we decided to go ahead with the collabora-tion, I thought it was important to leave our apartment and meet at some neutral location. So we made a date to have our first meeting at Ellen's coffee shop, just a block away. You came with the story of Abraham as the idol-breaker, the iconoclast. From my readings I had been struck by the story of the three strangers (actually angels) who come to visit Abraham while he recovers from his circumcision, and who foretell the birth of his son Isaac and the destruction of Sodom and Gomorrah. Not knowing who they are, but always showing hospitality towards strangers, we are told he runs to fetch a calf. At this point, the text leaves off and the oral tradition kicks in. He chases a calf into a cave and there he sees shadows. He knows intuitively that they are the shadows of Adam and Eve, as he also senses something verdant and lush, and again he intuits: this is the Garden of Eden. At that moment he knows that this is the place where he and his family will be buried, and he captures the calf and returns to feed his guests.

That story was magical to me because that simple act of fetching a calf to perform an act of hospitality for strangers connects Abraham to the prehistorical mother and father of all humanity, at least in the West. And the cave still exists, though underneath a partly Herodian, Byzantine and mostly Islamic structure today in Hebron, thirty miles south of Jerusalem.

SR: Abraham is about as radical and visionary a person as we've ever had. He lived in a world where people saw the forces of nature as the highest value. The sun, the moon, the stars, trees, various statues—they worshipped these things—Abraham said, "None of the above." There is a story in both the Midrash in Judaism and in the Koran in Islam about Abraham breaking the idols in his father's idol factory. He puts his life on the line by doing that and in both traditions is miraculously saved from the fiery furnace that King Nimrod throws him into. Here is a man who has a totally different conceptual take on the true focus for human worship—one that is unified, invisible and, ultimately, ethical.

BK: At the same time, we were listening to the news, this is late '80s, and beginning to feel that behind the political tension there was a religious conflict in the Middle East that most people weren't paying much attention to at the time. We thought it was too bad in the West, at that point, that people rarely knew the sources of what was, in a way, the ancient roots of their own culture.

SR: I felt that on a political level you couldn't really understand what was happening in the Middle East if you took it as a purely political situation minus thousands of years of religious conflict. And unless you had some background in that, you couldn't understand what was really happening. And I guess we wanted to get a better understanding ourselves, and the best way to do that was to go there and speak to Israelis, Palestinians, and then come back here. We organized a series of field trips and came up with a set of five questions to ask each of the interviewees in each of the three acts: Who for you is Abraham? Who for you is Sarah? Hagar? Ishmael? And Isaac? And out of those interviews we created the libretto.

BK: Also, it gave me a place to go to with my camera. The Cave in Hebron is a hot spot with an ancient history and at the same time we had the story of a family which seemed to be a good base for an opera. And it is also the only place on earth, albeit at different times, where Jews and Muslims pray in the same place.

SR: Yeah, a great story. An old man, an old woman, and they didn't have any children. And it was crucial to them that they have a child.

BK: One incident I like to remember. We were performing *The Cave* in Tokyo, and for the first time in the many tours of the work, we had a real technical problem. One of the video playback channels stopped playing. An announcement was made, and for fifteen minutes while the problem was being fixed, the audience remained quiet and in their seats, riveted to the libretto. I had often wondered, when thinking of performing in Japan, how this story basic to the West was pretty much unknown in Japan. And yet here, in this hall, a story about a barren woman and old man resonated with its universality. It was moving and memorable to witness.

And the tale is complex, even to include surrogate mothering.

SR: Yes, surrogate mothering existed at that point, in the Bronze Age. Sarah hasn't been able to have a child, so she says to Abraham, "Go into Hagar my handmaid, perhaps I will be builded up through her." And that's what happens. Hagar gives birth to Ishmael, which means "G-d will hear." Later, three angels appear to Abraham as strangers in the desert, and say to him, "A year from now Sarah will conceive and bear a child." And she does at the age of ninety. Abraham is almost a hundred when Isaac is miraculously born. But things are not smooth between the two women and eventually Hagar and Ishmael are forced to leave, but they get to what is now Saudi Arabia and to Mecca and are revered to this day by Muslims everywhere.

BK: So, the challenge was to make a work where this story would live through the words of contemporary people who knew the story, who would speak with vitality as if they knew these figures. And, in a sense, they really did. In the first two acts, ironically, the Israeli act and the Palestinian act, when the people were asked, "Who for you is Abraham? Sarah? Hagar? Ishmael? Isaac?" they all knew who these figures were and spoke of them very personally. Both Israelis and Palestinians, when asked, "Who for you is Abraham?" often answered, "He's my father." But in the third act, the American act, it was a more distant relationship, and in a lot of ways the responses became more imaginative, humorous and creative. Not so tied to the book.

SR: When we asked Richard Serra, "Who for you is Abraham?" he said, "Abraham Lincoln High School, high on a hilltop 'mid sand and sea. That's all I know about Abraham." Do you remember what was said about Hagar?

BK: Well, in the Palestinian section "She was a refugee." In the third act, in the American act, she became "the first single mother." I remember we were happy to come home to America. And actually, it's interesting given that the work began to be conceived in Vermont, we worked on it there a great deal. You had a studio upstairs and I had one downstairs.

SR: And we were wired.

BK: We were wired, yes, you could always trip over the wires coming downstairs from your studio to mine. What was the process?

SR: There was time code that kept us in sync.

BK: Oh, right, we were linked. I would start a tape deck that was striped with time code which would trigger the music in your computer upstairs and that would send me the music that would play on the Beta deck I had next to my computer. You could also print out a score you'd give me with time code.

SR: Yes. I had SMPTE time code numbers over every bar.

BK: You would give me a score that had the talking heads time coded and then I would look at the score. While you were working on the next talking heads, I would figure out where I wanted to place the still images I was creating for the five screen tableaus. We decided we would stick with the interview material as a basis for the entire work. We would stick with the documentary footage we recorded, which put me in a bit of a spot at the beginning. Photoshop was just getting released at that time with very few capabilities. I settled on a program called Hi Res QFX from Ron Scott, a software engineer in Texas. Essentially it was a big deal to be able to grab a single image from the video. I decided to develop ideas from my previous multiple-channel works, blow up the screens to fill a stage, have musicians and singers placed within this very frontal mise-en-scène, and take little aspects of the interviewees' image—a shoulder, a piece of hair, an earring—to create a kind of painting alongside the talking head images. In a sense, whenever you see somebody in the course of the work, they are presented in an aural and visual portrait of themselves. And that becomes the glue for the work, this five-channel tapestry with relationships between channels (1 and 3), and (2 and 4), and (1, 3 and 5) and so on that is the basic armature for conveying the narrative of three very different cultural views.

SR: Very different and very interlocking. It was a very long project. We began in, what, 1989, and we finished in 1993… It premiered in Vienna at the Wiener Festwochen. It was an amazing situation. Way back then we had thirty people in Vienna, a lot of rehearsal time in what had been the stables for Franz Joseph. It was called the Messepalast. Very interesting black box space where we put in bleachers and created a proscenium space.

BK: We were incredibly fortunate that they could fund such a large project at that time. Because we hadn't been able to properly tech the piece before we went on the road with it. We'd only had small musical rehearsals, really. There was a video installation in my studio where we would invite people to look at

five tiny monitors on racks in a room. We never had a chance
to really see how the whole thing would come together, how it
would be lit, how the musicians and singers would move in the
space, until we arrived for rehearsals for the month in Vienna.
It was a wonderful experience and brought together an amazing group of musicians, singers, theatrical and technical people.
Kind of created a perfect family, much less complicated than
the one in our piece.

SR: We were fortunate to present the work in the US, Europe, Japan, Hong Kong and Australia. And then there was a
long pause, when we both did our own work, until we were
asked to write another opera for the changing of the centuries
in 2000. Everybody was all wired up about Y2K, the beginning
of the twenty-first century. So we thought about it, and as I remember, we very quickly came up with the fact that technology was the driving force of the twentieth century. If you could
have looked at planet Earth in 1900 and then again in 2000, the
changes would have been enormous. Automobiles everywhere,
airplanes flying over the entire planet, movies, telephones, television and computers, wherever you look.

BK: And in our own work, our continued engagement with
technology from my being coeditor of the magazine *Radical
Software*, which focused on the information environment in the
early 1970s, to my early multichannel video installations and
your early tape pieces. But to make this opera, we needed em-
blematic stories from the twentieth century. Given our desire
to work with actual events, I needed film or video footage and
you needed recorded sound and speech.

SR: We wanted something memorable at the beginning of the
century, another in the middle and one at the end. Three Tales.
For the first one, *Hindenburg* quickly came to mind because it

was this enormous zeppelin, with swastikas on its tail fins, exploding into flames over New Jersey. I mean, that's an incredibly provocative image. I guess it was the first time something like that was caught on film.

BK: It was the first disaster caught on film.

SR: When the *Titanic* went down, there was no one shooting the action with their camera.

BK: To get the material for *Three Tales*, I went to the National Archive in College Park, Maryland. There was a great shot taken from the *Hindenburg* looking down at the ocean as it was being trailed in a way by an ocean liner. It was really an outgrowth of hot air balloons, coming out of the nineteenth century—a luxury liner in the sky.

SR: Right, except instead of hot air they filled it with hydrogen. They wanted to get helium, but Roosevelt wouldn't sell them helium. And so, Hitler—Hitler was already part of Hindenburg's government—said, "If we can't get helium, we'll fill it with hydrogen," and of course, that was an arrogant and dangerous thing to do. When the *Hindenburg* crashed, one of the officials in Germany said, "It could not have been a technical matter," but of course, that's exactly what it was.

BK: The captain of the *Hindenburg* was described in the *New York Times*, "Captain Ernst Lehmann gasped, 'I couldn't understand it' as he staggered out." The music for that was a setting of those words sung by three tenors.

SR: Yeah. I think that was some of the best music in the whole piece. We only recorded one interview for "Hindenburg," Freya von Moltke, who was the widow of James von Moltke. He was put to death when it was discovered that he had a plot to assassinate Hitler, and she had to flee Germany. She ended up not far from us in Vermont, near Dartmouth College in New Hampshire. We recorded her and she remembered seeing the *Hindenburg*. She was from that era.

BK: I don't remember. What did she say?

SR: She said, "Why do such a thing? Why have such a big silver cigar in the sky? Well, that's another matter."

BK: For me, what was interesting technically less than ten years after *The Cave*, it was now possible to incorporate video, film and photography all within a single frame. In *The Cave*, complexity came from the relationship between images on multiple screens. Here it came from being able to juxtapose all different kinds of sources on a single screen.

SR: It was a very wise decision in terms of practicality. *Three Tales* has been done a number of times and *The Cave* rarely. And the other thing for me that was essential was that instead of having speech melody determine the tempo of the music, I decided that in this piece, since we're not dealing with religious subject matter or the Holocaust where I didn't want to touch anything, this is about technology, and I certainly *do* want to touch it. I set one tempo for the benefit of the musicians and adjust the voices and the other sounds to fit in.

Now, in "Hindenburg" one of our favorite scenes is "Nibelung Zeppelin," which is basically me taking Wagner's Nibelung leitmotif from *Das Rheingold*, the hammering on anvils one, and arranging it for percussion samplers and strings. And with the video you did something quite different.

BK: Yeah, vastly different from having Wagner as a source. When I was looking at the footage of the building of the *Hindenburg*, I was struck by the gracefulness of the men who were walking on the scaffolding while they were building its shell and also the machinists as they were intensely working with different kinds of tools to create the giant zeppelin. It got me thinking about the Judson dance movement of the 1960s, which was all about everyday movements like walking, running and things like that. So, in a sense, I choreographed the workers to the music that you created based on the Wagner motif.

SR: And all of the "Hindenburg" footage is of that period, in black and white from the 1930s and '40s.

BK: The first act ends with a shot from an airplane of the charred remains of the *Hindenburg*'s giant carcass spewed across the ground while you see just the wing of the airplane, the future of aviation, looking down, in a sense, on the past.

SR: After that, we wanted to move to a major event in the middle of the century. Obviously, the atomic bomb was enormously important and had to be considered, but we felt that both Hiroshima and Nagasaki had been so well-documented that we looked to what we thought was less known, yet extremely significant, the hydrogen bomb tests at Bikini Atoll in the early 1950s. Bikini is part of the Marshall Islands in the Pacific Ocean. And to do these tests, the United States Navy had to go to the island, speak to King Judah of the Bikinian people.

BK: An absolutely idyllic atoll with plenty of fruit and the ability to grow food right on the island, plus unlimited fishing.

SR: The least technological people on earth confronting the most sophisticated technological device known to mankind at that time. Two extreme cases face-to-face.

BK: Kind of a heartbreaking tale of what happened.

SR: Yeah, they are sort of "persuaded" to leave. There's a US Navy spokesperson who's filmed saying, "The United States government wants to turn this great destructive power into something for the benefit of all mankind." Then a British radio announcer says, "The inhabitants have been taken away, transferred to another Coral Island, and given new homes." Of course, they could never return to Bikini to this day because of the radioactivity of the soil on the island.

BK: They allowed themselves, as if they had a choice, to be transferred to a new island much less hospitable to fishing, to incoming weather or to basic recreation. They did it with such naïveté and trust.

SR: Yes… When we were about to begin act 2, you suggested we organize "Bikini" very differently from the four scenes in "Hindenburg."

BK: Right. There are alternations of image-sound blocks that rotate between life on the islands, life in the air (meaning the bombers) and life on the ships.

SR: Most of the ships were the US Navy bringing out expendable warships because they knew they would be destroyed with radioactivity. So, it was a way of disposing of what was considered to be the antiquated part of the US Navy. And that is what happened.

BK: But people from governments all over the world were there on observation ships to watch this. The Americans may have arranged the show, but they weren't the only witnesses to what was going on.

SR: They certainly wanted the Russians to see.

BK: They wanted people to see how powerful this weapon was, and that it should never be used again.

SR: Right, or "our newest weapon." These image blocks that you suggested were rotated, and after three complete rotations, the actual…what is it, one second of the hydrogen bomb?

BK: Yeah, it's one second of incredibly degraded footage I found that I then captured in the computer and manipulated, pixelated, made painterly and then sent back to video with each frame slowly fading into the next, creating a different kind of extreme slow motion.

You end up getting closer and closer to the actual explosion. But you're not seeing the mushroom cloud. You're seeing the palm trees on the island almost blown away with this incredible orange background of the explosion, the fire.

SR: There's no sound of the explosion, just incredibly slow music and the countdown, "zero."

BK: At the very end I used my slow-motion technique on footage I found of the elders of Bikini when they had been brought back to see their homeland, where they could no longer live but which they still wanted to see. And so, it ends with these old people walking on the beach.

SR: King Judah of Bikini says, "It's all changed. It's not the same." It's very simple, very direct, and very heartbreaking. And then we turned to the end of the twentieth century.

BK: And we didn't immediately know what the third act was going to be about.

SR: Right. We didn't know and we were going through the newspaper and there was an article with a picture of this sheep, and the caption was "Dolly—the cloned sheep." And we looked at each other and said that's it!

BK: Indeed, that was it. It looks ahead to sequencing the human genome while simultaneously making huge advances in robotics and artificial intelligence. So, this suggested that we contact scientists involved in all this, who we interviewed about these very hot topics.

SR: We interviewed James Watson, who, along with Francis Crick, won the Nobel Prize in Physiology for their discovery of the structure of DNA. Then to Oxford in England to record Richard Dawkins, the Neo-Darwinist, and Ruth Deech, who was overseeing embryo research in the UK. Then trips to MIT, where we interviewed Marvin Minsky, considered the father of artificial intelligence, Ray Kurzweil, the inventor who invented the reading machine for Stevie Wonder, Bill Joy, who coauthored *The Java Language Specification*, Jaron Lanier, who coined the term "Virtual Reality," Henri Atlan of the Advanced Studies in the Social Sciences in Paris, Rodney Brooks, the Panasonic Professor of Robotics Emeritus at MIT, and Sherry Turkle, director of the MIT Initiative on Technology and Self.

BK: And they become our characters. They're our actors, in a sense, and they also critique, in their very individual way, what's going on technologically.

SR: We have a lot of examples here. Richard Dawkins, the biologist, *The Selfish Gene* was his famous book, says, "Once upon a time there was carbon-based life and it gave over to silicon-based life. I don't face the prospect with equanimity. Maybe I'm just sentimental." That came across as very characteristic of him. Which ones do you have?

BK: For Richard Dawkins I have, "I don't think there's anything that we are that is, in principle, deeply different from what computers are." And at the same time there's Rodney Brooks, who says, "At one point our brains were steam engines. When I was a kid they were telephone switching networks, then they became digital computers, then massively parallel digital computers. Probably out there now there are kids' books that say our brain is the world wide web. We probably haven't got it right yet."

SR: Well, here's one from Marvin Minsky, who was totally committed to technology. He's passed away. Brilliant man, very nice man, too, by the way. He said, "You go and buy this module at the Mind Store, and have it connected to your brain, and then you do four- or five-part counterpoint." (*laughs*) When I set that, I took up the challenge and wrote four- and five-part counterpoint using his voice and the voice of a student at MIT who had built a robot.

BK: In a funny kind of way, that's what *Three Tales* is about. It's all of these people that we've engaged in conversation, they are people very immersed in the future, in a sense, in creating the future and having a huge impact on it. And at the same time, there's a question; when Dawkins says, "Once upon a time there was carbon-based life that gave over to silicon-based life." What does "gave over" mean? Do we have control?

SR: He used the passive voice: it "just happened."

BK: Jaron Lanier had a good line. He remarked, "It's a terrible mistake to think of the spiritual impulse as resulting from cognitive weakness." So, with these incredibly intelligent characters in the third act, you have many different ways of framing the future, and in a sense, I think that's what's going on in *Three Tales*.

SR: Henri Atlan brings a biblical commentary: "The prophet Jeremiah decided to build an artificial man, he was perfect. He was able to talk. Immediately he talked to Jeremiah and he asked him, 'What did you do?' 'Look, I have succeeded.' 'No, no, no. It's not good. From now on, when people will meet other people in the streets they will not know whether you made them, or G-d made them. Undo me.' So, that's what Jeremiah did." This is a Midrash, a commentary about two thousand years old on the biblical text that is not to be found in the Bible itself. The idea of an artificial man, or a golem, goes way back. Atlan was framing this ancient perspective on an artificial man with what is actually going on in science now. And a couple of others that really go together. One from Ray Kurzweil, who says, "We can create things far faster than biological evolution, can create something more intelligent than ourselves. Intelligent machines." And a quote from Bill Joy, who says, "If we're going to create a robot species, we oughta take a vote first." I think (*laughs*) those quotes frame the poles of magnetic attraction and repulsion that energize *Three Tales*.

CHAPTER 18

COLIN CURRIE

Colin Currie: My first interaction with your music was seeing the single page that is *Clapping Music*. This was brought in to the Edinburgh Youth Orchestra that I was part of, and in fact, I straightaway attempted it with a friend of mine, my first ever performance of your music at the age of twelve or thirteen years old. A probably very entry-level performance of *Clapping Music* (*laughs*). But the first experience of hearing your music done correctly, properly, and fully would have been the seminal recording of *Music for 18 Musicians* with yourself and your own ensemble, which I would have heard shortly after that. And this was in the early days of CDs, compact discs, so it was one of my first CDs, and when more of your music became available, I realized there was a whole swathe of repertoire to get to know, so I would save up and would gradually buy CDs every few months and got to know many, many more of your pieces.

Steve Reich: When did you decide to form the group for *Drumming*?

CC: Well, this was linked to your seventieth birthday in 2006 when the BBC Proms approached me about curating a late-night prom of your music for a concert at the Royal Albert Hall. They kind of threw me the carte blanche and I thought, "Fantastic, this is a great opportunity!" And I knew that *Drumming* was on the cards. It was like, "Ding!" It was the first piece that came to my mind because I'd never played it and I felt that although it was a piece that I loved very much, it was perhaps the one I understood the least. I didn't really know how it fit together. I'd never looked carefully at the score; I didn't even know particularly how it was notated. I obtained the handwritten score of *Drumming* and I also had the Nonesuch recording as reference. I was absolutely starting from the beginning, but I knew I had a very good set of people around me to attempt this task. My other young colleagues at that time who now remain in the group, people you know like Sam [Walton] and Aidy [Spillett] and Owen [Gunnell] and all the gang. This first experience clarified the importance of tailoring any performance to the acoustic surroundings. During sound checks, musicians who are not playing in certain sections walk around the hall and work in tandem with our sound engineer and by giving comments to the musicians onstage playing. We frequently tweak tempi as a result, and also tailor the density of the "resulting patterns" on the tuned drums. Drier acoustics and smaller venues can encourage busier and more intricate patterns, whilst larger halls will engender due caution and require a broader brush. The program was *Clapping Music, Nagoya Marimbas, Music for Mallet Instruments, Voices, and Organ* and *Drumming*. That actually was the inaugural concert of my group because the very next day I called my agent and said, "Okay, this is now a thing (*laughs*). We're doing this. And this is the tip of the iceberg. That was just our first performance of *Drumming*. We have to do it again. We have the bug already, there's loads of other pieces we want to do, let's get this going."

SR: When I first heard you, I think it was at the South Bank.

CC: It was. It was Queen Elizabeth Hall in, I believe, 2011.

SR: Well, I'll tell you part of me was like, "These guys are unbelievable!" And as I told you before, I also wanted to strangle you at the same time (*laughs*) because I knew we could never have played it like that!

CC: Mixed emotions. (*laughs*)

SR: Mixed emotions, it was like, "Wonderful!—and we've really been replaced." (*laughs*)

CC: Well, I'll be honest with you, in a way I was quite nervous about performing to you for the first time. I think we all knew that we were playing it a bit differently from the version you were a part of yourself and others that you may have heard. Our version of this work has a wide dynamic range, and this was something we latched on to from the start. *Drumming* is famously and respectfully (it seems to me) relatively free of dynamic markings, and this allows musicians to bring a suitable range to the music. Exaggerated and sudden changes seem out of place, and we generally seek the proverbial "slow build." In terms of rhythm, questions abound surrounding phasing. For the most part, the mental process, as you know, combines a rock-solid certainty as to your contrapuntal destination, with an ability to guard against a premature arrival. It's also desirable to stay in that aurally chaotic place between patterns, but woe to you if you lose your bearings as to your arrival point. When we go around on international trips coaching students, we are often surprised by youngsters knocking out feisty and fantastic phases one after another. A fascinating development and a wonderful example of techniques trickling down through the generations.

SR: What you brought to the piece was a completely different take. I mean, we were very straightforward in our presentation.

You brought a kind of youthful enthusiasm and also a revelation, a whole new way of performing it with the expressive use of dynamics you mentioned. And that was very encouraging. It was saying, "Oh, the future lies in performances I can't imagine." Following this kind of thinking, what was your approach to *Music for 18 Musicians*?

CC: Well, I first performed *Music for 18 Musicians* in 2013 and I had very specific ideas about the piece. For me, the key was to get the musician to the role best suited to their musical/technical qualities. The vibraphone guru, central stage, needs a cool head, good judgment and a dash of soloistic flair. There are various types of "rocks" in the marimba department, and they need to be solid. Every single musician needs to be aware of the overarching line and their place within it. The piece is inherently democratic and everyone contributed to the rehearsals with questions about durations and articulation. Clarity of cuing needs to be absolutely fail-safe and I stress the necessity of having like-minded musicians assembled for this work.

SR: Looking ahead several years, many years, *Quartet* was a totally different cup of tea when you first opened up that score and midi.

CC: I recall it distinctly. I was in Toronto, in Canada, doing one of my weeks performing a concerto with the symphony orchestra there, and I remember getting the score and midi on my laptop and I called one of the pianists, Simon Crawford-Phillips. Our love of your music went way back to our student days when we would throw *Music for 18* parties at the house (*laughs*). I rang him and said, "Get ready. We've got this absolute gem that's just arrived in the in-folder this morning." I could see this energy coming off the page, all the key changes, the fast-paced action; but also the chamber music side of it. The second movement with these delicate textures and extraordinary bi-tonalities and dissonances. So, I do recall being very excited.

SR: It certainly sounded that way when you played it. Listening only to midi will eventually make you sick (*laughs*). When I flew over, I was feeling "What is this piece?" It starts ideas and then goes somewhere else and then goes somewhere else. And I was trying to figure out "What kind of apologies can I give to Colin? How can I put on a good face?" And then when I heard you guys, I thought, "You know, it's not so bad." With live musicians you suddenly hear reality.

Okay, now completely different yet again, *Tehillim*, which you did in Tokyo. Constantly changing meters and you're conducting, not playing. A little bit of backstory on *Tehillim*, it was done by the New York Philharmonic way back in the '80s. Zubin Mehta was conducting at the time, he was music director, and during rehearsals he was showing off that he could do all the changing meters. And at one point he looked over at me, smiling, and said, "One more subdivision and I quit!" (*laughs*)

CC: (*laughs*) And did he quit? And did you subdivide again?

SR: No, he didn't quit and the meter changes continued. Then the second part of the backstory is, it was the orchestra version, there were too many strings, the whole thing was lugubrious, and he was there, but the rest of the orchestra was not. The singers were operatically oriented and not the people I usually work with. There were four performances. At the end of the fourth, I went up to see him in his dressing room and he had just gotten the Brahms Gesellschaft medal. I looked at him, he looked at me and he said, "Steve, the Reich Gesellschaft medal: I ain't got." (*laughs*)

CC: Oh, blimey.

SR: So, I gave him a hug. I just said, "Thank you, Zubin, I know you really did everything you could do." But it was not to be, especially in the '80s, because in the '80s there were still many players who just saw a lot of triangles and slashes and "Why-are-we-doing-this?" So of course, generations matter. But anyway, you did *Tehillim* with the right chamber orchestration in Tokyo. What was it like for you?

CC: Well, I knew I wanted to do *Tehillim*. It's one of your largest-scale works, and one that I just think is beautiful and uplifting. I wanted to do it with my own group, for sure. I felt, perhaps rather audaciously, I could conduct it. I have only conducted your music, and at that point only with student groups and very low-key things, where the pressure wasn't particularly on. But all of a sudden there I was standing onstage in Tokyo Opera City, with my own ensemble, and Synergy Vocals, I was over-whelmed by the need to make sure that this sounded the way I wanted it to sound and that everyone felt comfortable and was able to enjoy themselves. But again, somehow the music took over and came together really nicely, and of course the acoustic in that hall is very, very good. It's a wonderful onstage sound. Everyone could hear each other very well. And it was totally thrilling. I think the best thing about being a conductor for that piece, and probably for many others, is it really is the best seat in the house. You're right by the string section, the chords are all there. You've got the singers coming at you over the top of the percussion. It was nerve-racking and it was thrilling.

SR: I loved the whole thing. I was also amazed. It's one thing to conduct in a constant meter, it's another thing to conduct this piece with every measure a different combination of threes and twos. A challenge to any conductor.

CC: Well, I think for everyone onstage, the overwhelming desire to just nail this thing trumped any of the challenges. It was like, "Okay, this has to happen right." (*laughs*)

SR: Oh, it did.

CC: And as I remember, the Japanese, who turned out to be a very expressive audience, went bananas. I remember the end especially of the second concert, they refused to stop applauding and cheering. It was amazing.

SR: You have a Hallelujah in D major, so there's a clear path all the way home. (*laughs*)

CC: It's a great way to bring it in, yeah (*laughs*). Noted.

SR: So, *Proverb*. A very different piece, a low-key piece. The vibes are there, but it's really not a "motoric piece." What was your take? Again, you were conducting in Paris.

CC: Yeah, I conducted two works of yours at that festival: *Pulse* and *Proverb*. *Proverb* was a piece that I'm also very fond of, partly because I was at the BBC Proms for the first (in progress) European performance in the midnineties with Ensemble Modern. So, I actually heard that piece in one of its first incarnations way back then when I was in my late teens. It put a light on in my head. A few years after that the recording came out and it did strike me as a very different work; on the one hand, quite austere, quite reverential with a cathedral-type atmosphere, but it also sets up a big space for the listener, the thinker and anyone taking part in the music. It's extremely thought-provoking. It was beautiful to do the piece. I found it astonishingly moving.

SR: And you were working with Micaela Haslam and Synergy Vocals and they really nailed it.

CC: They did indeed, and marvelously so.

SR: Well, now, most recently you conducted again with *Reich/Richter* at the Barbican, where this time you conducted with a film and having to keep track of time code and a whole different world. What was that like?

CC: Well, I think this is another one of your departure pieces. The scale of it is staggering, a large-scale work that begins with a certain amount of activity and slows down. And we just find ourselves floating in space and these heartbreaking slow-moving bass lines in the piano which are left precariously on their own with barely any other support. It's hanging by a thread. And then gradually, sure enough, elements coalesce again, and we have what I think is one of your most effective and brilliant conclusions to a work. It's strong, it's uplifting, and it's dissonant. It's quite wild. Emotionally, this was one of the deepest pieces to be a part of. Connecting it to the visuals was a challenge. It was a very steep learning curve. I found it quite difficult once or twice, but when I could get it right, I felt it was extremely rewarding and those musicians that I did see looking away from the score and looking up at the screen did, too. I actually loved the interaction between the sonority and the visuals, it was extremely well integrated.

SR: You also were not conducting your own group. You were conducting the Britten Sinfonia, who I had known of but had not worked with. I was enormously impressed with the quality of musicianship and their attitude.

CC: They were absolutely impeccable!

SR: It was as if you worked with them for a hundred years. It was quite remarkable.

CC: It was a very happy experience, but I think, again, what I would say to you is it was quite a smattering of players my age or younger, and again, it's a generation of people who know your music. You could mention a half a dozen pieces to them and they would either have known them or very likely have played them. So, they sit down in front of *Reich/Richter* and they know the style, and the string players make the right kind of sound. Not quite without vibrato, just a little bit in there. And that's in place immediately. The precision, the pianists and vibraphones playing with clarity but also that warmth in the pedaling. They were great.

SR: I'm glad to hear that. You know, it's interesting. You brought up something which I've discussed with other people. The aural tradition. When performers and composers work together— especially early on. My ensemble was a crucial part of my development. There are people now who "do it better," and you're one of them (*laughs*), but we're kind of like the original instruments.

CC: Absolutely, yeah.

SR: And that gets passed on. The musicians in your ensemble all have students. And students see the notation, but as importantly or sometimes more importantly, they'll have you showing them something or saying something. It's never just read the notation. That's not how it works at all.

CC: There's so much more to it. I think it's interesting because everyone in my ensemble, we absolutely revere your performances, especially the larger key works, and those recordings that we all grew up with. But you know, it's funny, in a way.

You say you couldn't do what we do, we couldn't do what you did. We couldn't! (*laughs*) We have a different background now and we've been through different experiences.

SR: Exactly.

CC: It wouldn't be us. So, it's sort of a mutual difference and respect, I believe, in the way we perform the music. It's bound to be different. I think that's a testament to the music, that it can work in a number of ways.

SR: Any music that can't work in a number of ways will shortly disappear.

CC: Hear, hear! And looking forward to a wonderful tour next year in a better time when *Traveler's Prayer* will premiere alongside a whole armada of your works.

SR: Count me in.

CHAPTER 19

BRAD LUBMAN

Brad Lubman: Ensemble Signal premiered *Reich/Richter* at The Shed and then performed over 100 performances in 2019. I'm very interested to talk about how the piece came about. Of course, there was a film with it, but earlier there was the Gerhard Richter book called *Patterns*.

Steve Reich: Right. To go back a little, in 2009 I was in Germany performing with Ensemble Modern, which we've both done. Usually, my role would be to play piano for *Music for 18* and play drums in *Drumming* Part 1. Richter wanted us, me and the Ensemble, to do *Drumming* Part 1 inside of his show at the Ludwig Museum in Cologne, which we did, and it went very, very well. The next day we did *Music for 18* at the nearby Cologne Philharmonie, and Richter and I met, and there was a nice feeling of mutual respect between us. Cut to 2016, I got a call, asking if I would meet him at the Marian Goodman Gallery, in New York, to talk about a new project. When we met there, he showed me his book *Patterns*. It starts off with an abstract painting which he put into a computer, scanned it, took the scan and divided it vertically in half, and then each half in half again. He then flipped two of the quarters to form mirror images. Then he repeated that, dividing in quarters, then eighths, sixteenths, etc., all the way to 4096ths. So, what you see is first an abstract painting and then, as it begins to divide, mirror and repeat, you see these "creatures," because the mirror images produce symmetry, and you get creatures who have two eyes, two arms, two legs, etc., and they get smaller and smaller as the divisions increase until finally there are just bands of color. He said that while he was working on it, he was listening to *Music for 18 Musicians* and he and Corinna Belz were going to make a film of it, would I be interested in composing new music for it? So, I said, "Please send me some of the film and I'll see." It turned out the film was the book backwards. He started with the bands of color, as you may remember—having had a peek over 100 times during performance (*laughs*). Then it multiplies, we would say augments, until he's almost back at the original, and then reverts to dividing and gradually goes back to the color bands. So, the film is kind of an arch form, which I've been enamored with since I heard the Bartók Fourth and Fifth Quartets back when I was at Juilliard. It was very interesting, because it allowed me to continue working, as it were, on what I had done before.

And you know very well that what I had done before was a piece called *Runner*, which you and Signal played so beautifully in Washington, DC. That piece ends with an oscillation between two tones in most of the instruments. It's kind of a surprise since it's also an arch form, so you think, "The fifth movement should be similar to the first movement." Well, harmonically and tempo yes, but otherwise, it isn't. It's this oscillation. So, I was intrigued by that ending and I thought, "Wouldn't it be great to start a piece like that and then see where it goes?" And lo and behold, the way the Richter film begins is technically with two pixels to make each band of color. And then it goes to four pixels, eight pixels and so on. So, I was able to start off with a two-note oscillation that goes to four, then eight, then sixteen, but at that point it was time to bring in longer note values, not just sixteenth notes, but eighths, then quarters and so on. That is sort of how it all got started.

BL: It's interesting that you said the word *surprise* in relation to the ending material from *Runner* in that it ends with these sort of dyads, because what I've long noticed with your music is there will always be something in one piece, but it's not the main part of the piece, it's a little germ of an idea that then comes back in another piece as a central idea. I'm not saying that that's something you're doing intentionally, but let's say *Double Sextet* just for a moment. The kind of constantly changing harmonic language might not appear in earlier pieces, but there's maybe a little hint of it in an earlier piece.

SR: Right.

BL: In *Reich/Richter*, the thing that doesn't appear in your previous pieces is that middle section where the pulse drops out and it's almost as if the chords are being slowly stretched and moved out of phase in slow motion. Not like in the phase pieces of yours in the early days. A number of people were very struck by that. I was wondering, was that literally just, "Okay, I'm following the Richter film and now seems like the right time to stretch something," or was it something that came directly from the music or the process that you were describing?

SR: Both. The gradual enlargement of the visuals in the film definitely needed a slower and slower tempo in the music. What happened was that as Richter was on his way back to larger images, the number of pixels involved is enormous. The equivalent of that is slower music. I was already slow... It's interesting, you said the pulse disappears. It doesn't disappear. What happens is that the tempo throughout the piece is quarter note equals 100 beats a minute. If the regular beat becomes a dotted half note, then the tempo is cut to thirty-three beats a minute. Try clapping or tapping your foot regularly at that tempo. It's very difficult. At more or less that point you say, "Well, that's not a pulse." When does a pulse cease being a pulse because it's so slow you don't perceive it as a pulse?

BL: Right. The pulse doesn't actually disappear, if one focuses just on the left hand of the piano…

SR: That's what's just barely holding everything together…

BL: That very slow bass line. At first it all feels like time stands still and we're all just floating.

SR: Yes, that's exactly right, and that's why I didn't want to subdivide further. I wanted to say, "Okay, let's deal with it." What's that going to force me to do that I haven't done before?

By the way, I just remembered a piece of mine, *Variations for Winds, Strings, and Keyboards* way back in the '70s…

BL: Yes, I know it.

SR: There are these two brass choirs, and one fades in a long, held chord and then the other fades in a different long, held chord, and the overlap is what's interesting. That is actually like what we're talking about now, where the harmonies in the strings and the woodwinds really overlap. That's what makes that long section work, but I certainly wasn't thinking about that piece from the '70s until this very moment. In other words, there are a lot of things that you have in your head, and who knows what effects they may have… I just work here. *(laughs)*

BL: *(laughs)*

In the *Reich/Richter* with those long chords, in terms of harmonic material, is that based on harmonies that we hear earlier in the piece? Because all of a sudden, it takes on this very different harmonic language.

SR: The whole piece keeps moving in a cycle of four different key signatures, always moving up a minor third. Notice I don't say D to F to A-flat to B because it may be major or minor or modal or chromatically altered. Within that series of scales, I'm free. That's the area, that's home, it's not D major or B minor, or E dorian, it's two sharps, or wherever I happen to be in the cycle. You can say it's a gamut.

BL: Right.

SR: I did work out a number of chord progressions that seemed right for this very slow section that were not heard before, and generally the individual chords are not dissonant at all compared to other parts of the piece. But if you hold the first chord and slowly overlay it with the second chord, then you create a whole new harmonic situation. That's a way of following what you're doing and getting surprising results.

BL: Yes, and very, very wonderful results, I may say.

SR: All our musician friends came over and said something like, "...and by the way, that very slow section..."

BL: Yeah, exactly. I remember working on that very carefully as if I was engineering it in Pro Tools or something like that, to make sure that when you hear the cross fade you really hear the overlap.

SR: Right. As a good conductor, you clarify that most interesting point.

BL: Thank you, I try to do that as much as possible. (*laughs*)

SR: Every composer is in your debt, believe me.

And by the way, I'd never done any film music before. This was the first and probably the last. Like all films, it had time code, as you know only too well; numbers that remind you of the minute and second and fraction of a second of where you're at at any given moment. I had a breakdown like, "Here's where it goes from so many pixels to twice that number, and here's where it goes to twice more that number." In other words, those were the "hit points," though Richter, Corinna and myself all agreed these would be approximate. And these points do not correspond to some shift in story line as in a narrative film. Richter and Belz were making a moving version of Richter's patterns now structured in time. That time structure and those images prodded me to do things I would not normally have done and one of them is the extremely slow section.

BL: This reminds me now, listening to you speak about how the piece is put together and the materials or the process. The one thing I've always been struck by in all of your music is the level of integrity, the level of craft, is so incredibly done. One doesn't listen to the music and go, "Oh, I hear what he's doing. He's doing this, this and this." It always comes off as an amazing experience. In other words, I don't think you're the type of composer that wakes up and says, "Today I'm going to write a piece about exaltation and joy."

SR: (*laughs*) I don't know anybody who would do that.

BL: Well, I think there are some composers who do start from that angle.

SR: I can think of a great French composer who thought about the ocean...

BL: Right. But I'm thinking about *Radio Rewrite*. When I listen to *Radio Rewrite*, I don't go, "Oh, I hear, it's that song by Radiohead but he's kind of done a pastiche or something like that." No, it's like, "Oh, cool! A new Steve Reich piece." It's fascinating to me how you're able to use the source material yet come out entirely as a new piece of your own, rather than being like, "Oh, yeah, he's based it on Radiohead." I always find that really fascinating.

SR: As we discussed once on an airplane, before I wrote *Radio Rewrite* I was in the middle of this monstrosity for two ensembles. It was an ensemble counterpoint, I mean, it was like two elephants that were fairly well trained... (*laughs*) And I finally said, "This is not happening." And I forget the sequence of events, but I started watching rehearsal videos of Radiohead. It probably had to do with meeting Jonny Greenwood and hearing him do *Electric Counterpoint* and thinking, "Everybody knows Radiohead, I know their name, but I don't know their music, I've got to hear their music." I watched the rehearsal tape. Two things came out of it. Number one: I just thought these guys are great. The rehearsal tapes are in black and white. Everybody is in T-shirts; they're not looking at the camera. They're rehearsing, and you can see when they really get into it. It's real music-making. It's not an MTV production in any way, shape or form. That was very moving for me. And there were a couple of tunes that I just felt were really great. "Everything in Its Right Place" is an interesting tune. It's three-chord rock, but like nothing you've ever heard before. Maybe modal Phrygian? The other tune, "Jigsaw Falling into Place," has a more standard but very attractive set of chords. I just started jotting the chords down and thinking, "Okay, I'll go with that structure." So, that part became the fast movement, and "Everything in Its Right Place," which is sort of a slow tune, sort of hazy, it never quite really resolves. "Everything in Its Right Place" but it's not really ever in its right place (*laughs*). So, it became again a five-movement piece with "Jigsaw" I, III and V, and II and IV being devoted to "Everything in Its Right Place." Once I decided to use those songs, I just wrote my piece, changing harmonies and augmenting durations, especially "Everything in Its Right Place," which changed everything.

BL: Right.

SR: It no longer moves along as a recognizable tune except for fragments, particularly the notes for the word *everything*, the tonic and dominant which might qualify as a shorthand for "everything." The tunes or their harmonies are sometimes partially there, usually not.

BL: No.

SR: And again, with the chords, I did what I wanted to do with them rhythmically. Their durations, the harmonic rhythm determines the perceived harmony. If that's drastically changed, which it is, then even if the chords are the same, you don't perceive them as the same.

BL: Right, exactly. Another thing, just compositionally speaking. Some composers go through great preplanning, and there are all sorts of charts and working it out and scribbles, and for others the pre-compositional stuff takes less time and then there's the actual composing with many revisions. Other composers, there are very few revisions. So, I'm thinking about you taking these chords from Radiohead and what was your process? You said you came up with your kinds of rhythms. Is there a typical process? It takes you a few hours, a day, and then you fool around with it until you say, "Aha! I've got it!" Or is it something with a lot of trial and error and things that are not used? Or does it depend on the piece?

SR: It does depend on the piece, but in general, beginning is the most difficult part until I hit something and feel, "That's it!" And that can happen improvising at the keyboard, it can happen by listening to some other music and saying, "Oh, wait a minute now," lots and lots of ways. Generally speaking, ever since *Music for 18 Musicians*, I've generally tried to get some idea of a harmonic ground plan that I'm going to use. And in *Radio Rewrite*, those tunes furnished me with that. Not the rhythm of those harmonies, but those harmonies, and I also had melodic material, particularly in "Everything in Its Right Place." So with that I felt, okay, let's just start. And immediately here comes the cycle of harmonies from "Jigsaw" played on two pianos with electric bass in constantly changing meters. Now, why start like that? Well, basically, musical intuition is at the bottom of every musical decision I make. In this case, it sounded good, it made good musical sense because the chords we talked about were there but somewhat altered and completely reenergized via the changing meters. That cycle is then repeated, adding strings and winds and vibes in increasing complexity to complete the first movement. Then time to go on with the rest of the piece, and very quickly I'll come up to a point where either I don't know what's next or I don't like what's happening. And, at this stage of my life, I've become a "save as…" composer (*laughs*). I'm working along, I hit a spot where I don't know what to do or don't like what I've done. And I say, okay, I'm going to save what I have and then try to figure out how to go on. Or let's say I have a minute and a half of music, and I'm trying to get the flow of the thing, I'm playing it back on midi, and at forty-five seconds I hear something and I feel, "…wait a minute. How did I ever let that happen?" And I will operate. So, by the time I get through with the whole piece, it has survived a thousand cuts (*laughs*). And when I get to the end I say, "Goodbye for now—see you in rehearsal," because that is another place where I make further, usually smaller, detailed revisions. During rehearsal I am all ears and open to everybody's thoughts. I would say to any other composers reading this, if you don't listen to what musicians have to say about your music, who are you going to listen to? That kind of well-informed, generally well-intentioned, practical criticism is solid gold. I take it seriously. Usually, it consists of practical questions about dynamics, interpretation, tempo, balance and so on.

BL: Right. But this leads to other questions. I'm thinking about the precomputer days. What you just said was that now when you're listening to the midi playback, something might strike you, as you said, "Oh, forty-five seconds in, how did I miss that thing?" But how did that happen for you in the days when there was no computer software, and you were writing in a manuscript book?

SR: Well, to tell you the truth, I have always written both in a manuscript book *and* worked in real sound. Earlier on I had tape recorders. For *Piano Phase*, I recorded the pattern, made a tape loop of it and then sat down and played against it. In *Drumming*, say in the marimba section, which phase position works best? One beat ahead, two beats? Try it. Record it. Overdub it. I have always worked in real sound. And during the process, I would play back those prerecorded sections and critique them, as well. When I was writing *Tehillim* and didn't play strings or winds, I would play them on a synth. Also, during that period of time I worked with my ensemble, I would compose so much and then we'd get into rehearsal right away. So, my music was rehearsed and corrections made while composing. That way of working continued up through *The Desert Music* in 1984, where I could only rehearse [a] small group of instruments. I started using computer notation in '85 with *Electric Counterpoint*. And I mocked up the guitar using a sampling keyboard with a guitar sample. Then, a couple of years later, I started using Sibelius computer notation software with midi playback. So, in a way, it's been smoothly continuous, always rooted in sound and always rooted in revision en route.

BL: Yes, you mentioned that once, it was amazing to me because I tended for many years to be old-school and traditional about certain things. To me, if you were a composer, you've got to be at the piano and working things out.

SR: I thought you'd say, "At your desk working things out in your head." Schoenberg's "Farben," the middle piece in *Five Pieces for Orchestra*, is incredibly beautiful, orchestrated to a turn. I've heard that he heard it all in his head. Stravinsky talks about composing at the piano. I, too, composed at the piano or marimba or drums along with a tape recorder. I think every composer has their own way of working. Ultimately, it's the finished music that matters. Music that musicians want to play and that audiences want to hear. How it was composed seems to me to be more or less interesting biographical shoptalk.

BL: Right. Well, as to our own working together, we have to go back to 1995. Bang on a Can started their chamber orchestra and I was the conductor. You came to that first concert. You wanted to meet me. You introduced yourself, said some very nice things, and you said, "I may have something for you." And the next day you called me up and said, "How would you like to do the New York premiere of *City Life*?"

SR: Right. And you did a great job conducting my ensemble.

BL: Thank you, it was indeed a great pleasure and a wonderful moment for me. Then, moving ahead to 2007, the June in Buffalo festival wanted to do *Daniel Variations* and *Tehillim*, and I was asked to put together the ensemble. So I said to Lauren Radnofsky, "We've got this great opportunity!" and I explained what June in Buffalo was, I said what the program was, and we put together the A-team of people we had worked with. We got to the first rehearsal, and during the break I said, "This is such an incredible group, there's such a special chemistry here, maybe we should do something else." Meaning we should repeat this concert someplace else. Lauren said, "I'm gonna make that happen. I'm gonna turn this into a group." And we did, Lauren became executive director and co–artistic director of Ensemble Signal, and you were a key figure, you even gave us our name.

SR: I had an ensemble for forty years, from 1966 to 2006. By 2006 I felt I couldn't handle the irreducible details, even with other people helping out, and Ensemble Signal has really proved to be incredible. If you are doing a piece of mine, I know it's going to be right. I don't have to worry.

BL: Ensemble Signal is a generation of people who grew up listening to things like *Music for 18*, *Tehillim* and *Eight Lines*. That stuff had long been recorded when most of the people in the group were teenagers. It's in their psyche. I felt like I was the link between what I learned working with your ensemble and then Ensemble Signal. It was always great when you would say, "You all know what to do." If you can present to a composer something and the composer says, "Yeah, let's make that a little bit louder, a little bit shorter there, and otherwise, you've got it." It's a very special thing for all of us.

So, we look forward to the next piece.

ACKNOWLEDGMENTS

This book would not have been possible without the enthusiasm and guidance of Peter Joseph, my editor at Hanover Square Press. From the very beginning he helped me arrive at the idea of conversations with other artists as a way of illuminating my own music, while at the same time letting them shed light on their own.

I would also like to thank Kerriann Otaño, who accurately transcribed all the recorded conversations—not an easy thing to do.

When it came time to begin the editing process, Grace Towery of Hanover Square Press was extraordinarily helpful and much appreciated.

Finally, many thanks to my longtime friend and associate Bob Hurwitz, president of Nonesuch Records. He was the first to respond to Peter Joseph's inquiries about me writing a book. Bob set the wheels in motion in the right direction.

ABOUT THE CONTRIBUTORS

David Lang is one of the most performed American composers writing today. He is acclaimed for his vocal music, including
his Pulitzer Prize–winning *the little match girl passion*, and for his
theatrical imagination, in his operas and in narrative music for
dance and film. Lang's 2015 score for Paolo Sorrentino's film
Youth received Academy Award and Golden Globe nominations,
among others. In June 2019 his opera *prisoner of the state* premiered at the New York Philharmonic, conducted by Jaap van
Zweden. It was co-commissioned by opera houses and presenters
in London, Rotterdam, Bochum, Bruges, Malmö, Copenhagen,
and Barcelona. Lang is a professor of music composition at the
Yale School of Music and is artist in residence at the Institute for
Advanced Study in Princeton. He is cofounder and co–artistic
director of New York's legendary music festival Bang on a Can.

Brian Eno is a musician, producer, visual artist, and activist who
first came to international prominence in the early '70s as a founding member of British band Roxy Music, followed by a series of
solo albums and collaborations. His work as producer includes
albums with Talking Heads, Devo, U2, Laurie Anderson, James,
Jane Siberry, and Coldplay, while his long list of collaborations

include recordings with David Bowie, Jon Hassell, Harold Budd, John Cale, David Byrne, Grace Jones, Karl Hyde, James Blake, and most recently with his brother, Roger, on *Mixing Colours*. His visual experiments with light and video continue to parallel his musical career, with exhibitions and installations all over the globe. To date he has released over forty albums of his own music and exhibited extensively, as far afield as the Venice Biennale, Saint Petersburg's Marble Palace, Ritan Park in Beijing, Arcos da Lapa in Rio de Janeiro, and the sails of the Sydney Opera House. He is a founding member of the Long Now Foundation, a trustee of ClientEarth, and patron of Videre est Credere. His latest album, *Film Music 1976–2020*, was released in November 2020.

Richard Serra is one of the most significant American artists of his generation. Beginning in the late 1960s to the present, his work has played a major role in advancing the tradition of modern abstract sculpture. His sculptures and drawings have been exhibited worldwide, including in the international exhibitions Documenta in Kassel, the Venice Biennale, and the Whitney Biennial. Serra has had solo exhibitions at and his works in the collections of the Museum of Modern Art, New York; Stedelijk Museum, Amsterdam; Centre Pompidou, Paris; Dia Center for the Arts, New York; Pulitzer Foundation for the Arts, St. Louis; Guggenheim Museum Bilbao; Metropolitan Museum of Art, New York; among others.

Michael Gordon is known for his monumental and immersive works. *Decasia*, for 55 retuned spatially positioned instruments (with Bill Morrison's accompanying cult-classic film), has been featured on the Los Angeles Philharmonic's Minimalist Jukebox Festival and at the Southbank Centre. *Timber*, a tour de force for percussion sextet, played on amplified microtonal simantras, has been performed on every continent, including by

Slagwerk Den Haag at the Musikgebouw and Mantra Percussion at BAM. *Natural History*, a collaboration with the Steiger Butte Drum of the Klamath tribe, was premiered on the rim of Crater Lake (Oregon) by conductor Teddy Abrams and is the subject of the PBS documentary *Symphony for Nature*. Gordon's vocal works include *Anonymous Man*, an autobiographical choral work written for The Crossing, and *What to Wear* with the legendary New York theater director Richard Foreman. Recent recordings include *Clouded Yellow*, Gordon's complete string quartets performed by the Kronos Quartet.

Michael Tilson Thomas is founder and artistic director of the New World Symphony, music director laureate of the San Francisco Symphony, and conductor laureate of the London Symphony Orchestra. In addition to conducting the world's leading orchestras, MTT is also noted for his work as a composer and a producer of multimedia projects that are dedicated to music education and the reimagination of the concert experience. He has won twelve Grammys for his recordings, is the recipient of the National Medal of Arts and the 2019 Kennedy Center Honors, and is an Officier dans l'Ordre des Arts et des Lettres of France.

Russell Hartenberger is professor emeritus and former dean of the Faculty of Music, University of Toronto. He has been a member of both the percussion group Nexus as well as Steve Reich and Musicians since 1971. He holds a PhD in world music from Wesleyan University. As a member of Nexus, he has performed with leading orchestras in North America, Europe, and Asia, and along with members of Nexus, he created the soundtrack for the Academy Award–winning full-length documentary *The Man Who Skied Down Everest*. With Steve Reich and Musicians, he recorded for ECM, DGG, and Nonesuch Records, and performed on the Grammy Award–winning recording of *Music for*

18 Musicians. In 2017 he was presented with the Leonardo da Vinci World Award of Arts by the World Cultural Council.

Robert Hurwitz served as president of Nonesuch Records from 1984 to 2017, where he worked with Steve Reich, John Adams, Philip Glass, Laurie Anderson, Louis Andriessen, Kronos Quartet, Brad Mehldau, Chris Thile, Joshua Redman, Gidon Kremer, Richard Goode, Dawn Upshaw, Jeremy Denk, Stephen Sondheim, Audra McDonald, Mandy Patinkin, Randy Newman, Stephin Merritt, Caetano Veloso, and k.d. lang. He has served as chairman emeritus of Nonesuch Records since January 2017.

Stephen Sondheim is an American composer and lyricist whose major works include *A Funny Thing Happened on the Way to the Forum, Company, Follies, A Little Night Music, Pacific Overtures, Sweeney Todd, Merrily We Roll Along, Sunday in the Park with George, Into the Woods, Assassins,* and *Passion,* as well as the lyrics for *West Side Story, Gypsy,* and *Do I Hear a Waltz?* He has been awarded eight Tonys, the Pulitzer Prize, the Presidential Medal of Freedom, the Kennedy Center Honors, and an Academy Award. His collected lyrics with attendant essays have been published in two volumes: *Finishing the Hat* and *Look, I Made a Hat.* In 2010 the Broadway theater formerly known as Henry Miller's Theatre was renamed in his honor.

John Schaefer is an American radio host and author. A longtime host at WNYC, Schaefer began hosting the influential radio shows *New Sounds* in 1982 and *Soundcheck* in 2002, and has produced many different programs for other New York Public Radio platforms. Schaefer is also the author of the book *New Sounds: A Listener's Guide to New Music,* first published in 1987; *The Cambridge Companion to Singing: World Music;* and the TV program *Bravo Profile: Bobby McFerrin* (Bravo Television, 2003). In 2003 Schaefer was honored with the American Music Center's prestigious Letter of Distinction for his "substantial contributions to advancing the field of contemporary American music in the United States and abroad." In May 2006 *New York* magazine cited Schaefer as one of "the people whose ideas, power, and sheer will are changing New York" in its *Influentials* issue.

Jonny Greenwood is a musician, a composer, and the lead guitarist and keyboardist of the alternative rock band Radiohead. He has been named one of the greatest guitarists of all time by publications including *NME*, *Rolling Stone*, and *Spin*. Greenwood has composed for orchestras, including the London Contemporary Orchestra and the BBC Concert Orchestra, and has scored the films *There Will Be Blood* (2007), *Norwegian Wood* (2010), *We Need to Talk About Kevin* (2011), *The Master* (2012), *Inherent Vice* (2014), *Phantom Thread* (2017), and *You Were Never Really Here* (2017).

David Harrington is the artistic director, founder, and one of the violinists of the Kronos Quartet. For more than forty-five years, San Francisco's Grammy-winning Kronos Quartet and its nonprofit Kronos Performing Arts Association have reimagined and redefined the string quartet experience through thousands of concerts, over sixty recordings, collaborations with composers and performers from around the globe, more than one thousand commissioned works, and education programs for emerging musicians.

Elizabeth Lim-Dutton is a New York City–based violinist who has been a member of Steve Reich and Musicians and the Steve Reich Ensemble since 1991. She has performed the world premieres of *The Cave*, *Three Tales*, and the New York premiere of *City Life*. She has performed extensively with the Orchestra of St. Luke's, has toured the US as concertmaster for the New York City Opera National Company, and has recorded over seventy film scores and performed in over forty Broadway shows, most recently as a member of the Lincoln Center Theater production of *My Fair Lady*. Her solo recordings have been on the ESS.A.Y label for Philharmonia Virtuosi and for Steve Reich on Nonesuch, which include *The Cave, City Life, Three Tales, Daniel Variations*, and *Music for 18 Musicians*, a 1998 Grammy Award winner for Best Performance by Small Ensemble.

David Robertson is a conductor, artist, thinker, American musical visionary, and occupies the most prominent podiums in opera, orchestral, and new music. He is a champion of contemporary composers and an ingenious and adventurous programmer. Robertson has served in numerous artistic leadership positions, such as chief conductor and artistic director of the Sydney Symphony Orchestra, a transformative thirteen-year tenure as music director of the St. Louis Symphony Orchestra, with the Orchestre National de Lyon, BBC Symphony Orchestra, and as protégé of Pierre Boulez, the Ensemble Intercontemporain. He appears with the world's great orchestras, including the New York Philharmonic, Royal Concertgebouw Orchestra, and many major European, Asian, North and South American ensembles and festivals. Since his 1996 Metropolitan Opera debut, Robertson has conducted a breathtaking range of Met projects, including the 2019–20 season opening premiere production of *Porgy and Bess*, for which he shared a Grammy Award, Best Opera Recording, in March 2021. Robertson serves as director of conducting studies, distinguished visiting faculty, of the Juilliard School.

Micaela Haslam is a UK-based soprano and the preeminent coach of Steve Reich's *Music for 18 Musicians*. She is the director of Synergy Vocals, well-known for performing all of Reich's vocal music with orchestras and ensembles all over the world. The ensemble has also worked with other well-known composers, including Luciano Berio, John Adams, Louis Andriessen,

Steven Mackey, and Sir James MacMillan. Micaela was a member of the Swingle Singers and the BBC Singers, and has performed and recorded with many other leading vocal ensembles, including The Sixteen, Tenebrae, and The Deller Consort. She has also sung backing vocals for The Heritage Orchestra, Jacob Collier, Goldie, Anna Calvi, These New Puritans, and Rob Reed.

Anne Teresa De Keersmaeker (b. 1960) created *Asch*, her first choreographic work, in 1980, after studying dance at Mudra School in Brussels and Tisch School of the Arts in New York. Two years later came the premiere of *Fase, Four Movements to the Music of Steve Reich*. De Keersmaeker established the dance company Rosas in Brussels in 1983 while creating the work *Rosas danst Rosas*. Since these breakthrough pieces, her choreography has been grounded in a rigorous and prolific exploration of the relationship between dance and music. She has created with Rosas a wide-ranging body of work engaging the musical structures and scores of several periods, from early music to contemporary and popular idioms. Her choreographic practice also draws formal principles from geometry, numerical patterns, the natural world, and social structures to offer a unique perspective on the body's articulation in space and time. *Drumming* (1998) and *Rain* (2001), two compelling group choreographies with the minimal motivic music of Steve Reich, mark the high midpoint in the curve of Anne Teresa De Keersmaeker's career as a choreographer and remain iconic and definitive of Rosas as a dance company. In 1995 De Keersmaeker established the school P.A.R.T.S. (Performing Arts Research and Training Studios) in Brussels in association with De Munt/La Monnaie.

Julia Wolfe is a composer whose music is distinguished by an intense physicality and a relentless power that pushes performers to extremes and demands attention from the audience. The 2019 world premiere of *Fire in my mouth*, a large-scale work for orchestra and women's chorus commissioned by the New York Philharmonic, received extensive acclaim. The work is the third in a series of compositions about the American worker: *Steel Hammer* meditates on the story of the John Henry legend and human against machine, and the 2015 Pulitzer Prize–winning work, *Anthracite Fields*, is a concert-length oratorio for chorus and instruments, which draws on oral histories, interviews, speeches, and more to honor the people who persevered and endured in the Pennsylvania anthracite coal region.

In addition to receiving the 2015 Pulitzer Prize in Music, Wolfe was a 2016 MacArthur Fellow. She received the 2015 Herb Alpert Award in Music, and was named Musical America's 2019 Composer of the Year. Julia Wolfe is cofounder/co–artistic director of New York's legendary music collective Bang on a Can, and she is artistic director of NYU Steinhardt Music Composition.

Nico Muhly, born in 1981, is an American composer who writes orchestral music, works for the stage, chamber music, and sacred music. He's received commissions from the Metropolitan Opera—*Two Boys* (2011) and *Marnie* (2018)—Carnegie Hall, Los Angeles Philharmonic, Australian Chamber Orchestra, Tallis Scholars, and King's College, Cambridge, among others. He is a collaborative partner at the San Francisco Symphony and has been featured at the Barbican and the Philharmonie de Paris as composer, performer, and curator. An avid collaborator, he has worked with choreographers Benjamin Millepied at the Paris Opera Ballet, Bobbi Jene Smith at the Juilliard School, and Justin Peck and Kyle Abraham at New York City Ballet, as well as artists Sufjan Stevens, The National, Teitur, Anohni, James Blake, and Paul Simon. His work for film includes scores for *The Reader* (2008) and *Kill Your Darlings* (2013), and the BBC adaptation of *Howards End* (2017). Recordings of his works have been released by Decca and Nonesuch, and he is part of the artist-run record label Bedroom Community, which released his first two albums, *Speaks Volumes* (2006) and *Mothertongue* (2008).

Beryl Korot is an internationally exhibited artist and a pioneer of video art and multiple-channel work in particular. Working in video and weaving simultaneously, her work brought the ancient and modern worlds of technology into conversation. She was coeditor of *Radical Software* (1970), the first publication to focus on video as a new art form. Two early video installation works, *Dachau 1974* (1974) and *Text and Commentary* (1976), are in major museum and private collections, including MoMA/NYC, the Kramlich Collection, and the Thoma Foundation. In 1980 she coded a language painted onto her handwoven canvas, which recently extended to drawings on paper with digitized threads and large-scale paper tapestries. Two video opera collaborations with Steve Reich, *The Cave* and *Three Tales*, brought video installation art into a theatrical/musical context. Her works have been exhibited at the Leo Castelli Gallery, Documenta 6, MoMA/NYC, Tate Modern, SFMOMA, Reina Sofía, Kunsthalle Düsseldorf, Whitney Museum of American Art, Art Basel, ZKM/Center for Art and Media, bitforms gallery, The Whitworth Gallery, and The Aldrich Museum, among many others.

Colin Currie is a solo and chamber artist, hailed as "the world's finest and most daring percussionist" (*Spectator*). Currie is the soloist of choice for many of today's foremost composers and performs regularly with the world's leading orchestras and conductors, including the New York Philharmonic, Royal Concertgebouw, Royal Stockholm Philharmonic, London Philharmonic, and The Cleveland Orchestra. Colin founded the Colin Currie Group in 2006 to perform the music of Steve Reich, and the Colin Currie Quartet in 2018 to present more diverse works written for percussion quartet.

Brad Lubman, conductor/composer, is one of the foremost conductors of modern music and a leading figure in the field for over two decades. A frequent guest conductor, Lubman has led many of the world's most distinguished orchestras, including the Bavarian Radio Symphony Orchestra, Royal Concertgebouw Orchestra, Los Angeles Philharmonic, San Francisco Symphony, Danish National Symphony, NDR Symphony Orchestra Hamburg, DSO Berlin, SWR Sinfonieorchester, WDR Symphony Cologne, Orchestre Philharmonique de Radio France, and the Netherlands Radio Philharmonic Orchestra. In addition, he has worked with some of the most important European and American ensembles for contemporary music, including Ensemble Modern, London Sinfonietta, Klangforum Wien, and Steve Reich and Musicians. He has conducted at new-music festivals across Europe, including those in Lucerne, Salzburg, Berlin, Huddersfield, Paris, Cologne, Frankfurt, and Oslo. Lubman was the recipient of the 2019 Ditson Conductor's Award, in recognition of his distinguished record of performing and championing contemporary American music. Lubman is founding co–artistic director and conductor of the New York–based Ensemble Signal. Since its debut in 2008, the Ensemble has performed over 350 concerts and coproduced ten recordings. Their recording of Reich's *Music for 18 Musicians* on harmonia mundi was awarded a Diapason d'Or in June 2015 and appeared on the Billboard Classical crossover charts. Brad Lubman is on faculty at the Eastman School of Music and the Bang on a Can Summer Institute.

INDEX